THE DOLPHIN GUIDE
TO SAN FRANCISCO
AND THE BAY AREA

Present and Past

". . . San Francisco is not only, in its way, western; it is young, and the young are affirmative . . . There is a paradox here, however. For San Francisco is an old city too, rich in history, and its youth and age both lie near the surface. The San Franciscan walks arm-in-arm with his busy present and his full-packed past, brisk enough as he goes about his affairs but willing to pause and recollect the yesterdays that meet him at every corner.

"So much has happened in San Francisco, so fast and only a short while ago . . ."

JOSEPH HENRY JACKSON—*My San Francisco*

Restaurants – pg. 235
Muir Woods – pg. 210

Curt Gentry, author of THE DOLPHIN GUIDE TO SAN FRANCISCO AND THE BAY AREA, has been a resident of the city by the Golden Gate since 1954. Born in Lamar, Colorado, in 1931, he attended the University of Colorado and worked on various newspapers until joining the United States Air Force in 1950. Following his return from Korea, he was graduated from San Francisco State College and worked in local bookstores until 1961, when he began devoting full time to his writing.

His other books include *The Madams of San Francisco; John M. Browning: American Gunmaker* (with J. Browning); *The Vulnerable Americans; Frame-Up: The Incredible Case of Tom Mooney and Warren Billings; The Killer Mountains: A Search for the Legendary Lost Dutchman Mine;* and *The Last Days of the Late, Great State of California.*

THE DOLPHIN
Guide to San Francisco
AND
The Bay Area
PRESENT AND PAST

———◆———

by Curt Gentry

DOLPHIN BOOKS
DOUBLEDAY & COMPANY, INC.
GARDEN CITY, NEW YORK
1969

For WILLIAM HOGAN: journalist, friend, and (although born in Oakland and a resident of Mill Valley) San Franciscan, in the best sense of each of these words.

ACKNOWLEDGMENTS

Acknowledgment is made to the following publishers and authors who have graciously granted permission to quote from the books indicated: Appleton Century, Charles Caldwell Dobie, *San Francisco Chinatown*; John Day, Arnold Genthe, *I Remember*; Doubleday & Co., Inc., Harold Gilliam, *San Francisco Bay*, Harold Gilliam and Phil Palmer, *The Face of San Francisco*, Irving Stone, *Men to Match My Mountains*; Alfred A. Knopf, Inc., Herbert Asbury, *The Barbary Coast*, Oscar Lewis, *Silver Kings*, Oscar Lewis and Carroll D. Hall, *Bonanza Inn*; and Viking Press, John Steinbeck, *East of Eden*.

Contents

PART III: SAN FRANCISCO RESTAURANTS, ENTERTAINMENT, SHOPPING, AND TRANSPORTATION GUIDE

Introduction

"I do not know that in all my travels I ever visited a city less interesting to the normal tourist," wrote English novelist-of-manners Anthony Trollope in 1875. "There is almost nothing to see in San Francisco that is worth seeing."

Rudyard Kipling thought otherwise. Little more than a decade later he was to find San Francisco "a mad city—inhabited for the most part by perfectly insane people whose women are of a remarkable beauty."

A half-starved young Armenian writer, William Saroyan, added his comment in the midst of the great depression: "If you're alive, you can't be bored in San Francisco."

The three impressions are neither totally false nor totally contradictory. It all depends on your point of view. Even less than most cities does San Francisco lend itself to pat classification. For each general statement made about it, there is sure to be a completely contradictory opinion.

It is sophisticated, at times. It offers a remarkable flowering of the arts, but rarely gives them adequate support. It is Western, but lacks a well-stocked Western apparel store. It is a rich city—its per capita income (and, alas, outgo) among the highest in the world, yet to many of its residents poverty is a constant reality. It is uncommonly beautiful, but avoids facing the problems of its large skid row. It is a world apart from Los Angeles, but is, on occasion, also afflicted with smog.

Which, for all intents and purposes, leads to two conclusions: 1. San Francisco is a city of contrasts; 2. There is no one San Francisco. Each of us—resident, visitor, or exile—sees reflected here mostly what he or she wants to see. San Francisco is not, as sometimes described, a state of mind; it is many states of mind, not only varying among individuals, but depending upon our moods and momentary desires.

This might apply equally well to any major city or town

but for the additional fact that "the city" is particularly evocative. It lends itself to interpretation. Perhaps therein lies the secret of its particular magic, its distinctive charm.

Therefore, a guide to San Francisco and the Bay Area can of itself be only an introduction, an encouragement to personal viewing and discovery. In an effort to balance my own prejudices I have leaned rather heavily on other writers who once or often walked the city streets. Some, like Ambrose Bierce, disliked what they saw, but expressed themselves uncommonly well. Others, like Kipling, were impressed but didn't want to really admit it, though Kipling did depart saying: "San Francisco has only one drawback. 'Tis hard to leave." A favorite source has been journalist Frank Soule's *Annals of San Francisco*, published in 1854. Soule's fat history was written when the city was officially only seven years old, but portions of his work, often strangely prim and proper for a newspaperman, provide a remarkable insight into twentieth-century San Francisco. For example, what better moral advice could one offer a young woman visiting the city for the first time than Soule's caution that "It is difficult for any woman, however pure, to preserve an unblemished reputation in a community like San Francisco, where there is so great a majority of men, and where so many are unprincipled in mind and debauchees by inclination . . ."?

Take this book lightly; it is neither the first nor the last word on what to see in San Francisco. Your most vivid impressions of the city will not be found in these pages; they will come from your individual, often accidental, explorations and discoveries.

THE DOLPHIN GUIDE TO SAN FRANCISCO AND THE BAY AREA is so arranged that, by following the suggested tours mapped out in the book, you will see a maximum of the city and adjacent areas in a minimum of time. But there is a fallacy in such an arrangement, for this, while definitely not a history, is a guide to the present past of San Francisco. And there is a toll required if you want to travel in the past; you must spend a little time. You must be willing to look around you, stop and listen whenever curiosity or fancy dictates. There is a story behind every odd-shaped building, each unusual expression or habit, each street name. There are also many fine stores, bars, and restaurants not listed in this guide; they are yours to find, patronize, covet, or share. They are a part of your San Francisco.

The author would like to make the following special acknowledgments: to Laura, for advice and editing, for most of the exploration in Part III, and, above all, for understanding affection; to Irene Simpson and the Wells Fargo History Room, for permission to use the photographs of Black Bart, Lillie Hitchcock Coit, and Emperor Norton; to Stuart Nixon and the Redwood Empire Association, for permission to use the contemporary photographs in this volume; to Albert Harmon of the San Francisco Maritime Museum, for sharing his incredible maritime lore; to Guido Viglizzo, for introducing me to the authentic side of Fisherman's Wharf; and to Harold Gilliam and Oscar Lewis, whose books were doors into San Francisco.

CURT GENTRY

PART I:
THE CITY

*"Make no mistake, stranger, San Francisco
is West as all hell."*

BERNARD DE VOTO

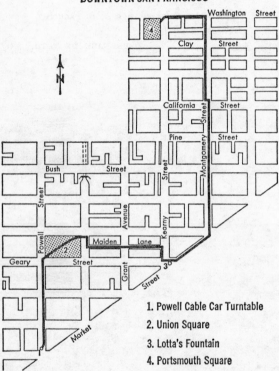

DOWNTOWN SAN FRANCISCO

1. Powell Cable Car Turntable
2. Union Square
3. Lotta's Fountain
4. Portsmouth Square

CHAPTER ONE

DOWNTOWN SAN FRANCISCO

A Walking Tour into the Present Past of San Francisco, back to the sleepy village of Yerba Buena. Starting at the Powell Street cable-car turntable and including: Union Square — Maiden Lane (alias notorious Morton Street) — Lotta's Fountain — the Palace Hotel — Montgomery Street, the Wall Street of the West, but once the city's least staid thoroughfare — and Portsmouth Square. Plus such unorthodox-but-typical-of-San Francisco characters as Joshua Norton, Emperor of the United States and Protector of Mexico — Black Bart — renegade Mormon Sam Brannan — financier and mint robber William Ralston — the San Francisco vigilantes — Captain John Lawson, champion scuttler of ships — and the gentlemanly gamblers of early San Francisco.

Powell, Market, and Eddy streets.

THE CABLE CAR. Since its first trial run in 1873, the San Francisco cable car has fascinated both residents and visitors. "The cable cars have for all practical purposes made San Francisco a dead level," wrote young India-born journalist Rudyard Kipling, while visiting the city in the 1880's. "They take no count of rise or fall . . . They turn corners almost at right angles; cross other lines, and, for aught I know, may run up the sides of houses . . ." Early San Franciscans were no less impressed; a Chinese resident put his amazement even more succinctly: "No pushee, no pullee, allee samee go like hellee!"

The cable car was born, according to a persistent local

legend, on a rainy evening in the year 1869, as Scottish wire-cable manufacturer Andrew Hallidie was climbing one of the city's many steep hills. Alongside Hallidie four horses were laboriously pulling a cart full of passengers toward the crest. Suddenly, while the Scotsman stood helplessly by, the horses slipped and fell, the car's weight dragging them down to the foot of the hill. The passengers escaped injury, but the horses had to be shot. It is said that Hallidie thereupon resolved to invent a more humane means of transportation.

Which he did. In the early-morning hours of August 1, 1873, Hallidie's first cable car sat waiting on the peak of the steep Clay Street hill for its first experimental run. Hallidie had laid out the almost mile-long course—seven blocks on Clay, from Leavenworth to Kearny—under pressure of a deadline. A successful run had to be made before midnight of August 1, else Hallidie would lose his franchise for the line.

At five in the morning the passengers—Hallidie and a half-dozen assistants—boarded the car, followed by Jimmie the gripman. Suspense mounted, the cable moved noisily in its slot under the street, and Hallidie gave the command to start. Jimmie put his hand on the grip, stared down into the thick fog that had settled in the valley below, and quickly stepped off the car. Everyone else might be mad; he wasn't.

Inventor Hallidie took the controls; without fanfare (except for a bouquet, tossed by a Frenchman from a nearby window) the car moved slowly over the crest of the hill, speeding at a breath-taking twelve miles per hour into the fog and its place in history.

The first cable car was successfully launched. Within a few years it would provide transportation in most major American cities. In San Francisco, at the peak of its popularity, there were more than a dozen lines. Today only three remain. Two turn on this turnstile: the Powell Street car, which goes up and down Nob Hill, along the edges of Chinatown and North Beach, to halt three blocks from Fisherman's Wharf; and the Hyde Street car, which follows the same route over Nob Hill but turns to climb Russian Hill and dive down Hyde Street to Aquatic Park. The turntables for the California Street line, shortest of the three remaining lines, are at California, Drumm, and Market streets, and, one and a half miles away, at California and Van Ness Avenue.

All three trips are memorable and the fare is the same as on the city's modern busses. Ride them while you can. Recent city administrations, the indifference of many residents, and confused ballot propositions have eliminated all but these lines in the interests of a more progressive transportation system.

Recently a very stubborn young lady—backed by the courts—brought to an end one of the last exclusively masculine prerogatives. For years the right to stand and ride on the steps outside the cable car was strictly limited to men. No more.

The corner of Powell and Market streets, now one of the busiest in the city, took little part in the activities of the village of Yerba Buena, the sleepy trading port that between 1835 and 1847 grew up close to the shores of Yerba Buena Cove (now the city's financial district), and that on January 30, 1847, was officially christened the City of San Francisco. During most of these years this windy corner was a desolate little valley that lay between two immense sand dunes, populated only by rabbits and that persistent creature the San Francisco flea. For a time it was known as St. Ann's Valley, and was the site of a botanical exhibit, but that it was considered far from the community itself is evident in a clipping from the San Francisco *Bulletin* of December 6, 1855, when editor James King of William wrote, answering a challenge to a duel:

"We pass every afternoon about 4½ to 5 o'clock along Market Street from Fourth to Fifth. The road is wide and not so much frequented as those streets farther in town. If we are to be shot or cut to pieces, for Heaven's sake let it be done there. Others will not be injured, and in case we fall our house is but a few hundred yards beyond and the cemetery not much further . . ."

It was not until the 1870's, when Comstock millionaire E. J. "Lucky" Baldwin decided to build here a luxury hotel to rival the Palace, that it attained notable prominence.

The Baldwin Hotel, housing also Baldwin's Academy of Music, was opened in March of 1876, on the northeast corner of Powell and Market. It was an immense structure for that time, six stories high, covering most of a block. Its furnishings, which were lavish, included a $25,000 clock from Tiffany's which Mark Twain described as telling "not only the hours, minutes and seconds but the turn of the tides, the phases of the moon, the price of eggs and who's got your umbrella." The theater was the scene of some of the finest performances of the drama-laden eighties and nineties, though most were to forget these and remember only that young San Franciscan David Belasco got his start here, as stage manager; that each morning during Anna Held's stay a horse-drawn milk truck unloaded fifty ten-gallon cans at the Powell Street entrance for the actress's famed milkbaths; and, most impressive of all, that a monstrous fire in 1898 burned the three-million-dollar theater to the ground.

Its owner, E. J. "Lucky" Baldwin, deserves more than passing mention, for he possessed many traits and patterns common to the more renowned millionaires of the period, the "Big Four," who built the Central Pacific, and the "Silver Kings" of the Comstock Lode. He came onto the San Francisco scene at a time when opportunity was not just around the corner but ever present for the man sharp enough to seize it. Baldwin was a shrewd businessman, totally unscrupulous in his dealings, whose success was due in equal measure to skill and fraud. And once he had made his fortune he spent much of it foolishly and ostentatiously, in an effort to erase the frontier crudity of his past.

He was also something of a character. When he died in 1909 he left behind him a strange and varied list of accomplishments. Among other things he had made fortunes in landholding in Alaska and California; he had founded Santa Anita Race Track (perhaps his most permanent achievement); he was the first president of the Pacific Stock Exchange (now the San Francisco Stock Exchange); and he brought from Japan the first oriental acrobats to appear in this country. (This same troupe was later to provide the inspiration for *The Mikado*, by Gilbert and Sullivan.)

He disclaimed his nickname; there was no such thing as luck, he asserted, perhaps too often and too loud. They called him Lucky because, on the eve of sailing for a big-game hunt in India, he instructed his broker to sell all of his Comstock Lode stock. Not until after sailing time did the broker discover that Baldwin had neglected to leave the key to his safe; on his return the stocks were worth four million additional dollars.

Luck did eventually desert him, for a time. His hotel and theater burned, uninsured. His belief in Lake Tahoe as a resort area—he built another large hotel there—was not confirmed during his lifetime. He died with much land but heavily in debt, only to have oil discovered on his land and his estate zoom upward to thirty-five million shortly after his death.

THE FLOWER STANDS. As old as the cable cars are the street-corner flower stands of San Francisco. Visitors commenting on the high cost of living in the city are often told by prideful hosts, "Yes, but flowers are so much cheaper here than in the East." No one knows for sure when the first stands appeared. Bookseller Tro Harper, after questioning old-timers in the business, discovered that in the late 1870's there were a dozen or more stands in the vicinity of Kearny and Market streets, catering primarily to gay blades on their way to visit professional lady friends on the Barbary Coast.

Walk north on Powell Street three blocks to Geary Street and Union Square.

POWELL STREET was named for a Dr. William J. Powell. Historians disagree as to whether he was accorded this honor because he was surgeon on the U.S. sloop *Warren*, which took part in the conquest of California; because he was later a popular entertainer and ventriloquist; or because he just happened to live in the same building (near the present site of Union Square) as city surveyor Jasper O'Farrell, who named the city's streets.

O'FARRELL STREET was named for the Dublin Irishman O'Farrell, who made the first comprehensive survey of San Francisco in 1847. Showing what we today in hindsight term great foresight, when he laid out Market Street he made it unusually wide, believing that one day it would be a much-trafficked route. Early residents were less impressed. When his map was first published, a lynching party headed for O'Farrell's lodgings. Forewarned, O'Farrell caught a ferry to Sausalito and remained in hiding until tempers cooled.

GEARY STREET was named after a most remarkable man, John W. Geary, who lived in the city for a total of only three years but during this time was San Francisco's first postmaster, its last alcalde (mayor) under the Spanish system, the first mayor under the American system, and a member of the state constitutional convention. He was just as active after leaving the city in 1851, going on to become a one-term governor of Kansas, a general in the Union Army, and a two-term governor of Pennsylvania.

The condition of San Francisco's civic government upon Geary's assumption of office as alcalde on August 1, 1849 (when the gold rush was well under way), is best described in his own words:

"At this time we are without a dollar in the public treasury, and it is to be feared the city is greatly in debt. You have neither an office for your magistrate, nor any other public edifice. You are without a single police officer or watchman, and have not the means of confining a prisoner for an hour; neither have you a place to shelter, while living, sick or unfortunate strangers who may be cast upon our shores, or to bury them when dead. Public improvements are unknown in San Francisco. In short, you are without a single requisite necessary for the promotion of prosperity, for the protection of property, or for the maintenance of order. . . ."

UNION SQUARE. Geary, Powell, Post, and Stockton streets.

Union Square is a moderately quiet, well-kept oasis in the midst of San Francisco's downtown shopping area. On sunny days the benches offer rest for weary shoppers, a convenient meeting place, and a temporary haven for the aged. During lunch hours attractive young ladies and eligible young men pour out of nearby office buildings to share the grass, the sun, and occasional glances, while below ground, the four-floor Union Square Garage (the first of its kind, built during World War II) fills with automobiles. Flower festivals are held here year round, each July 4 there is a cable car bell-ringing contest, and at Christmas time there are a huge tree and elaborate decorations (as there have been since San Francisco's mad Emperor Joshua Norton so decreed it in the 1860's).

There are always more pigeons than people in the square; the latter do not necessarily appreciate the former, but most of the suggested remedies (such as that of San Francisco's poet laureate columnist Herb Caen—to ship them all to Oakland) have been branded as inhumane. The square is often the scene of peace rallies, band concerts, and placard-bearing harbingers of the world's end or salvation. Proponents of free speech won an important victory in 1959 when the court ruled against attempts to restrict public speaking in the square, basing its decision on a Supreme Court decision which states that parks are traditionally used for "communicating thoughts . . . and discussing public questions."

Most of Union Square's history was standard and, for this city, uneventful. The 2.6-acre block was presented to the city by Mayor Geary in 1850 for use as a public square. It gained its name on the eve of the Civil War, following a series of violent pro-Union demonstrations held here. For a time it was the site of several large rambling pavilions that housed skating rinks and band concerts. The ninety-seven-foot high naval monument in the center of the square, commemorating "the Victory of the American Navy under Commodore George Dewey at Manila Bay, May First, MDCCCXCVIII," was dedicated by President Theodore Roosevelt in 1903. Then came the earthquake and fire of April 1906, and the square, thus far unendowed with either glamour or sentiment, suddenly possessed both.

Actor John Barrymore was staying in the nearby St. Francis Hotel when, at 5:12 on the morning of April 18, 1906, the first shock of the earthquake was felt. "Tradition has it that he was entertaining a young lady—the fiancée of another man—in his suite at the time," William Bronson remarks in his book *The Earth Shook, the Sky Burned.* Tradition also has it that Barrymore was slightly inebriated and that after convincing himself that the cause was not bad malt he wandered out of the hotel into Union Square, where he sat and surveyed the damage around him. Sometime later, after martial law was declared, the militia put him to work stacking bricks in the square. It is said that when his uncle, the famed actor John Drew, heard of his plight he uttered a classic couplet: "It took an act of God to get Jack out of bed and the United States government to get him to work."

During the four days of inferno that followed the quake, Union Square was transformed into a crowded campsite, inhabited mostly by residents of the St. Francis Hotel, which was destroyed on the fire's second day. Later a temporary replacement for the hotel was built on the square, serving until a new building was finished on the site of the old.

THE ST. FRANCIS HOTEL. Powell, Geary, and Post streets.

Fire was no new thing to the St. Francis. The original Hotel St. Francis, built in 1849 and located at the corner of Grant Avenue and Clay Street, had burned on October 22, 1853, in one of the most spectacular blazes of that fiery year. The old St. Francis had had its moments. It was built on the site of the first wooden building in San Francisco, the home of Jacob Leese; in its basement ballots were counted during the state's first election; and it was the first hotel in the city to put sheets on its beds.

"This was the fashionable house of the day," noted *The Annals of San Francisco*:

"Here the elite of the city either boarded, or were accustomed to congregate, and it became the theatre of many rare and amusing scenes. The chambers were separated by the thinnest sort of board partitions, without either lath or plaster, and consequently but little privacy could be enjoyed by the lodgers. These by whispering too loudly, or talking too plain, frequently and unconsciously gave their neighbors intimations of facts it was not intended, and, indeed, which it was quite improper should be known abroad . . ."

Though its walls are thicker, and the gossip mostly that of society matrons lunching in the famed Mural Room, the present-day St. Francis Hotel is still one of the city's most fashionable hostelries. It also contains several of San Francisco's best restaurants and bars.

At one time Union Square was surrounded by churches: Calvary Presbyterian, where the St. Francis Hotel now stands; Trinity Episcopal, at the corner of Powell and Post streets; Temple Emmanu El, on the site of the 450 Sutter Medical Building; the First Unitarian Church, where I. Magnin stands. One wonders, looking back in time, whether all were built here by chance or as an attempt to balance good and evil, for in those days Maiden Lane was known as Morton Street.

Cross Stockton Street at Post Street, walk one-half block south to Maiden Lane, follow Maiden Lane two blocks to Kearny Street.

Today MAIDEN LANE is one of the most attractive streets in downtown San Francisco. About its terraced walkways, tasteful shops, restaurants, and bars there is a feeling of elegant informality. The street, always a little fresh and impudent, turns unusually bright in spring, when the merchants block off all traffic and hold an annual Daffodil Festival on its thoroughfare. Whatever the season, you can walk the two blocks of Maiden Lane without so much as a hint of its bawdy past.

To appreciate the depravity of Morton Street from the 1870's until its purgation in the fire of 1906, we might note that in his book *The Barbary Coast* author Herbert Asbury —after more than two hundred pages of documented sin— introduces the street with this line: "The worst cribs in San Francisco were probably those which lined both sides of Morton Street . . ."

Asbury elaborates:

". . . not only were the Morton Street cribs the lowest in San Francisco's red-light district, they were also the most popular, partly because of the great variety and extraordinary depravity of the women to be found there, and partly because the police seldom entered the street unless compelled to do so by a murder or a serious shooting or stabbing affray. Ordinary fights and assaults were ignored . . ."

The women were of all nationalities and ages. From dusk to dawn they leaned from their windows, naked to the waist, in the dim red light loudly competing as they solicited passers-by with explicit promises. The street had a gross feature that distinguished it from more sedate places such as Chinatown and the Barbary Coast. For a dime a passing male could fondle one breast, for fifteen cents two. Inside prices were little higher, ranging from twenty-five cents to one dollar. On busy nights each girl often had from eighty to one hundred customers. And for a long time the two blocks averaged a murder per week.

This too was a part of San Francisco, a heritage of the gold rush that was a long time in dying. The forces of righteousness succeeded in closing it only once, for a few months in 1892; it took the fire of 1906 to make it respectable.

In 1909 it was renamed Union Square Avenue; in 1921 Manila Avenue, in honor of Admiral Dewey; and then in 1922, in the crowning irony of all—those intent upon forgetting something often go to opposite extreme—it was renamed Maiden Lane, after the center of New York's silver and jewelry trade.

From Maiden Lane walk one-half block south on Kearny Street to the intersection of Market, Geary, and Kearny streets.

KEARNY STREET was named after one of the most controversial personages in California history, General Stephen Watts Kearny. Following the Bear Flag Rebellion, Kearny played an important though not altogether commendable part in the American conquest of California, during the campaigns of the winter of 1846. In the early half of 1847 he engaged in a power play with Commodore Robert F. Stockton and Lieutenant Colonel John C. Frémont (Frémont having been appointed military governor of California by Stockton, and Kearny at the same time appointing himself to the post), which in turn led to the court-martial of Frémont and one of the century's greatest *causes célèbres*.

There was a time—from 1890 to 1924—when two of the city's largest rival newspapers, the *Chronicle* and the *Examiner*, faced each other across this stretch of Market Street. Had it occurred a quarter century earlier, such proximity would probably have led to fatalities, for San Francisco's journalism was for many years in the frontier tradition, both the pen and the revolver being essential tools of the trade.

THE SAN FRANCISCO CHRONICLE was founded in 1865 on a borrowed twenty-dollar gold piece and the youthful hopes of Charles (twenty) and Michael (seventeen) de Young. The two brothers quickly proved that what they lacked in age and experience they made up for in ambition and ability. Before *The Dramatic Chronicle* was three months old they scooped their longer-established competitors with the news story of the decade. On the morning of April 15, 1865, Michael de Young was visiting in the telegraph office when a startling dispatch announced that "His Excellency President Lincoln was assassinated at the theatre last night." Within two hours the *Chronicle* had the first extra on the streets. By day's end it was one of the few newspapers still publishing in the city. An irate mob had reacted to the news by destroying the pro-Confederate papers, then, forgetting their reason, as mobs are prone to do, they set upon any other papers where opposition languished.

Libel laws were not clearly defined in the *Chronicle's* early days (one San Francisco court ruled against a plaintiff on the grounds that his character was such that he could not be libeled) and the de Young brothers were quick to discover that a verbal attack boosted circulation. Politicians and opposition editors were considered the best game. The result was usually a counterattack, a duel, or an ambush. In 1879, not long after Charles de Young attacked, both in print and physically, the Workingmen's-party candidate for mayor, he was shot and killed in the *Chronicle* office by the candidate's son.

In 1890 the *Chronicle* moved from 417 Clay Street to another location, the new De Young Building, the northeast corner of Market, Geary, and Kearny streets. It was the city's first steel frame structure, surviving both the efforts of an incendiary mob in 1905 and the earthquake and fire of 1906. In 1924 the paper was moved to its present location on the southwest corner of Fifth and Mission streets. (The De Young Building remains at the old spot, but well hidden, under two new stories and the façade of a savings and loan company). Today the *Chronicle* is one of the West's leading newspapers, its assortment of local columnists—some of them syndicated—equal to that of any paper in the United States.

THE SAN FRANCISCO EXAMINER, the *Chronicle's* major competitor, was for many years located in the Hearst Building, on the southeast corner of Market and Third streets.

Wealthy miner George Hearst purchased the old pro-Confederate *Examiner* in 1880 to lend support to his senatorial ambitions. In 1887 his son William Randolph Hearst wrote from Harvard a letter which included these lines:

"I have begun to have a strange fondness for our little paper—a tenderness like unto that which a mother feels for a puny and deformed offspring . . . in fact, to tell the truth, I am possessed of the weakness, which at some time or other of their lives, pervades most men. I am convinced that I could run a newspaper successfully . . ."

Hearst presented the paper to his son, and several million dollars with which to run it.

Young Hearst spent the money wisely, gathering to the paper some of the finest journalistic talent in America. Early contributors included Ambrose Bierce, Lincoln Steffens, Gertrude Atherton, R. D. Milne, Edwin Markham, Bud Fisher, and Joaquin Miller, to name only a few. Hearst in his early years was willing to experiment, with the result that the *Examiner* was to claim a long list of notable journalistic firsts, including foreign correspondents and the comic strip. And from the *Examiner* grew the powerful newspaper chain that bears the Hearst name.

Today the *Chronicle* (morning) and the *Examiner* (evening) share the same Fifth and Mission street building, as well as a combined Sunday edition. There are more than a few San Franciscans who feel both were far more lively when they were still feuding.

The first California newspaper, incidentally, was the *Californian,* first published in Monterey August 15, 1846, later moving to San Francisco. The following editorial taken from one of the early handouts explains some of the problems of the pioneer publication:

"OUR ALPHABET.—Our type is a spanish font picked up here in a cloister, and has no VV's in it, as there is none in the spanish alphabet. I have sent to the sandvvich Islands for this letter, in the mean time vve must use tvvo V's. Our paper at present is that used for vvapping segars; in due time vve vvill have something better: our object is to establise a press in California, and this vve shall in all probability be able to accomplish. The absence of my partner for the last three months and my buties as Alcadd here have dedrived our little paper of some of those attentions vvich I hope it vvill hereafter receive."

VVALTER COLTON

LOTTA'S FOUNTAIN. Between the de Young and Hearst buildings, on a small island set off from the north side of Market at its junction with Geary and Kearny streets, is one of the ugliest and most beloved monuments in the city, Lotta's Fountain. Connected with the monument are the stories of three unusual women who charmed San Francisco: Lola Montez, Lotta Crabtree, and Luisa Tetrazzini.

LOLA. When Lola Montez stepped onto the Long Wharf at the end of Broadway Street on a May morning in 1853, the city of San Francisco had been in official existence for six years, the gold rush had been on for five, and California had been in the Union for three. It was a rough, loud, dirty, boisterous town she saw, combining the many vices and few virtues of a frontier settlement and a world port.

A young army lieutenant named Ulysses S. Grant arrived about the same time. Having been away from the city for a year, he set down his new impressions:

"San Francisco presented the same general appearance as the year before, that is, eating, drinking and gambling houses were conspicuous for their number and publicity. They were on the first floor, with doors wide open. At all hours of the day and night in walking the streets, the eye was regaled, on every block near the waterfront, by the sight of players at faro."

Grant himself won forty dollars, enough to buy a good dinner and a night on the town. He goes on to mention that the streets and houses were now "built out on piles where the year before the largest vessels visiting the port lay at anchor . . .

"Often broken pieces were found in the street, large enough to let a man down into the water below. I have but little doubt that many of the people who went to the Pacific Coast in the early days of the gold excitement, and have never been heard from since, or who were heard from for a time and ceased to write, found watery graves beneath the houses and streets built over San Francisco Bay . . ."

The lieutenant arrived in the city without fanfare or welcome; he was fortunate that he was an officer and trusted to have a pass into the city, for the military were deserting for the gold fields in great numbers.

Lola Montez was not so quietly received, nor did she find the city gloomy. It bestowed upon her its greatest adulation; bidding went as high as sixty-five dollars per seat for her first performance at the American Theatre.

By all impartial accounts, Lola Montez was not a good dancer; her voice was not at its best when singing; her acting was not mediocre, it was bad—but as overcompensation, she was a very beautiful woman with a scandalous reputation. "I have always been notorious, never famous," she once commented in a mixture of unhappiness and pride.

In as much as, in 1853, the majority of the women in the city were of dubious reputation, it was probably the renown of her conquests that singled her out for scandal; included among her many past lovers was King Ludwig of Bavaria. Also, word of her shocking Spider Dance had preceded her, but San Franciscans found her contortions in shaking the large whalebone-and-rubber spiders from her costume less than indecent. She was a novelty; in time she married a local editor and moved to the mountain settlement of Grass Valley.

LOTTA. It was here that a small girl named Lotta Crabtree wandered into her garden. Lotta was a precocious little charmer of eight, and Lola taught her to dance and sing. Samuel Dickson describes her in his *Tales of San Francisco* as "the very quintessence of San Francisco's love of life, a vivacious, an irresistible minx of a girl, winsome as a Kate Greenaway drawing, whimsical as a character in 'Alice in Wonderland'—pretty as a canary bird set free." Accompanied by her mother, Lotta toured the mining camps of California, singing, dancing, perpetually laughing. There were few children in these areas, or in San Francisco, in the 1860's, and when she appeared on stage the miners happily tossed nuggets and sacks of gold dust at her feet.

Unlike many of the city's favorites who in time moved into the domain of legend, Lotta Crabtree lived a long, successful life. She appeared on the New York stage as a delightful young lady of seventeen, was prominent in the theater until she retired at forty-four, and when she died in 1924, at the age of seventy-seven, left an estate of over four million dollars.

Lotta's Fountain was given to the city while she was still alive, however, in 1875, in a ceremony so boisterous that two companies of soldiers had to be called to dispel the riot.

LUISA. Luisa Tetrazzini made her first appearance in San Francisco in 1905, as Gilda in *Rigoletto*. Samuel Dickson, who was there on her opening night, described it as follows:

"She sang 'Caro Nome' and at the end the audience did not, as it so often did, burst into applause before the last note was ended. The last note faded into absolute silence, there was a breath-taking pause, and then they went mad.

"They shouted and stamped and stood up; all the audience stood up and cheered, and the orchestra men stood up and cheered. Men stood on the seats of their chairs and threw their hats in the air; women tore flowers from their dresses and threw them on the stage. And when that mad pandemonium had finally stilled . . . Tetrazzini sang the 'Caro Nome' again."

Lola Montez had charmed the city with her beauty and reputation, Lotta Crabtree with her freshness and spontaneity, Luisa Tetrazzini, representing still another stage in the city's cultural evolution, did it through her great talent.

This was her first but not her most memorable perform-ance. After being discovered in San Francisco she went on to be acclaimed in New York. And, during a contract argu-ment with Oscar Hammerstein, she made a statement that forever endeared her to San Francisco: "I will sing in San Francisco if I have to sing there in the streets, for I know the streets of San Francisco are free."

It was Christmas Eve, 1910, when she fulfilled her prom-ise. She stood, not far from Lotta's Fountain, on a platform built over the steps of the De Young Building. She sang only three songs, to an adoring crowd said by newspaper esti-mates to number three hundred thousand. The attendance was undoubtedly exaggerated, the magic effect on those who heard her was not.

To commemorate the event, a plaque was added to Lotta's Fountain. On Christmas Eve, 1960, the ceremony was re-created, with another singer, but the crowd was not large. Those who remembered knew it couldn't be the same. Luisa Tetrazzini, in the meantime, had died in poverty in a garret in Florence, Italy, in 1940.

Another ceremony takes place here each year. Every April 18, at 5:12 A.M., the South of Market Boys (proud boosters of the city's working-class Mission District) gather and hang a black wreath on the monument, in memory of an earth-shaking event that moved the city even more than the tal-ents of Mesdames Montez, Crabtree, and Tetrazzini.

Walk east on Market Street one block to Montgomery Street, opposite

THE PALACE HOTEL (now the Sheraton-Palace), Mar-ket and New Montgomery streets.

To appreciate the curious esteem in which residents of San Francisco held the Palace Hotel during its construction and after its opening in 1875, we must know something about the times in which it was built and the people who were so awed by it.

Our source is *Bonanza Inn*, by Oscar Lewis and Carroll D. Hall, the definitive history of the Palace Hotel.

The city:

"To unprejudiced eyes the town was crude, noisy, unkempt, its sidewalks littered and in wretched repair, its streets lined with buildings reflecting the worst features of the debased architectural taste of the period. In the downtown area every third structure was said to be an eyesore; on the newer residential streets the percentage was much higher . . ."

And the people:

"The town had been in existence less than three decades; of course it had neither background nor taste. It had grown far too rapidly; too much had happened in too short a time. By the middle '70s the spare simplicity of the frontier village had given place to the ostentation of the suddenly rich. Consequently the place was full of contradictions, not only in its physical aspects but in the behavior of its citizens. Captains of industry in stovepipe hats and Prince Alberts were known to scrawl their illegible signatures to checks made out in six figures, then carefully wipe the pen-point on a leg of their beautifully tailored trousers. Grand ladies five years removed from washtub or boarding-house kitchen paraded down fashionable Kearny Street, holding the trains of their Paris-made dresses above the sidewalk while jets of muddy water fountained upward between the planks at each descent of their ample feet. Citizens picked their way through streets filled with mud-holes and littered with horse-dung, entered a bank that was an inexact copy of a Venetian palace, and in the marble and bronze office of its president discussed the art of Edwin Booth in sentences sprinkled with oaths. Ex-teamsters married the daughters of brothel-keepers and shouldered their way into society, while men with degrees from ancient universities scoured cuspidors in Pacific Street dives, and women of refinement tended the tables of squalid boarding-houses . . ."

It was in this atmosphere that the Palace Hotel first opened. It was truly America's first great luxury hotel. But even more important, it was San Francisco's own. No one could accuse the city of being crude, unkempt, unsophisticated when it had a hotel seven stories high, with eight hundred rooms, covering two and one half acres, where a decade earlier there had been a large, desolate sand dune, and a few decades before that, where General Mariano G. Vallejo, wealthy Mexican landowner and friend to the first settlers, had shot a bear. Beneath its glass-domed rotunda its Grand Court was paved in marble; horses and carriages entered its luxurious confines through an arched driveway that opened onto New Montgomery Street. Its decorations and furnishings were the ultimate in ostentation. It towered over and dominated the skyline of San Francisco. It was, again quoting Messrs. Lewis and Hall, "at least four times too large for its period and place, but the town had never had a sense of proportion and no one was disturbed."

With the construction of the Palace, San Franciscans began taking themselves and their city seriously. The Palace was not merely the grandest building in the city, it was a pace setter, it encouraged change, not only in newer buildings, but in habits and manners and intentions. It pushed the city forward, at the cost, of course, of part of its rowdy past.

Lest the foregoing give the impression that San Francisco changed into a mannerly city overnight we will insert the impressions of Mr. Kipling, who wrote of checking into the Palace in 1889:

"When the hotel clerk—the man who awards your room to you and who is supposed to give you information—when that resplendent individual stoops to attend to your wants, he does so whistling or humming, or picking his teeth, and pauses to converse with someone he knows. These performances, I gather, are to impress upon you that he is a free man and your equal. From his general appearance and the size of his diamonds he ought to be your superior . . ."

As a hostelry, the Palace drew its share of the great figures of the time: a thin, anemic-looking young man who wore a large carnation and registered as "O. Wilde and servant"; a parade of Civil War generals—Sheridan, Sherman, and Grant, the last-mentioned in the midst of the grand balls given in his honor, undoubtedly remembering his unnoticed visits as a lieutenant; King David Kalakaua of Hawaii, who died here in 1891; Warren G. Harding, who did the same in 1923; and Enrico Caruso, who fled the Palace and San Francisco on April 18, 1906, badly frightened and swearing never to set foot in the city again, a promise he kept.

The Palace survived the quake but not the fire. Many who watched it burn later noted that only with its destruction did they really believe that San Francisco was doomed.

A new Palace arose where the original hotel stood, a little smaller, a little less grand, but maintaining its luxury hotel tradition.

Cross to northeast corner Market and Montgomery streets.

MONTGOMERY STREET is "Wall Street of the West." Its dozen or so square blocks of skyscrapers serve as the financial nervous system of most of Western America and a good portion of the Pacific Far East. Perhaps the most compact description of this area is that of Harold Gilliam, who, in his book *The Face of San Francisco*, calls the street a "center of power."

"Out of the Montgomery Street area come no usable commodities, no steaks or shoes or houses or automobiles or television sets. Its main products are decisions . . .

". . . To make a decision is to exert power. And the skyscrapers of Montgomery Street are centers of power. From the top floors of the downtown buildings of San Francisco lines of power reach out to all parts of the state and the West—power to provide money and communications and transportation and electric energy, power to mobilize the resources of mines and oil fields, forests and farmlands, and to direct the labor of millions of employees in ways that are socially wise or foolish. The towers of Montgomery Street are the colossi of Western economy."

Montgomery Street first became a "center of power" well over a hundred years ago. The decisions reached here often affected the whole city of Yerba Buena-San Francisco, sometimes the whole state of California. Things were less complex, more direct in those days. There was no need for a bevy of secretaries, administrative assistants, or vice-presidents to communicate a decision. No need for ticker tapes, telephone and telegraph wires, or the media of modern advertising. These were times when action often followed decision as quickly, and literally, as firing followed the unholstering of a gun.

Continue north on Montgomery, cross Sutter Street.

SUTTER STREET was named for Johann (John) Augustus Sutter, a courageous and ambitious Swiss adventurer who first arrived in Yerba Buena in 1839. On a grant from the Mexican Government, Sutter established a fort and a colony in the Sacramento area. Less than ten years later he had opened a large part of Northern California to settlement, built a prosperous community, and seemed well on his way to a comfortable prosperity on the new frontier.

The ruin of John Sutter began on January 24, 1848, when carpenter James Marshall, building a sawmill for Sutter on the south fork of the American River (about 150 miles from San Francisco), made a remarkable discovery.

From the diary of John Sutter:

"January 28th. Marshall arrived in the evening, it was raining very heavy, but he told me he came on important business. After we was alone in a private Room he showed me the first Specimens of Gold, that is he was not certain it was Gold or not, but he thought it might be; immediately I made the proof and found that it was Gold. I told him even that most of all is 23 Carat Gold; he wished that I should come up with him immediately, but I told him that I have to give first my orders to the people in all my factories and shops.

"February 1st. Left for the sawmill . . . I examined myself everything and picked up a few Specimens of Gold myself in the tail race of the Sawmill . . . I have a talk with my employed people all at the Sawmill. I told them that as they do know now that this Metal is Gold, I wished that they would do me the great favor and keep it secret only 6 weeks . . . unfortunately the people would not keep it secret . . ."

Events then moved swiftly toward the tragic downfall of empire-builder Sutter.

"March 7th. The first party of Mormons, employed by me left for washing and digging Gold and very soon all followed, and left me only the sick and the lame behind . . .

"March 21st. Threatened by a band of robbers . . .

"April 2d. . . . Some of the neighbors, while the Mormons left, became Likewise the Goldfever and went to the

mountains prospecting and soon afterwards moved up to digg and wash Gold, and some of them with great success.

"*April 18th.* More curious people arrived . . .

"*April 28th.* A great many people more went up to the Mountains . . .

"*May 19th.* The great Rush from San Francisco arrived at the fort, all my friends and acquaintances filled up the houses and the whole fort . . . The Merchants, Doctors, Lawyers, Sea Captains, etc. all came up and did not know what to do, all was in a Confusion, all left their wives and families in San Francisco, and those which had none locked their Doors, abandoned their houses, offered them for sale cheap, a few hundred dollars for House & Lot . . .

"*May 25th.* The travelling to the Mines was increasing from day to day, and no more Notice was taken, as the people arrived from South America, Mexico, Sandwich Islands, Oregon, etc. All the Ships Crews and soldiers deserted . . ."

John Sutter lost everything. Squatters pre-empted his land, killed his crops and animals, tore down his buildings to make sluice gates. His empire disappeared as he watched, helpless. A broken man, he appealed repeatedly to the courts and the Government, but they ruled against him. He died in 1880, heavily in debt.

On the southwest corner of Montgomery and Sutter streets is the 111 Sutter Building, standing where once stood one of San Francisco's most famous early hotels and restaurants, the LICK HOUSE, built by James Lick in 1862 on a site that cost him three hundred dollars. The hotel was, in relation to its time, as grand as the Palace, though on a much smaller scale.

It was sufficiently opulent for the satiric pen of Mark Twain, who describes a ball there in his *Washoe Giant in San Francisco* (for purposes of identification, Benicia and

San Jose are Bay Area communities; Goat Island is an island in the bay):

". . . the ball was a grand success. The Army was present and also the Navy. The nobility was represented by his Grace the Duke of Benicia, the Countess of San José, Lord Blessyou, Lord Geeminy, and many others whose titles and whose faces have passed from memory. Owing to a press of imperial business, the Emperor Norton was unable to come.

"The parlors were royally decorated, and the floors covered with a rich white carpet of mauve domestique, forty dollars a yard, imported from Massachusetts or the kingdom of New Jersey, I have forgotten which. The moment I entered I saw at a glance that this was the most extraordinary party ever given in San Francisco. I mentioned it to Benish (the very friendly, not to say familiar, relations existing between myself and his Grace the Duke of Benicia, permit of my addressing him in this way without impropriety) and he said he had never seen anything like it where he came from. He said there were more diamonds here than were displayed at the very credible effort of the Messrs. Barron, recently. This remark revived in his breast a reminiscence of that ball. He observed that the evening before it came off, he visited all the jewelry shops in town for the purpose of leasing some diamonds for his wife, who had been invited; but others had gone before him and 'cleaned out' (as the facetious nobleman expressed it) every establishment. There was but one shop where a diamond remained on hand; and even there, the proprietor was obliged to tell him—though it cost him pain to do it—that he only had a quart left, and they had already been engaged by the Duchess of Goat Island, who was going to the ball and could not do without them . . ."

But perhaps the most memorable event involving the Lick House was not a ball but a court case, concerning one of the doughnuts from the bar's free lunch counter.

In 1896 two sportsmen, Lord Talbot Clifton, a British nobleman, and White Hat McCarty, a gambler and horse player, drove a team of grays up to the Lick House, descended, then looked in vain for a hitching post. Finally McCarty hit upon a solution; entering the Lick House bar, he took a doughnut from the free lunch counter, came back outside, and fastened it to the reins. Numerous drinks later, upon leaving the bar, McCarty was arrested for violating the run-away-horse ordinance, not having tied his horses to a hitching post or a heavy weight.

McCarty decided to take the case to court. The judge— acting in the same spirit as an earlier magistrate, who used to declare a recess by announcing, "The court's dry. Let's all go get a drink"—ruled in McCarty's favor, declaring that no horse tied to a lunch-counter doughnut could possibly run away. The judgment was rendered with all due solemnity; this was, the judge stated, undoubtedly his weightiest case.

Continue north on Montgomery to Bush Street.

Montgomery Street lives in its own time. It awakens early; while most of the city is still sleeping, chauffeur-driven limousines deliver well-dressed stockbrokers to their offices in time for the opening of the New York Exchange. By eight-thirty busses and taxicabs are releasing thousands of office workers who move into the elevators to fill the tall buildings. Activity is constant from that time on. By two the sun has set on Montgomery Street; the skyscrapers make a dim canyon of the street. Activity is intense again at four-thirty and five; by seven, except in the vicinity of the bars and restaurants, the street is quiet once more. And it grows increasingly deserted by the hour.

This is the time when one walking here thinks most of the street's past, though the well-ordered quiet bears little resemblance to old Montgomery Street.

To see the street as it was during the gold rush, you must remember that it was built on a mud flat, and that for days after it rained . . . But we'll let Civil War General William Tecumseh Sherman describe it:

"Montgomery Street had been filled with brush and clay and I always dreaded to ride on horseback along it, because the mud was so deep a horse's legs would become entangled in the bushes below, and the rider was likely to be thrown and drowned in the mud. I have seen mules stumble in the street and drown in the liquid mud . . ."

Sherman was not exaggerating. A sign at a nearby corner expressed it more pointedly: "THIS STREET IMPASSABLE: NOT EVEN JACKASSABLE."

Sidewalks were, for many years, cookstoves, bags of cotton, tobacco, even in one place a grand piano; whatever couldn't be used or sold was dropped in the mud to provide a steppingstone, although all too often these too sank out of sight.

Now add to your image the ramshackle wooden buildings and canvas tents along the sides of the street, the smell of unbathed miners and mountain men, horses, some loud curses and oaths, the inevitable drunks, an occasional gunshot or two, the noise of building, the ever-present bustle of trading and commerce, one or more fights (in the mud) and you'll get the feel of gold-rush Montgomery Street.

Later this area became less muddy and more respectable. In the 1870's and 1880's it became fashionable to promenade along portions of Montgomery and Kearny streets. It was not much quieter, there were as many drunks as ever, but the people were better dressed. Men got gold by digging for it with their hands; most San Franciscans who made fortunes in silver did so on the stock market.

Let's look now at some of the men who walked this street, this block between Bush and Pine, focusing on two in particular; the first a monarch, the second California's greatest highwayman.

SAN FRANCISCO'S EMPEROR. Unlike most of the men who came to San Francisco in 1849, Joshua Norton arrived with the start of his fortune already made. Thirty-four years old when he stepped onto the Long Wharf, he had in his possession forty thousand dollars, saved from various trading ventures in Africa and South America. By 1854 he had turned his savings into a quarter of a million dollars and was, in a single transaction, ready to make his first million. He bought up all the rice on the West Coast, cornered the market, then waited while the price soared. But the unexpected happened. Three unannounced ships sailed in through the Golden Gate, their holds bulging with rice. The man they jokingly called "Emperor," because in his business dealings he showed the daring of an empire builder, became a pauper and was quickly forgotten.

One afternoon in September 1859, a strange-looking man in a uniform "vaguely military" walked into the office of the San Francisco *Bulletin* and handed editor Deacon Fitch a piece of paper. Newspaper offices attract characters, and several hours passed before Fitch looked at the paper the man had left. It read:

"At the peremptory request and desire of a large majority of the citizens of these United States, I, Joshua Norton, formerly of Algoa Bay, Cape of Good Hope, and now for the last nine years and ten months past of San Francisco, California, declare and proclaim myself Emperor of these United States; and in virtue of the authority thereby in me vested, do hereby order and direct the representatives of the different states of the Union to assemble in Musical Hall, of this city, on the 1st day of February next, then and there to make such alterations in the existing laws of the Union as may ameliorate the evils under which the country is laboring, and thereby cause confidence to exist, both at home and abroad, in our stability and integrity.

NORTON I
Emperor of the United States"

Fitch not only read it; yielding to his sense of humor, he printed it.

With this proclamation began the twenty-three-year reign of Norton I, Emperor of the United States (and later, through his own thoughtful consideration, Protector of Mexico), a reign that was not only to be unofficially recognized by the legislature of the state of California and by the city government of San Francisco, but, more important, was to be accepted by his subjects, the people of the city, who with amusement took the strange little man into their hearts.

Periodically the *Bulletin* issued Norton's proclamations. Some were completely mad—for example, Norton urged the city supervisors to pour land into the bay, to fill in the mud flats and extend the Embarcadero, adding hundreds of acres of building land to the city. Everyone smiled, forgot it, then years later did it. Norton asked for funds to build a large bridge connecting San Francisco and Oakland. The people laughed for days! Undaunted, the Emperor issued still another proclamation—this time calling for funds for a second bridge, spanning the Golden Gate, connecting San Francisco with Sausalito and Marin County. The city was convulsed.

Norton issued proclamations for every type of civic improvement, including razing buildings to widen the most congested streets, laying down paving and putting up gas lights, so that decent women could go out at night. One proclamation declared that Christmas would henceforth be a holiday for children and ordered the people to light a huge Christmas tree in Union Square. The people bought the tree and decorated it, and have done so every year since.

Merchants and restaurateurs vied for his patronage. A local printer turned out the Emperor's own currency (bills in denominations of ten, twenty-five, and fifty cents, payable, prophetically, in 1880), which merchants honored without question. He was allowed to review the troops at the Presidio, the cadets at the University of California. Early in his reign Norton adopted two of the ugliest mutts in canine history, named unrespectfully Bummer and Lazarus. With his cane as a weapon Norton rescued Bummer from a brutal miner; Lazarus was a near-dead stray that Bummer and Norton nursed back to health. The pair went everywhere Norton went, along Montgomery as he made his daily inspection of his kingdom, into the offices of the wealthy where he made monthly assessments of billions, settling, of course, for two or four bits. On the opening night of every theater performance the management would reserve three seats in the first row of the balcony for the Emperor and his two friends. The audience would rise to its feet as the Emperor and his royal dogs entered the theater.

He was invited to sit on the speaker's platform during most major addresses. (He broke up two such meetings. He rose, at a meeting of the National Woman's Suffrage League, to tell the women to go home, clean their houses, tend their children, and leave the making of laws to men. At another gathering anti-Chinese riots broke out, with agitators attempting to hang the Chinese by their queues. In the midst of the uproar Norton stepped gravely to the center of the speaker's platform, bowed his head, and began reciting the Lord's Prayer. The people left in shame.)

He attended each session of the state legislature in Sacramento, making from the floor his suggestions, which that august body always promised duly to consider. At the start of one such trip his currency was refused on the steamship; the newspapers rallied to his defense and the president of the company issued him a lifetime pass. The Southern Pacific followed suit, adding dining-car privileges.

But his interests were not confined to California, or even the United States and Mexico. Periodically he sent cablegrams to the Czar of Russia, the Kaiser, various heads of state, suggesting solutions to their problems, including a world peace organization. At a moment of weakening Anglo-American relations he wired President Lincoln, ordering him to marry the widowed Queen Victoria. Lincoln, with characteristic good humor, replied, promising to give the matter his careful consideration. He also cabled Jefferson Davis, Grant, and Lee in an attempt to mediate an end to the Civil War. He believed that his dispatches successfully terminated the Franco-Prussian War. (Though Lincoln's reply was real, most of the others were bogus cablegrams sent to the Emperor by local newspaper wags. Norton carried them bulging from his pockets wherever he went; they were found on him when he died.)

His was not an uneventful reign. If service was poor in a restaurant he would deny it patronage, until the owners begged him to return. Several restaurants proudly bore signs: "Emperor Norton Eats Here." Once, walking along Montgomery Street, he saw in a window a cartoon ridiculing him and his two royal canines. He smashed the window with his cane. The merchant not only publicly repented; he thereafter sent the city the fees for the dogs' licenses.

When Bummer died the newspapers used their front pages for his obituary; Mark Twain wrote a eulogy in Virginia City's *Territorial Enterprise;* and more than ten thousand people marched in the funeral procession.

Then, in the 1870's, the Emperor's newspaper, the *Bulletin,* noting his threadbare costume, ran the following:

"His Majesty's full dress never-mention-'ems have lost their seat, and there is dangerous risk of the Empire being brought into contempt."

Norton considered that a most scurrilous attack and immediately transferred to the *Examiner* the honor of printing his royal proclamations.

"Whereas the Evening Bulletin newspaper has been goosey enough to join proscriptive traitors against our Empire of the United States and Protectorate of Mexico: Therefore, we Norton I, Gratia Die Emperor, do hereby fine the said Bulletin $2,000; the amount to be appropriated for our Royal Wardrobe."

The other papers joined the fun, but turned their good-natured ire on the city officials; it was their responsibility! The mayor and the board of supervisors met, dug into their pockets, and declared that Norton I, Emperor of the United States, was thereafter to receive each year the sum of thirty dollars for new uniforms, as a gift from his subjects, the grateful people of San Francisco. The city celebrated noisily.

At eight-fifteen, on a foggy evening in January 1880, Emperor Norton climbed the California Street hill on his way to a meeting of the California Academy of Sciences, where he had been asked to speak. He paused on the corner across from Old St. Mary's Church, as the cable car went by, its occupants waving and saluting happily. Emperor Norton smiled, leaned for a moment against the building behind him, then slipped to the ground.

The flags of California flew at half mast. His funeral was the largest the city had ever seen. While Bummer had drawn a crowd of ten thousand, Norton himself drew three times that number. Many were to write of him. Among them was Robert Louis Stevenson, whose words were also a tribute to the Emperor's city:

"In what other city would a harmless madman who supposed himself Emperor of the two Americas have been so fostered and encouraged? Where else would even the people of the streets have respected the poor soul's illusion? Where else would bankers and merchants have received his visits, cashed his cheques, and submitted to his small assessments? Where else would he have been suffered to attend and address the exhibition days of schools and colleges? Where else, in God's green earth, have taken his pick of restaurants, ransacked the bill of fare, and departed scatheless? They tell me he was even an exacting patron, threatening to withdraw his custom when dissatisfied, and I can believe it, for his face wore an expression distinctly gastronomical . . ."

He was given two grand funerals, one immediately after his death, another in 1934, when the old cemetery was moved. On the last occasion Mayor Angelo Rossi placed a wreath on his grave, a battalion of soldiers fired three volleys, and he was given a new headstone of granite. The inscription reads:

NORTON I

EMPEROR OF THE UNITED STATES

AND

PROTECTOR OF MEXICO

JOSHUA A. NORTON

1819–1880

BLACK BART. In the middle of the afternoon of Monday, November 8, 1883, two men walked down Bush Street to Montgomery, crossed the street, then walked up Montgomery to California, and from there to the Wells Fargo offices at California and Sansome. Passers-by did not pay them undue attention. There was nothing unusual about either man. Both were quiet, well dressed, and of apparently calm demeanor, though we know now, in retrospect, that each would have given a great deal to know the other's thoughts and intentions.

One, the hunter, Special Detective Harry N. Morse, later described his companion and quarry, who went under the name of C. E. Bolton, as follows:

"He was elegantly dressed, carrying a little cane. He wore a natty little Derby hat, a diamond pin, a large diamond ring on his little finger, and a heavy gold watch and chain.

He was about five feet, eight inches, in height, straight as an arrow, broad-shouldered, with deep-sunken bright blue eyes, high cheekbones and a large handsome gray moustache and imperial; the rest clean shaven. One would have taken him for a gentleman who had made a fortune and was enjoying it. He looked anything but a robber."

But robber he was, the most notorious of California's highwaymen, and Mr. Morse was escorting him to the Wells Fargo office of Chief of Detectives James B. Hume, who had been tracking him since the meek-mannered gentleman committed his first crime seven years and twenty-eight robberies ago, signing his calling cards, "Black Bart, the Po8."

Bart's message, left at the scene of his first stagecoach holdup, read:

> "I've labored long and hard for bread,
> For honor and for riches,
> But on my corns too long you've tred
> You fine haired sons of bitches."

His second message, left at the scene of another robbery a year later, started:

> "Here I lay me down to sleep
> To wait the coming morrow,
> Perhaps success perhaps defeat,
> And everlasting sorrow."

Then Bart repeated his first poem, concluding with these lines:

> "Let come what will I'll try it on,
> My condition can't be worse;
> And if there's money in that box
> Tis munny in my purse."

The fear-inspiring highwayman, who wore a white flour sack for disguise (but never harmed anyone), finally made one serious error. Fleeing his last crime, he dropped a hand-kerchief. Its laundry mark led to the tobacco shop of a Mr. Ware at 316 Bush Street. Mr. Ware also acted as a laundry agent; he not only identified the mark but said he knew its owner well, the distinguished Mr. Bolton. And it was here that Morse met him. Though the two talked of mining matters Bart must have known the jig was up when Morse suggested they walk together to the office of Mr. Hume. Bart was tried and convicted; he served six years. His short sentence and immediate disappearance after release led imaginative reporters to conjecture. Some were convinced Bart had returned to the road. Others believed he had made a deal with Wells Fargo, a short sentence and a life-long annuity on condition he never rob another company stage. Both were guesses; no more was ever heard of Black Bart.

Before moving from the vicinity of Bush Street we must briefly note one unmarked historical site two blocks to the east, at the corner of Battery and Bush, where stood the Oriental Hotel. Most local histories recall that February 11, 1854, the Oriental Hotel was the scene of a huge banquet, celebrating the lighting of the city with coal gas. Resisting the temptation to play on the words "lit" and "gassed," we will simply state that here, sometime in the 1860's, famed bartender "Professor" Jerry Thomas invented a drink that he called the "Martinez" and that we today know as the "martini."

Walk north on Montgomery to Pine Street.

THE MILLS BUILDING, 220 Montgomery Street, was built in 1891 by Darius Ogden Mills, one of the founders of the Bank of California, a stern-faced no-foolishness kind of man who listed his occupation in the San Francisco City Directory as "capitalist." In earlier times this was the site of Platt's Hall, a public auditorium. Here the oratorical reverend Thomas Starr King brought fame to Bret Harte by reading his poem *The Reveille;* here too appeared such stellar attractions as Henry Ward Beecher, and General Tom Thumb and his wife.

THE RUSS BUILDING, across the street, was, when erected in 1927, the tallest building in the city (436 feet) and the largest office building on the West Coast. Christian Russ purchased the lot in 1847 for $27.50, built a home here and later a hotel, the Russ House.

THE PACIFIC COAST STOCK EXCHANGE BUILDING, one block to the east, at the southwest corner of Pine and Sansome streets, is one of the most impressive buildings in the area, both externally and internally. It houses the Pacific Coast Stock Exchange, which traces its activities back to the San Francisco Stock and Exchange Board, founded in 1862.

The visitors' gallery, which overlooks the trading room, is open to the public weekdays 7–2:30, entrance at 155 Sansome Street.

Today a wave of excitement is generated when a stock unexpectedly moves up several points. Trading in gold-rush days was subject to much wilder fluctuations. A commodity almost worthless in the East might here have brought a fortune. Butcher knives, favored for digging out gold, brought twenty or thirty dollars apiece. For some months plain tacks, used in building the canvas shanties, were literally worth their weight in gold; one pound of gold buying one pound of tacks. A few months later so many tacks had been imported by enterprising merchants that, rather than pay to have them unloaded from incoming ships, they were dumped into the bay. And a month later there was again a market for them when it was discovered they could be melted down and used for bullets.

Land prices varied too. A vacant lot on the corner of Montgomery and Washington streets was offered the day prior to the opening of the Broadway Wharf for five thousand dollars, with no sale. The next day the same lot sold readily for twice that amount. One pioneer died fifty thousand dollars in debt; by the time his estate was settled in the courts two years later it was worth one million dollars.

"The price of provisions being exceedingly unsteady, customers soon learned not to be surprised at anything in the way of prices," historian Hubert Howe Bancroft notes, and goes on to tell the story of one wag who, on learning that eggs were six dollars a dozen, chided his grocer friend for his low prices, claiming that down the street they were charging eighteen dollars a dozen. Not only did the grocer immediately raise his prices, his customers paid the new price without question.

Of such dealings was many an early San Francisco fortune made. As author Richard Dillon so well put it, many preferred "to dig the gold from pokes and pockets rather than seams and riffles."

North on Montgomery Street, crossing Pine Street.

THE BANK OF AMERICA, whose new headquarters covers the block bounded by Montgomery, Pine, Kearny and California streets, is another institution of financial importance to California and the West. Founded in 1904 as the Bank of Italy by Italian commission merchant A. P. Giannini, it has since become the largest commercial bank in the world, with over nine hundred branches.

North on Montgomery Street to California Street.

While in this vicinity and on the subject of bankers, it might be well to tell the story of banker, visionary, mint robber WILLIAM CHAPMAN RALSTON.

Lewis and Hall remark in *Bonanza Inn* that "there was more than a touch of Roman emperor about William Chapman Ralston.

"Better than any other citizen Ralston typified the city's flamboyance, its headlong ambition to accomplish this year, or next, what prudently might be delayed a decade. Self-assured, energetic, brash, he never doubted his power to do whatever he set out to do—and to do it a bit more splendidly than it had been done before."

Ralston moved from being clerk on a Mississippi river boat into the steamship business, then into banking with apparent ease. Together with conservative capitalist D. O. Mills, Ralston helped found the Bank of California, whose first office was at the corner of Washington and Battery streets, and which was soon to become the most important bank in California, owning at one time, largely through Ralston's efforts, a good part of the Comstock Lode. Ralston lived well and extravagantly; special trains carried his guests from San Francisco to his estate at Belmont and back. The Palace Hotel was his child (his folly, some said), though he died before it was completed.

Tales about him are numerous and already legendary. Among the more fantastic is the true story of how one foggy September midnight in 1869, William Ralston and two friends robbed the United States Subtreasury of a million dollars, a crime that won him no punishment but only civic respect.

In the fall of 1869 rumors began circulating around the city that the banks had overloaned and that widespread bank failure was imminent. Curiously the banks had plenty of gold, but all in bullion. President Grant had temporarily suspended the minting of gold coin; despite efforts of the bankers, he would not rescind his order.

The Bank of California at this time was located on the northwest corner of Sansome and California streets, one block east of where you are standing. The United States Subtreasury was about a block and a half to the north, at 608 Commercial Street, in a narrow street off Montgomery. One night just after midnight Ralston and two business associates walked to the Subtreasury, found the door unlocked (undoubtedly a guard had been bribed), removed large sacks of gold coins, dragging them down Montgomery to California and to the bank; on the return trip they dragged back sacks of bullion. By morning, without even attracting attention, they had substituted one million dollars in ore for a like amount in coin. Ralston's move had been timed perfectly. By the time the bank opened, the streets for two blocks around were packed with bank customers; the run was on. But when the first men entered the bank and saw the huge stacks of gold coin, which the clerks had been instructed to pile high on their counters, panic subsided. By Ralston's going to each of the other banks and telling the crowds the Bank of California would honor all accounts, wherever deposited, the run was broken. In time, Grant rescinded his order; no criticism or complaints were ever brought against Ralston.

The bank did fail later, for other reasons, closing its doors on August 25, 1875. Two days later William Ralston went swimming in the bay off what is now known as Aquatic Park, and drowned. Even time hasn't settled the verdict: accident or suicide?

Ralston's escapade was not the first time a million dollars moved down this street. In 1851 the customhouse at the corner of Montgomery and California burned, and on May 28 its contents were moved to the new location, a building at the corner of Kearny and Washington.

The Annals of San Francisco describes the humorous moving day:

"Some thirty gigantic, thick-bearded fellows, who were armed with carbines, revolvers and sabres, surrounded the cars containing the specie, while the Honorable T. Butler King stood aloft on a pile of ruins with a huge 'Colt' in one hand and a bludgeon in the other, marshalling his men and money . . . The extraordinary procession proceded slowly along Montgomery Street to the new customhouse. Mr. King, marching, like a proud drum-major, at the head of his miniature grand army. The people, meanwhile, looked on with astonishment . . . But immediately the farcical nature of the whole exhibition struck the most phlegmatic, and peals of laughter and cries of ironical applause accompanied the brave defenders of 'Uncle Sam's interests' to the end of their perilous march . . ."

A good joke was worth savoring and the overcautious King took the town's fancy. A young man named Frank Ball wrote a satirical song about the march and drew capacity crowds wherever he appeared to sing it.

King proved himself no fool. Summoning Mr. Ball to his office, he asked him if he would like a desirable post in the customs. Ball, expecting punishment, gasped out his pleased acceptance. "Then, Sir, it is yours," said the collector gravely. And, for some reason, Mr. Ball never again sang his famous song.

Cross Montgomery at California Street.

THE PARROTT BUILDING, situated where the United California Bank now stands, on the northwest corner of California and Montgomery streets, was the first stone—and first fireproof—structure in San Francisco, built in 1852 of granite blocks imported from China. These curious stone blocks, one of which is on display in the Wells Fargo History Room, fit together like a giant jigsaw puzzle. When the Chinese masons hired to assemble them struck for higher pay, they won their strike handily, since no one else could read the directions on the blocks. Wells Fargo and Company had offices here. And it was here, on Friday the thirteenth, April 1866, that San Francisco learned of the new experiments of chemist Alfred Nobel. A Wells Fargo employee became curious about the contents of a medium-sized can that had arrived by ship a few days before and that was now oozing a sticky black substance. While several others looked on, he applied a chisel and hammer to the lid. Results were immediate: sixteen dead, one express office demolished, the building next door moved two inches off its foundations. The contents had been plainly labeled on the can, though few at that time knew the meaning of the word "nitroglycerine."

The Parrott Building was well built. It survived both this event and the efforts of firemen to dynamite it during the fire of 1906. It was finally torn down in 1926 to make way for the present building.

It isn't necessary just to imagine the colorful past of this lively street. You can see part of it if you walk into the HISTORY ROOM of Wells Fargo Bank, 420 Montgomery Street (open 10–3 on regular banking days).

WELLS FARGO. Few businesses played as lively a part in the development of San Francisco and the West as the company established by Vermonter Henry Wells and New Yorker William G. Fargo on March 18, 1852, to supply banking and express service for gold-rush California.

The first local office of the firm, opened the same year, was on Montgomery, between Sacramento and California streets. Before long there were offices in most of the gold-rush communities. Express services included carrying passengers, mail, goods, and gold, as well as fending off predatory highwaymen. Billions in Sierra gold and Comstock silver were carried into San Francisco by the armed, two-man, six-horse Concord stages of Wells Fargo, one of which is on display in the History Room.

Shipments East went either overland by stage or by one of two sea routes: Clipper ships sailed around the Horn; Pacific Mail steamships docked at Panama, the cargo then being carried across the isthmus to another ship, bound for Eastern ports. To assure safe delivery of funds, firsts, seconds, and thirds of exchange were issued. One certificate was sent by land, two by sea; the first to arrive in the Wells Fargo office in the East was honored.

The bimonthly departure of the mail for the East, by way of Panama, gave rise to the custom of "Steamer Day," during which San Franciscans settled all financial accounts, a practice observed until the turn of the century.

The permanent collection in the History Room covers the period from the company's beginning in 1852 to the 1906 fire, and includes mementos of some of San Francisco's most fascinating characters—Joshua Norton, Emperor of the United States, Protector of Mexico; Lillie Hitchcock Coit, fire buff and society matron; Charles E. Bolton, alias Charles E. Boles, alias highwayman "Black Bart"; Samuel Langhorne Clemens, alias Mark Twain—as well as of the famous, or infamous, Vigilantes.

North on Montgomery to Sacramento Street.

The following story is necessarily long; it occurred not in one place but in many parts of San Francisco, though a good many of the incidents took place on Montgomery Street and the last chapter occurred about four blocks east on Sacramento, between Front and Davis streets. If you are reading this for the first time as you follow this route, this would be an excellent time to find a nearby coffee shop or restaurant and take a break while you peruse it.

THE SAN FRANCISCO VIGILANTES. The lure was gold. Within three years from the onset of the rush, over two hundred thousand strangers had poured in and out of San Francisco, whose pre-gold-rush population, in 1847, was 459. They came from every part of the world, men of all kinds and women of mostly one. There were gamblers, thieves, murderers, con men, financiers, and some honest men. As Bret Harte put it, "the less said about the motives of some of our pioneers the better; very many were more concerned in getting away from where they were, than in going to any particular place."

Early San Francisco was wild, make no mistake about it. But it was also young; *The Annals of San Francisco* notes that four fifths of the total population was under forty years of age, over one half between the ages of twenty and forty, and adds, especially fitting here, "These circumstances must be borne in mind when the reader considers the restless enterprise, energy and capability exhibited by the comparatively small population of the town."

Curiously, those men whose acts first forced the public to take the law into its own hands had been, for the most part, in California long before Marshall discovered gold.

THE HOUNDS

Nearly all of them were former members of the regiment of Colonel Jonathan D. Stevenson, recruited in New York to fight against Mexico but arriving in California in March 1847 after the fighting was done. The majority took their discharges in California, and in the fall of 1848, some fifty to a hundred of them banded together into a group first known as the "Hounds," later as "The Society of Regulators." (Their background showed in the name of their headquarters, a large canvas tent at Kearny and Commercial streets, which they christened Tammany Hall.) Their objectives were not only fraternal, though, being ex-soldiers, they gave themselves rank and often wore military dress. They gathered mostly for the purpose of committing crimes and general maliciousness. Their special delight was

Sunday-afternoon raids against the Chilean quarter, an area on the southern and eastern slopes of Telegraph Hill where natives from Mexico and Central and South America resided. Here lived most of the city's "pioneer prostitutes," as Herbert Asbury fittingly described them (although probably to the discomfort of some of the members of The Society of California Pioneers). The Hounds periodically and methodically attacked this quarter, raping, robbing, and killing, then burning the crude shanties. Their slogan, of course, was "California for Californians." Other San Franciscans ignored these raids for a time—horrible, yes, but after all, what can *we* do about it—which encouraged the Hounds to expand their base of operations.

Before long their crimes and bloodshed took no accounting of geographical area or skin color. Asbury writes:

". . . during the early summer of 1849 they became bolder. It was about this time that they began to call themselves Regulators and brazenly announced that they expected the people of San Francisco to support them, and to pay them well for protecting the city against the Spanish-Americans. Thereafter no man's life and goods were safe. The Hounds roamed the streets in small and large bands, robbing men and stores in broad day, and beating and stabbing merchants and others who ventured to dispute their right to take what they wanted without payment . . ."

Residents were slow to anger. When finally they did, they acted fast. In a particularly vicious raid on Sunday, July 15, 1849, the Hounds destroyed most of the Chilean quarter, pursuing the survivors as they fled through the streets of the city. The next morning when the renegade Mormon and city leader Samuel Brannan mounted a whiskey keg on the busy corner of Montgomery and Clay streets, exhorting the citizens to action, the city's long-suffering outrage found a direction. At three that afternoon they packed Portsmouth Square, listening to Brannan and other prominent businessmen and shouting their approval. A few

Hounds attempted to break up the meeting but were quickly routed. Many of the others, now attempting to flee the city, were caught, duly tried by a "people's court," and convicted. But the nature of the city government at the time was such that within a few days all were released. Most of them left San Francisco.

At this point a few words describing the courts, police, and officialdom of early San Francisco are in order. They were lax, corrupt, graft-ridden, as they have often been found to be in the city's history. As *The Annals of San Francisco* put it:

". . . It would be unjust to individuals and to human nature, to challenge *every* public officer in San Francisco with gross peculation and corruption in office; yet it was confessed on all sides that almost every citizen, who had a *chance* of preying upon the corporation means, unhesitatingly and shamefully took advantage of his position."

The routing of the Hounds marked the first mass public action against crime in San Francisco, and the first public recognition that the established agencies of justice were ineffective.

Crime did not diminish with the fall of the Hounds, since the few operative police were still loath to arrest and the courts to convict. Consider for a moment these statistics: (1) Between 1819 and 1846 there were only six murders committed among the white residents of California; (2) Between 1850 and 1854 there were twelve hundred murders committed in San Francisco alone, but only one legal execution, a Spaniard hanged for killing a Mexican.

THE SYDNEY DUCKS

The Hounds were amateurs, the Sydney Ducks professionals.

In the late 1840's Australia temporarily solved its criminal problem by encouraging its ex-convicts to migrate to California. There grew up in the heart of San Francisco, in the area later to be known as the Barbary Coast, a band of criminals known, because of their place of origin, as the Sydney Ducks. Here one could find specialists for every crime, operating without fear of retribution, knowing that if they were caught (unlikely) and the judge could not be rendered accommodating (even more unlikely) there would be a barrage of witnesses testifying to the presence of the accused in Chico or Stockton on the day of the alleged crime.

The Sydney Ducks terrorized the people of the city as the Hounds had never done. As a convenient cover for their more blatant atrocities they resorted to arson. Six times between 1849 and 1851 the largely wood and canvas city of San Francisco was burned almost to the ground.

Efforts were made to halt the crimes through legal means. In August 1849, Alcalde John W. Geary obtained funds to buy a deserted ship, the brig *Euphemia,* for use as the city's first jail. A sheriff and a city marshal were elected. The insufficiency of these efforts is apparent in the following, from Herbert Asbury:

"During the half-dozen years that followed Alcalde Geary's first attempt to form a reputable municipal government, an average of almost two murders a day were committed in San Francisco . . . Robberies, assaults, and other crimes were so numerous that no effort was ever made to determine their approximate number . . ."

Several particularly vicious crimes against respected citizens almost brought the people to mob action. In February of 1851 a storekeeper was robbed and brutally beaten by two men. Two men answering the description were arrested by the legal authorities and held in jail. A mob in Portsmouth Square, numbering between eight and nine thousand, demanded action. Under the leadership of William T. Coleman the accused were tried *in absentia.* It was a fair trial, of the people's court, and, to the disgust of the crowd, resulted in a hung jury. The mob then attempted to storm the jail but was repulsed. It was fortunate that they did not succeed, and that the vigilantes did not come into being over the issue of these two men, for both were innocent.

But steps in the direction of public action had already been taken: there were indignation meetings; the forming of a shopkeepers' militia to patrol and protect the stores at night; the appointment of a "Committee of Fourteen" to assure that the men charged with assaulting the storekeeper were not released on bail; and, of course, the recollection of success in disbanding the Hounds. As many writers have noted, "Vigilance was in the air."

In the meantime the Sydney Ducks again burned the town.

Early in June 1851 some two hundred citizens met secretly in a building (owned by Brannan) at Battery and Pine streets and formed the first Committee of Vigilance. On June 9 they drafted a constitution that began:

"WHEREAS, it has become apparent to the citizens of San Francisco, that there is no security for life and property, either under the regulations of society as it at present exists, or under the law as now administered:

"THEREFORE, the citizens, whose names are hereunto attached, do unite themselves into an association for the maintenance of the peace and good order of society, and the preservation of the lives and property of the citizens of San Francisco, and do bind themselves, each unto the other, to do and perform every lawful act for the maintenance of law and order, and to sustain the laws when faithfully and properly administered; but we are determined that no thief, burglar, incendiary or assassin, shall escape punishment, either by the quibbles of the law, the insecurity of prisons, the carelessness or corruption of the police, or a laxity of those who administer justice . . ."

The first criminal to encounter vigilante justice was a dull-witted Australian convict named John Jenkins. Jenkins had been seen fleeing a burglary with a safe on his back and was apprehended dumping it into the bay. His crime occurred on the afternoon of June 10, 1851; by midnight he had been tried and convicted by the vigilante court; by 2 A.M. he was swinging over Portsmouth Square, each man on the committee taking his turn at holding the rope, which had been thrown over a beam projecting from the second floor of an adobe house situated on the western side of the square.

When officials threatened action against the vigilantes the group published a list of its entire membership, which included many of the most prominent citizens of San Francisco, stating that all were responsible. No action was forthcoming.

During the coming weeks the fire bell of the Monumental Engine Company tolled many times, the signal for convening the vigilante court. Most of the crimes were minor; many of the accused were found not guilty and released. A month passed, after the first hanging, before another occurred. On July 11, 1851, "English Jim" Stuart, after confessing to murder and a great variety of other crimes (including the assault on the storekeeper), was tried, convicted, then hanged on a derrick near the waterfront.

The following month the committee captured, convicted, and sentenced to death two more Sydney Ducks, Sam Whittaker and Robert McKenzie, who had been members of Stuart's gang and were implicated in his confession. But this time the law came back into motion. Governor John McDougal (later convicted of election fraud), together with the mayor and sheriff of San Francisco and a band of newly appointed deputies, stormed vigilante headquarters and rescued the two men. A few days later thirty-six armed vigilantes rushed the jail, took the prisoners, and, seventeen minutes later, hanged them.

This was the last major action of the first Vigilance Committee. Never officially disbanded, it considered its work done when ships departed San Francisco packed with fleeing residents of Sydney Town.

THE SECOND VIGILANCE COMMITTEE

Of course the Sydney Ducks didn't stay away long. Civic corruption increased rather than diminished. Perhaps the officials saw the handwriting on the wall and decided to grab what they could while there was still time. In October 1854 "Honest Harry" Meiggs—assistant alderman and one of the most respected and beloved local citizens, founder and booster of North Beach, builder of Meiggs Wharf— filled a ship with imported wines and delicacies and fled to South America, leaving his friends and the city treasury approximately one million dollars poorer. He also took the city's records with him, which complicated all civic transactions, land claims, etc., for a year or two. (Years later, when Harry became a multimillionaire in Peru, he repaid a large part of his "debt," was sentimentally forgiven by the people of the city, and was preparing to return home, when the governor refused to sign his legislative pardon.)

Before long Sydney Town was back in business, not "as usual," but on a greatly increased scale. As one contemporary writer put it, "Sydney Ducks were again cackling in the pond."

On the evening of November 15, 1855, General W. H. Richardson, United States marshal for the Northern District of California, was attending the theater with his wife. Charles Cora, an Italian gambler, was also in attendance, with his mistress, Belle, a minister's daughter who ran a high-class house of prostitution on Waverly Place. Richardson, seeing Belle, complained to the management that such women should not be allowed in polite society. The manager refused to throw her out, and the Richardsons departed after exchanging insults with Cora.

The following day the two men met again, had a drink together, agreed to forget the incident, had a few more drinks, and swapped new insults. Richardson swore that the next time he saw Cora he would slap his face.

Two days later, as Cora was leaning an elbow against the

bar in the Blue Wing Saloon, Richardson entered and invited him outside. What follows differs with each account. Some say Richardson drew first, both a knife and a pistol; others say he was unarmed. No one disputes what then happened: Cora shot him dead. Cora was arrested and tried. The jury disagreed and he was held for a second trial.

Then onto the scene came James King of William, described by Stanton A. Coblentz in *Villains and Vigilantes* as a "reformer fighting perilously for an ideal in a world that recognized no final argument except a pistol shot." James King of William (the "of William" was his own addition, his father's surname, to distinguish him from the other James Kings in the city where he was born) was a crusading newspaper editor associated with the *Bulletin*. He set as his target no less than the purging of vice from San Francisco. He hit, and hard, a corrupt banking firm, ballot-box stuffing, prostitution, gambling, the city administration, the police, numerous individuals, his rival editors, and those who schemed to keep Cora from punishment. Surprisingly, he lived to make these attacks for all of seven months. Then he chose as his target James P. Casey, an editor, a member of the Board of Supervisors, and a graduate of Sing Sing.

A particularly strong attack on Casey appeared in the *Bulletin* of May 14, 1856, released on the streets about three in the afternoon. As King was leaving the *Bulletin* office at five o'clock (crossing Montgomery at the corner of Washington Street), Casey appeared, pointed a gun at King's chest, and fired. This act, which drew thousands into the streets outside the jail where Casey was held, led to the formation of the Second Committee of Vigilance. Newspapers the following morning carried this announcement:

THE VIGILANCE COMMITTEE
The members of the Vigilance Committee, in good standing, will please meet at No. 105½ Sacramento Street, this day, Thursday, 15th instant, at nine o'clock A.M.
By order of the Committee of Thirteen

Again under the leadership of William T. Coleman the committee drew up a constitution and accepted recruits. Two thousand were signed up by nightfall. Feeling was so high that the militiamen guarding the jail where Casey was held wrote a letter of resignation to the governor, stacked up their arms, and joined the vigilantes. The local unit of the National Guard disbanded, then immediately reorganized as the Independent National Guard and offered their services.

King did not die for six days. Business was practically suspended as the people of the city filled the streets, awaiting bulletins of his condition. Rumors were in the air; Casey, they said, was to be rescued from the jail by his political friends. On the morning of Sunday, May 18, the vigilante bell rang. At noon twenty-six hundred men, fully armed, marched west from committee headquarters along Sacramento to Montgomery Street, then on to the jail. The sheriff had thirty men. The vigilantes took Casey. Then, as an afterthought, they went back and got Cora too.

On Tuesday, May 20, at quarter-past one in the afternoon, James King of William died. Two days later, while King was being buried on Lone Mountain, with about half the city in attendance, the other half stood outside vigilante headquarters and watched as Cora and Casey swung from the same beams on which, a few years before had died Whittaker and McKenzie.

FORT GUNNYBAGS

On June 3 Governor J. Neely Johnson issued a proclamation declaring "the county of San Francisco in a state of insurrection." Thus began one of the strangest wars in the history of the state. The vigilantes obtained a large building between Front and Davis on Sacramento Street (on the site now numbered 243 Sacramento), fortified the stone walls with sandbags and heavy arms. Two cannons, loaded and manned at all hours, were kept on the roof. Though officially named Fort Vigilance it was popularly called Fort

Gunnybags. Its armory grew as ships bearing the governor's supplies of arms to the military in the city were seized, one before the ship had even docked.

It was a strange war. There were indications that the governor was on both sides.

For two months following the hanging of Cora and Casey there was not a single murder reported in San Francisco, and only a few minor robberies. The vigilantes were not inactive, however. In the interim they tried and banished a good portion of the city's political riffraff. On July 29, 1856, two murderers were hanged (one for a murder committed two years before, which must have frightened more than a few of the denizens of Sydney Town) on a gallows set up near Sacramento and Davis streets. Still the military didn't act.

The vigilantes also tried State Supreme Court Justice David S. Terry for assault and several other crimes, but their catch was bigger than they wanted to risk handling; admitting that the usual punishments were not applicable in the present instance, they released him.

Then, ever conscious of public feeling, which was no longer solidly behind them, they made one final parade through the city's streets and disbanded. Many, realizing that crime would decrease only after the honest election of honest officials, banded together in the People's Party, which manned the polls, elected a good number of former vigilantes to office, and was a potent force until the start of the Civil War, when it split on the issue of slavery. (Their effectiveness is evident in comparing municipal expenditures for 1855, $2,500,000, with those for 1857, $354,000.)

Were the Committees of Vigilance good or bad? More than a hundred years after the events occurred, historians and writers are still debating this question, still divided as to which was worse, the Hounds and Ducks or the unlawful vigilantes.

Walk north on Montgomery one-half block to Commercial Street.

Not all of the diggings were in the Sierras. In 1849 twenty-four-year-old New York *Tribune* correspondent Bayard Taylor, sent West by publisher Horace Greeley to get the real story of the gold rush, paused here, on his second day in San Francisco, before the United States Hotel:

"Walking through the town the next day, I was quite amazed to find a dozen persons busily employed in the street before the United States Hotel, digging up the earth with knives and crumbling it in their hands. They were actual gold hunters, who obtained in this way about $5 a day. After blowing the fine dirt carefully in their hands, a few specks of gold were left, which they placed in a piece of white paper. A number of children were engaged in the same business, picking out the fine grains by applying to them the head of a pin, moistened in their mouths . . ."

Walk north on Montgomery one-half block to Clay Street.

A number of notable sites are in this area. The plaque on the southwest corner of Clay and Montgomery streets reads:

"SOCIETY OF CALIFORNIA PIONEERS ORGANIZED ON THIS SITE. In a building which stood on this site, known as the Mellus and Howard warehouse, erected in 1848, the Society of California Pioneers was organized August 31, 1850, its object to collect and preserve the history of California . . ."

Those resident here prior to January 1, 1849, were considered members of the "first class"; those who arrived the following year were members of the "second class." Though honorary memberships were sometimes given, these divisions were strictly adhered to and for a good many years provided the basis for what little society there was in San Francisco. The Society of California Pioneers is still active today, maintaining an extensive library and historical collection at 456 McAllister Street, bordering Civic Center. Open to the public.

Two important events occurred across the street, on what is now the southeast corner of Clay and Montgomery streets, but was, in the days of the village of Yerba Buena, the shoreline of the city.

Here in July 1839, John Sutter anchored his brig *Clementine*, little suspecting that in less than a decade he would indirectly cause the greatest mass movement in the history of this continent, forever changing the face of Yerba Buena-San Francisco.

It was here, too, that Captain John B. Montgomery docked his ship U.S.S. *Portsmouth*, on July 9, 1846, and with seventy men and fife and drum marched west to the plaza of Yerba Buena (henceforth Portsmouth Square), there to raise the American flag and claim this city for the United States of America.

If you walk one block east to Sansome Street, you will pass over a graveyard of ships. Some lie buried beneath the sidewalk and street, others provide the foundations for buildings in this area.

Early San Francisco grew, not toward the hills, as one might expect, but out over the bay. Though there was a rough road to the Mission Dolores and another to the Presidio, Yerba Buenans stayed close to the waterfront, where all commerce occurred. The hills were wild and desolate, and between them were acres of shifting sand.

Expansion over the cove began gradually. Piles were sunk

in the mud at low tide, piers erected, and, on top of them, buildings. Ships pulled in and secured from the tides were used for warehouses and lodgings, and many, as the land was filled in around them, became permanently landlocked. The waterfront moved east, away from Montgomery Street. On July 5, 1849, the ship *Niantic* was anchored at what is now the northwest corner of Clay and Sansome streets, for use as a hotel, her crew having deserted her for the more fickle mistress gold. Its sign read: "Rest for the Weary and Storage for Trunks." The topside burned in the fire of 1851, but the hull was used as a foundation for the Niantic Building and part of it still lies beneath the building that stands here today. The city's first prison, the brig *Euphemia*, was moored nearby, at the northeast corner of Sansome and Sacramento streets. And then, not long after, Captain John Lawson came onto the scene.

THE CHAMPION SCUTTLER OF SHIPS. During the gold rush, Yerba Buena Cove was a forest of masts; hundreds of ships lay at anchor, deserted by their gold-hunting crews. By 1851 there were well over eight hundred in the bay. Some of these vessels sailed again. Others were used as warehouses and living accommodations. Many were scrapped for lumber; some of the world's finest woods went into the building of early San Francisco shanties. And a good number were left to burn or rot.

One of the most practical uses for the ships was hauling them in to that portion of the cove which was then being filled in, and sinking them. At this task there was one un-disputed pioneer and champion, Captain John Lawson, one of the least remembered but most colorful characters in early San Francisco.

Lawson began his career as champion scuttler when he bought two lots and found that they were under thirty-five feet of water.

The expense of hauling rocks and dirt was considerable; moreover it was hard to place such fill accurately. Lawson hit upon the idea of taking deserted ships, loading them with ballast, hauling them directly over the lots, then sinking them with carefully placed explosives. By the time his two lots were above water he was in the business.

His methods became more accurate and refined with practice. Divers were sent down to ascertain the depth of the water, the solidity of the bottom, the drift of the tides, the pull of the undercurrents, and the draw of the boat. Then Lawson worked each detail out on charts before commencing operations.

Among the ships he sank was the *Euphemia;* the thousand-ton bark *The Fair Agatha;* the mystery ship *Roma,* a snow-white vessel with baroque gilt fittings, said to have been an official Russian craft, romantically reputed to have carried a load of grand dukes, on their way to the mines.

It was not a problem-free occupation. Owners would turn up unexpectedly from the diggings. The *Cordova* sank beautifully, but, as Lawson soon learned, on the wrong lots. By 1853 there were few ships left and they were in demand. One night Lawson went to sleep aboard the *Noble,* which was to be sunk at the corner of Jackson and Davis streets the following morning. He awoke to find a tug hauling the ship out through the Golden Gate. Crawling to the bow, he cut the rope under a hail of gunfire. One of the pirates' bullets tore his cheek, another plowed his scalp.

Lawson was a good employer—for the purposes of getting the job done, perhaps too good. He paid his crews five dollars a day and all they could drink. He personally made sure there were always more than enough cases of whiskey aboard. His generosity backfired when he attempted to sink the *Alida* at Market and Davis streets. His crew of fifteen began drinking and reminiscing. By nightfall they refused either to sink or leave this fair old ship. Lawson pleaded, cajoled, threatened, then left under a hail of empty bottles. Irritated, he came back at midnight, affixed a barrel of gunpowder to the side, lit the fuse, and rowed away. Accounts of the sinking are most unsatisfactory; they make no mention of the fate of the crew.

Lawson is not remembered too fondly by some, particularly engineers and builders. The *Roma,* for example, which he sank at the corner of Market and East streets (now Market and the Embarcadero) had to be removed piece by piece when nearby buildings began sagging.

In all Lawson sank over one hundred ships, his competitors a like number, a ghost fleet of the past, now lying at anchor under the streets of downtown San Francisco.

From Montgomery and Clay streets, walk north one-half block.

Two plaques are on the southwest corner of Montgomery and Merchant streets, one commemorating the arrival of the first Pony Express rider, the other marking the Western headquarters of Russell, Majors, and Waddell, agents for the Pony Express.

THE PONY EXPRESS

"I agree not to use profane language, not to get drunk, not to gamble, not to treat animals cruelly, and not to do anything else that is incompatible with the conduct of a gentleman."

Thus swore "Buffalo Bill" Cody and eighty other men as they became riders in one of the most exciting undertakings in the taming of the West, the Pony Express, founded April 3, 1860.

"In itself, the Pony Express was an unsuccessful venture," wrote Joseph Henry Jackson in *The Western Gate:*

"It operated for only eighteen months or so, and it lost its promoters something like a million dollars. Nevertheless it accomplished an all-important thing; the Pony pioneered the Central Route to California, demonstrated that it was practical, and, by so doing, swung Congress over to that belief. Further, the pony was drama; his hoofs pounding the trails that led through dangerous Indian territory and over man-killing mountains and deserts, drummed the challenge of pioneering so loudly that all the world heard it. The courage and stamina of the Pony's riders gave America some tremendously good theatre; there was no resisting the excitement men felt when the Pony, flying over the prairie like 'a belated fragment of storm,' as Mark Twain put it, carried mail from Missouri to California in only ten days. That was an accomplishment to thrill the most cynical. The Pony's run actually ended at Sacramento. But the first pony came all the way down to San Francisco, abroad the steamer *Antelope* for those final eighty miles or so, and the city celebrated nobly as it should."

Across the street, cornered by Montgomery, Merchant, and Washington streets is (at the time of the writing) a parking lot. But pause here just a moment, listen and imagine, for the building that stood here is not long past, and it was haunted by the spirit of old San Francisco.

THE MONTGOMERY BLOCK. In summing up the outstanding achievements of the year 1853 the *Annals* noted:

"The magnificent structure known as Montgomery Block was completed toward the close of this year. This is the largest, most elegant, and imposing edifice in California, and would attract especial attention in any city, though it occupies a site that was partially covered by the waters of the bay as late as 1849. It has a front of 122 feet on the west side of Montgomery Street, from Washington to Merchant Street, along which streets it extends 138 feet, presenting an unbroken facade on these three streets of nearly 400 feet . . ."

Almost everything about the building was unorthodox. For the foundation its builder, Henry W. Halleck (later general in chief of the Union Army), used large redwood logs, which were sunk into the muddy tidelands, quickly earning the building the nicknames "Halleck's Folly" and "The Floating Fortress" by those who predicted it would sail across the bay. It *was* designed as a fortress, outside; inside the four connecting buildings overlooked a Florentine court. Unlike other city buildings at the time, it had four stories instead of three. It was, for many years, the largest building in California.

The second floor had a curious attraction for historic events. It was here (in Room 207) that editor James King of William died, six days after he was shot on the street outside by James P. Casey. Here, in the summer of 1888, Robert Louis Stevenson made arrangements to obtain the hundred-foot yacht *The Casco*, which was to take him on his final voyage to the South Seas. And it was on this floor, too, that Sun Yat-sen and Wong Sam Ark (world leader of the Chinese Masons) plotted the overthrow of the Manchu dynasty and the founding of the Chinese Republic.

On the Washington and Montgomery corner of the ground floor was the most famous saloon in San Francisco, the Bank Exchange, 1853–1918, where Duncan Nicol ("Pisco John") invented and served his legendary Pisco Punch.

Originally known as Parker's Bank Exchange, then as Duncan Nicol's Bank Exchange (and, informally, around the world, as "Pisco John's"), the bar was the center of much of the political and stock-market activity of the city from the 1850's to the 1880's. It was also the first cocktail lounge in the city to serve ladies. But it was Pisco Punch that brought it fame.

Its ingredients were (and alas remain) a secret, though there have since been many drinks bearing the name. Old-timers say it was the grandest drink ever created, and one might have a second but never a third. Nicol mixed it in the basement, then hauled it up to the bar via dumb-waiter. To the day its inventor died, shortly after the start of prohibition, he refused to divulge its components; as he told one reporter, "Even Mr. Volstead can't take the secret from me." One ingredient is known, Peruvian brandy, which was also used in perhaps the second most popular drink of the time, Button Punch. Rudyard Kipling described the latter as:

"the highest and noblest product of our age. No man but one knows what is in it. I have a theory that it is compounded of the shavings of cherub's wings, the glory of a tropical dawn, the red clouds of sunset, and fragments of lost epics by dead masters . . ."

On the Montgomery-Merchant corner of the block was one of the most famous restaurants in San Francisco, "Papa" Coppas, a refuge for writers, artists, and bohemians attracted by the genial surroundings, the trusting credit of Papa, and the twenty-five-cent special, which included a huge plate of spaghetti with sauce, a half loaf of French bread, and a bottle of wine. There were more expensive meals, too, for the tourists attracted here by the artists or their strange murals, which covered the walls.

In the 1890's Coppas was unofficial headquarters for most of the local literary lights: Jack London, Frank Norris, Charles Norris, Charles Caldwell Dobie, Ambrose Bierce, George Sterling, Will and Wallace Irwin; all came here, many had rooms or studios in the building.

It was here Gelett Burgess wrote the lines that were to plague him most of his life:

> "I never saw a purple cow,
> I never hope to see one;
> But I can tell you anyhow
> I'd rather see than be one."

until, in exasperation, he finally wrote a sequel:

> "Ah, yes, I wrote the 'Purple Cow'—
> I'm sorry, now, I wrote it;
> But I can tell you Anyhow
> I'll kill you if you quote it (!)"

The Montgomery Block, or the Monkey Block, as it later was affectionately but inexplicably known, survived the fire of 1906 only because an occupant drew out his revolver and threatened to shoot the first man to lay dynamite to it. The wind shifted, the fire moved on, and the building was saved, to stand for another five decades.

After most of its residents had moved out, and shortly before the building was razed in 1958, stories began circulating that the building was haunted. People still living here, or making one last visit, reported hearing strange conversations in empty hallways. They also experienced sudden, almost overpowering smells—not the musty odors of the corridors or the faint scents from the few illicit hot plates still remaining—but the unmistakable aromas of great and grand banquets. And there was unaccountable music and laughter, from rooms long vacant. Then the building was torn down.

Walk north on Montgomery one-half block to Washington Street.

On this corner was the city's first post office, located in the C. L. Ross & Co. store. In April 1849, Postmaster John W.

Geary slid a pane of glass out of a front window and began handing out mail. The line outside, since the previous day, had been over a block long; some, however, waited until delivery began, then paid ten or fifteen dollars for a good place in line.

Walk one block west on Washington Street to Portsmouth Square.

PORTSMOUTH SQUARE. Washington, Kearny, and Clay streets.

Yerba Buena and San Francisco grew up around "The Plaza," as Portsmouth Square was originally known. Located less than five hundred feet from the waterfront, the square became the city's first civic center—a place of buying and selling, politicking, debating, and loafing—crowded at most hours of the day with all manner of men, animals, and cargo.

Back in the quiet pastoral days of the Mexican occupation, one Candelario Miramontes, who lived at the Presidio, grew potatoes here. It was a fine, isolated location for a crop. But by the mid-1840's the square's solitude was gone.

When Captain John B. Montgomery hoisted the American flag over the Plaza on July 9, 1846 (on the spot, near the northeast corner of the square, where the Montgomery Flag Pole now stands), the square was already the center of what civic activity there was in Yerba Buena, whose habitations then numbered less than thirty. The adobe custom-house on the northwest corner of the square, where Montgomery's troops were quartered and from whose beams, less than five years later, would hang John Jenkins, housed Yerba Buena's municipal government, such as it was.

A half block to the west (midway between Washington

and Clay, on the east side of what is now Grant Avenue) was the city's first tenement, a large tent supported by four redwood pillars, the dwelling of harbor master Captain W. A. Richardson, constructed in 1835. And not far south of it (the southwest corner of Grant Avenue and Clay Street) was the first permanent home in the city (excluding the buildings at the Presidio and Mission Dolores), that of Jacob Leese.

Leese had arrived in the city in May of 1836, with intentions of starting a mercantile business. He began his house soon after his arrival, completing it on the morning of July 4. It was a rather grand structure, made of frame, sixty feet long and twenty-five feet broad. Richardson, meantime, sailed across the bay, inviting everyone he saw to his new neighbor's housewarming and Independence Day celebration. There was lots of bunting, American *and* Mexican flags, and an orchestra, which the *Annals* tells us consisted of "clarionet, flute, violin, drum, fife, and bugle; besides two small six pounders to form the bass, and to add their emphatic roar to the swelling din, when a toast of more than usual importance should be given . . ."

There was also a great deal to eat and drink, according to the same chroniclers:

"The abundance and variety of liquors at table seemed to tickle the Californians (Spaniards) amazingly. One worthy gentleman took a prodigious fancy to lemon syrup, a tumbler full of which he would quaff to every toast. This soon made him sick . . ."

The last word on the party was supplied by Mr. Leese in his diary: ". . . our fourth ended on the evening of the fifth."

Thus began a fine San Francisco tradition.

A year after Montgomery's landing the first school was built, on the west side of the square; it also served as jail, courthouse, church, and town hall. It was here that Judge William B. Almond, Esq., held court in 1849. From the *Annals*:

". . . the novel and summary manner in which he conducted his business and disposed of sometimes very important cases, was a source of as much merriment to some and mortification to others as anything else then transpiring in the town . . . His Honor . . . had a sovereign contempt to Buncombe speeches, legal technicalities, learned opinions, and triumphantly cited precedents. He was a man of quick discernment and clear judgement; and his opinion once formed, and that sometimes occurred before even the first witness was fully heard, his decision was made . . . The judge sat upon a rickety old chair, with his feet perched higher than his head upon a small mantel over the fireplace . . . and employed himself in paring his corns, or scraping his nails, while the 'learned counsel' briefly presented the case . . ."

On January 30, 1847, when the name of the city was officially changed from Yerba Buena to San Francisco, it was here, in the square, that the proclamation was read. And in 1848, when gold was discovered in the millrace of Sutter's mill, it was to the square that Sam Brannan ran, shouting, "GOLD! GOLD! GOLD from the American River!" (Sam had arrived in Yerba Buena on July 31, 1846, with a shipload of disgruntled Mormons, seeking a Zion outside the limits of the United States, where the Saints had been much persecuted. He arrived less than a month after Montgomery, and, it is said, upon seeing the American flag over the square threw down his hat, stamped on it, and cried, "There's that damn rag again!") And it was here, on October 18, 1850, that San Franciscans came to make speeches and celebrate after the mail ship *Oregon* sailed through the Golden Gate firing her cannons, announcing California's admission to the Union.

Picture for a moment the buildings that then surrounded the square.

Across the street to the north (moving from west to east) was the *Alta California* office, and atop it, on the second floor, Washington Hall, where the city's first play was held in January 1850, a double bill of *The Wife* and *Charles II*. Next to it was Monumental Engine Company, whose bell was to herald vigilante action; then the fruit stand of John Piper, later to make his fortune as the impresario of Piper's Opera House in Virginia City; and finally the Bella Union, the largest building of the lot and the city's most notorious gambling establishment (where Buddha's Universal Church now stands).

Across the street to the east, on the southeast corner of Kearny and Washington, was the El Dorado, another gambling house of some ill repute. On the main floor was Dennison's Exchange Saloon, where the first meeting of the Democratic party in California was held, October 25, 1849. Next door was the Parker House.

This corner was to be plagued by fire. The city's first fire broke out here, in December 1849, destroying both buildings. During the following year the Parker House was twice rebuilt and twice destroyed. Thomas Maguire then built the Jenny Lind Theatre on the same spot; during 1851 it burned twice, the third structure surviving only because it was made of stone. In 1852 Maguire sold it to the city of San Francisco for a city hall, at a price far in excess of its fair value. The Hall of Justice, built here in 1895 to house the city prison, police department, morgue, and courts, was destroyed in the fire of 1906. The new building was longer-lasting, housing these same offices until they were moved to the new Hall of Justice building in 1961. The rest of this block, in the early 1850's, was devoted to saloons and gambling houses.

To the south of the plaza, on the southeast corner of Kearny and Clay streets, was the city's first hotel, the Vioget House, built by surveyor John Vioget. With Montgomery's arrival its name was changed to Portsmouth House. Across the street, on the southwest corner of the same intersection, was the one-story adobe home and store of William Alexander Leidesdorff, American vice-consul under Mexican rule; it later became the City Hotel.

The gambling houses predominated—the El Dorado, the Bella Union, the Rendez-vous, the Empire, the Parker House, the Verandah—and from dusk to dawn they were the scene of frantic activity. For an account of their doings our source is Hubert Howe Bancroft. Bancroft was a bookseller during the gold rush. Fascinated with California's history, he began amassing books, documents, accounts —hoping someday to write a complete history of the state, soon realizing that no one man ever could. He did the next best thing. He built a "history factory" on Market Street, where he supervised the writing and publishing of what was to become a thirty-nine volume work.

Scholar though he was, Bancroft had an undisguised fondness for the gamblers who inhabited early San Francisco:

"Wherever found, in the city or in the mines, one can almost always pick them out in a crowd. They are the best-dressed men one meets; their pale, careworn, imperturbable faces wear an absent but by no means greedy air, and as they stand listlessly on the corner, or slowly and carelessly walk the street, by no means indifferent to a pretty female ankle, their calmly observant eyes, which are somewhat sunken in their sockets, seem to possess the faculty of looking through people while not looking at them . . ."

He goes even further, telling us that despite "his lonely disposition" this gentleman, the gambler, "is not quarrelsome, and never murders except professionally."

But it is fitting that the description of the gambling establishments that surrounded the square come from one with a prejudiced eye, for most of the early residents of the city took great delight in the sport.

Many of the halls, he notes, were decorated "with oriental splendor. . . .

"In one the ceiling, rich in fresco and gilt, was supported by glass pillars, pendant from which were great glass chandeliers. Around the walls were fine large paintings of nude female figures, and mirrors extending from floor to ceiling. Entering at night from the unlighted dismal street into an immense room lighted with dazzling brilliance, and loud with the mingled sound of musical instruments, the clink of coin and glasses, and the hum of human voices, was like passing from the dark depths to celestial brightness.

"There were long rows of leather-covered mahogany tables on which were tempting spread out heaps of glittering gold and silver coin, nuggets, slugs, bars, and bags of dust, and where the votaries of chance might choose from every game known to the civilized gambling world."

These were the surroundings. But it was the people, courting the goddess chance, which endowed them with life. "With difficulty one elbowed one's way through the promiscuous crowd that here nightly congregated. There were men in black clothes, immaculate linen, and shining silk hats, merchants, lawyers, and doctors, Chileans, and Mexicans; Irish laborers, Negroes, and Chinamen, some crowded round the tables intently watching the games, others lounging about, smoking, chewing, spitting, drinking, swearing, now and then dropping a dollar or a five, or ten, or twenty, or fifty dollar piece, with real or well-feigned indifference as to the result. Now and then the games were momentarily interrupted by the crack of a pistol, and the loungers became a little demoralized as the ball whistled past their ears and lodged in the wall. If a man was killed or wounded he was taken out, but the nature of the affray was left to be learned from the morning papers, and in a few moments all was as before."

After 1852, Bancroft notes sadly, "as a more refined civilization crept in and overwhelmed the low, the loose, and the vicious, gambling sank into disrepute. Law drove it behind doors and into windowless rooms. Then the gay gamblers of the olden times left the profession to a different class, and sought out new fields of distinction, perhaps in politics, law, or speculation."

As the years passed the square stayed very much the same, almost unmarked by time, a witness to, but not really a part of, the tremendous changes in the city around it, a city that was growing away from its beginnings. There were slight changes in the landscaping of the square. A permanent flagpole was erected on the site where Montgomery first flew the American flag. And much later still another monument was added, in memory of a tall, sickly young man who came here in 1879 to lounge on the grass, absorb the sun, and write. The bronze ship atop the simple granite shaft of the Robert Louis Stevenson Monument is the *La Bonne Aventure*.

But change finally came. In the words of Acting Mayor Harold Dobbs, "Progress must come and San Francisco must proceed if we are to keep our position as the Queen City of the West." Progress in this case was the uprooting of the square to build a large underground garage. The day was November 15, 1960, and Dobbs added a few other words before the first shovel of dirt was turned: "I can assure you that the surface of the park and the monuments so dear to all of us will be restored." It was not until some months later that San Franciscans discovered what city officials had known from the time the final plans were submitted, that to restore the square as it was would be unfeasible and impractical.

So change came to Portsmouth Square, as it has to most of the landmarks of the almost forgotten village of Yerba Buena.

Yet there is a certain quality about the city that provides its own continuity in change, that survives even progress, the razing of buildings, the uprooting of land. If you have seen San Francisco at night, from the Top of the Mark, the bridges, or from across the bay, you will catch a glimpse of this in this last quotation from Bayard Taylor, written in 1849:

"The appearance of San Francisco at night, from the water, is unlike anything I ever beheld. The houses are mostly of canvas, which is made transparent by the lamps within, and transforms them, in the darkness, to dwellings of solid light. Seated on the slopes of its three hills, the tents pitched among the chapparal to the very summits, it gleams like an amphitheatre of fire. Here and there shine out brilliant points, from the decoy-lamps of the gaming houses; and through the indistinct murmur of the streets comes by fits the sound of music from their hot and crowded precincts. The picture has in it something unreal and fantastic; it impresses one like the cities of the magic lantern, which a motion of the hand could build or annihilate."

One suspects there will always be a little of Yerba Buena about San Francisco.

For Additional Exploration:

BONANZA INN. By Oscar Lewis and Carroll D. Hall. The life and times of the Palace Hotel.

MEN TO MATCH MY MOUNTAINS. By Irving Stone. A monumental account of the opening of the Far West, 1840–1900.

THE FACE OF SAN FRANCISCO. By Harold Gilliam and Phil Palmer. A portrait of modern San Francisco, told through memorable photographs and a perceptive text.

THE WESTERN GATE. Edited by Joseph Henry Jackson. A San Francisco reader, from Fray Francisco Palou to Herb Caen.

BAGHDAD BY THE BAY. DON'T CALL IT FRISCO. NEW GUIDE TO
SAN FRANCISCO. ONLY IN SAN FRANCISCO. SAN FRANCISCO—
CITY ON GOLDEN HILLS. The collected works of columnist
Herb Caen.

SAN FRANCISCO: THE BAY AND ITS CITIES. Compiled by the
workers of the Writers' Program of the Work Projects Administration in Northern California. Although outdated,
the most comprehensive guide to San Francisco and the
Bay Area.

THE EARTH SHOOK, THE SKY BURNED. By William Bronson.
By far the finest book, both pictorially and textually, thus
far published on the earthquake and fire of 1906.

CHAPTER TWO:

TELEGRAPH HILL AND NORTH BEACH

A Walking Tour Through one of the Most Colorful Sections of the City — the Telegraph Hill-North Beach Area. Beginning with a moral journey through what once was that sink of depravity and "loud bit of hell," the Barbary Coast — on to Broadway, the night-club belt — North Beach, Italian and Bohemian — Washington Square — Telegraph Hill — and Fisherman's Wharf. With impersonal introductions to the Girls of the Coast — Shanghai Kelly, the friendly crimp — Calico Jim — temperate Dr. C. G. Cogswell and fire buff Lillie Hitchcock Coit — with a digression on the islands in the bay.

From Portsmouth Square walk east one block on Washington to Montgomery Street, cross to the northeast corner, walk north on Montgomery.

Despite the frequency and severity of its fires, accidental and man-made, San Francisco was never swept completely clean. Many of the buildings in the next few blocks date from gold-rush days. Most structures (those along the east side of Montgomery and the north side of Jackson Street) also stand on what was once the shoreline of Yerba Buena Cove.

THE CALIFORNIA STEAM AND NAVIGATION COMPANY, the second building from the corner, was built in 1859 as headquarters for the steamships that supplied the chief means of travel on the Sacramento and San

TELEGRAPH HILL
AND NORTH BEACH

1. Portsmouth Square
2. Washington Square
3. Coit Memorial Tower
4. Fisherman's Wharf

Joaquin rivers between 1854 and 1871. Prior to the formation of this company, independent competition was fierce; a boat would sometimes ram and sink another, rather than let it arrive at their common destination first.

The building in which DORO'S RESTAURANT is now located (714–720 Montgomery), known as the Ship Building, is a decade older. The schooner *Georgean*, abandoned in the bay in 1849 with a full load of cotton and Kentucky twist, was beached here and converted into offices and studios. For many years a Chinese laundry was set up in its fo'c's'le head.

Walk into the courtyard of the BELLI BUILDING (722–728 Montgomery). Here is an excellent example of the attractive use to which old San Francisco buildings are sometimes, though unfortunately not always, put. On the third floor of an earlier building California's first Masonic Lodge held its first meeting October 17, 1849. The present building, known as the Melodeon Theatre Building (722–724 Montgomery), was erected in 1857 and was for a time the scene of minstrel and musical shows. The Genella Building (728 Montgomery) was built in 1854 and contained, among other things, an early bank and a chinaware shop.

The building at 732 Montgomery was the site of the GOLDEN ERA BUILDING. The weekly *Golden Era* was a "family newspaper," devoted to "Literature, Agriculture, the Mining Interest, Local and Foreign News, Commerce, Education, Morals, and Amusements." Unlike most of the city's early newspapers, especially those periodicals with some literary pretensions, the *Golden Era* had a long life, being published for nearly forty years after its founding in December 1852. Among its contributors were Bret Harte (whose first published work, a slight poem called *The Valentine*, appeared in its pages in 1857); Mark Twain; poetess Ina Coolbrith; temperamental charmer Joaquin Miller; Charles Warren Stoddard, who, out of shyness, signed his early work, "Pip Pepperpod"; and young Unitarian minister

Thomas Starr King, whose inspired oratory was said to have kept California in the Union.

Progress takes various forms. The Pioche and Hotaling Warehouse, built in 1860 and located on the southeast corner of Jackson and Montgomery streets, was razed to make way for the San Francisco Playboy Club. And with the old building went a plaque which read:

"On this site the first San Francisco bridge was constructed in 1844 by order of William Sturgis Hinckley, alcalde of Yerba Buena. It crossed a creek which connected Laguna Salada with the Bay and was regarded as a remarkable structure and great public improvement as it shortened the distance to the town's embarcadero at Clarke's Point."

Obviously this called for a celebration. The *Annals* notes that the whole town, all thirty-odd residents, assembled to jump up and down on the bridge to test and marvel at its strength.

Walk east on Jackson Street.

JACKSON SQUARE.   Don't look for a square; there isn't one. The designation refers to the single block of Jackson Street bounded by Montgomery and Sansome streets, and came into use just a few years ago, when this run-down block of old warehouses and distilleries was remarkably renovated as a center for interior decorators' showrooms (wholesale only). Most of the buildings in this area were erected in the early 1860's and survived all subsequent fires.

THE HOTALING WAREHOUSE, on the southeast corner of Jackson Street and Hotaling Place, a whiskey distillery for the Barbary Coast, not only escaped the fire of '06 but was immortalized by it. In answer to the frequent assertions of San Francisco ministers that the city had been destroyed for its wickedness, Charles Field wrote these much-quoted lines:

> "If, as they say, God spanked the town
>   For being over-frisky,
> Why did He burn His Churches down
>   And spare Hotaling's whiskey?"

Walk east on Jackson to Sansome, cross the street, and walk back to Montgomery on the other side.

In addition to the decorators' showrooms there are several fine galleries and art shops in the vicinity of Sansome Street and Pacific Avenue.

The building on the northeast corner of Jackson and Montgomery streets predates most of the others in the vicinity. Once the bank of Lucas Turner and Company, it was built in 1854 by William Tecumseh Sherman, a man not usually remembered as a creator.

Continue west on Jackson to Columbus Avenue, then follow Columbus northwest for one block.

This area bounded by Montgomery, Pacific, Washington, and Kearny (now intersected by Columbus Avenue) has, almost since the beginning of San Francisco, housed one or another of the city's minority groups. Today they are the Filipinos, and the area is known as "Little Manila." In 1851, according to historian Bancroft, this was:

"a hollow filled with little wooden huts planted promiscuously, with numberless recess and fastnesses filled with Chileans—men, women, and children. The place was called Little Chile. The women appeared to be always washing, but the vocation of the men was a puzzle to passers-by. Neither the scenery of the place nor its surroundings were very pleasant, particularly in hot weather . . . Notwithstanding, it was home to them, and from their filthy quarters they might be seen emerging on Sundays, the men washed and clean-shirted, and the women arrayed in smiling faces and bright-colored apparel. They could work and wallow patiently through the week provided they could enjoy a little recreation and fresh air on Sunday. Whenever a vessel arrived from a home port, the camping grounds presented a lively appearance. Round the chief hut or *tienda* lounged dirty men in parti-colored serapes and round-crowned straw hats, smoking, drinking and betting at monte. Most of these were either on their way to, or had lately returned from, the mines."

The pastoral scene Bancroft described was, during the same decade, to pass forever from existence. From the 1850's, when this area marked the southern boundary of Sydney Town, to 1907, when political boss Abraham Ruef left his office in the Columbus Tower to spend fourteen years in prison, these blocks and those surrounding were to be one of the world's most infamous cesspools of vice and crime, known during the last thirty of these years as the Barbary Coast.

COLUMBUS TOWER, at Columbus Avenue and Kearny Street, is one of a number of flatiron buildings on this avenue, perfectly described by Herb Caen as "sharp edges of a city that grew in too many directions at once." Built in 1905 (superbly remodeled in 1959) the Tower was for several years the headquarters of the last of the great political bosses of the city, Abe Ruef.

One cannot credit Abraham Ruef with all the municipal corruption that occurred during his half-dozen years behind the San Francisco political scenes (1902–07). In part, acknowledgment must be made to an established tradition that during the nineteenth century was only occasionally interrupted by short eras of clean government. And more than a little of the credit belongs to Ruef's associates, often called "the paint eaters," after Ruef once remarked that in their greed they would even eat the paint off City Hall. (When that august building collapsed less than sixty seconds after the first shock of the 1906 earthquake, most residents were sure they hadn't stopped with the paint.)

Ruef came into power in 1902, with the election of Eugene E. Schmitz as mayor. Schmitz, a member of the Musicians' Union, was the candidate of the Union Labor party. Labor's friend soon proved to be its worst enemy, acting in the interests of both Ruef and the railroad lobby, interests that, as later trials proved, were all too often synonymous.

It was perfectly appropriate that Ruef's office, on the top floor of the Tower, overlooked all of the Barbary Coast and most of Chinatown, for he was in complete control of most of the vice in these areas. Largely due to the crusading efforts of Fremont Older of the *Bulletin,* graft prosecutions against Ruef, Schmitz, and a host of their cohorts were begun in November 1906. Schmitz fled to Europe and escaped punishment. Ruef, after hiding out for several months, was captured and sent to San Quentin. These events were to be important factors in the subsequent death of the Barbary Coast.

Walk east on the south side of Pacific Avenue.

THE BARBARY COAST

California folk song:

> "The miners came in forty-nine,
>   The whores in fifty-one;
>   And when they got together
>   They produced the native son."

French traveler Albert Benard de Russailh, 1851:

". . . There are also some honest women in San Francisco, but not very many."

Hinton Rowan Helper, *The Land of Gold*, 1855:

"I may not be a competent judge, but this much I will say, that I have seen purer liquors, better segars, finer tobacco, truer guns and pistols, larger dirks and bowie knives, and prettier courtezans, here in San Francisco, than in any other place I have ever visited; and it is my unbiased opinion that California can and does furnish the best bad things that are obtainable in America."

As these three quotations should indicate, the Barbary Coast did not spring up overnight. It had its roots in the gold rush, though it was not until the mid-1860's, after its era as Sydney Town, that it was christened, by person or persons unknown, the Barbary Coast, probably in honor of that infamous stretch of African coastline well known to sailors of the day.

Herbert Asbury, in his book *The Barbary Coast,* mapped out its area as occupying:

"a greater or lesser portion of the territory bounded on the east by the waterfront . . . ; on the south by Clay and Commercial Streets; on the west by Grant Avenue and Chinatown; and on the north by Broadway, with occasional overflows into the region around North Beach and Telegraph Hill."

Asbury notes that "Owing to periodic spasms of civic virtue, to the encroachments of residential and business developments and to other causes, its limits naturally varied with the years. . . . Its most iniquitous features," he adds, "were confined within the rectangular district limited by Broadway and Washington, Montgomery and Stockton Streets."

Here were saloons, dance halls, dives, cheap hotels, lodging houses, and brothels, the last far outnumbering all the other establishments combined. The brothels were of three types—cribs, cowyards, and parlor houses, each with numerous gradations of quality.

A crib was a room just large enough for a small but strong iron bed. A number of cribs grouped together under one management, in one or several connecting buildings, made up a cowyard, which often accommodated up to three hundred working girls, whose favors sold for two bits to one dollar.

(The expressions "one bit," "two bits," etc., had their origin in gold-rush San Francisco. Gold dust was measured in "bits" and "pinches." More than a few bartenders were hired for the length of their fingers, not for their facility at mixing drinks. The bartender who could reach into a leather poke and extract a good-sized "pinch" between his thumb and forefinger was never without an offer of a job. Thus was born the expression "How much can you get in a pinch?")

The parlor houses were much more lavish and sedate than the cribs and cowyards. Often they were furnished with thick rugs, red plush furniture, and ornate fittings worth their weight in gilt. Each had a large living room where the madam presided, often against a piano background. The asking prices here were five to thirty dollars, for the parlor houses had the pick of the girls.

Often a madam prided herself on the gentility of her establishment. One, that of Bertha Kahn, on Sacramento Street, had signs in every room declaring:

"NO VULGARITY
ALLOWED
IN THIS ESTABLISHMENT"

Madame Kahn's bagnio, according to Asbury, had a historical distinction. Here was born the traditional call by which harlots ever since have been summoned into the parlors of American houses of prostitution.

"When visitors entered her brothel, Madame Bertha, who was a huge woman with a tremendous contralto voice, strode to the foot of the stairs and shouted: 'Company, girls!'"

Another madam on Sacramento Street achieved a measure of local fame when she posted the following sign outside her establishment:

"MADAME LUCY
YE OLDE WHORE SHOPPE"

Indignant neighbors protested to the police, who made her return to the traditional advertising media, the discreet red light.

There were few parlor houses within the heart of the Coast; establishments here drew a different clientele. Most of the customers and habitués of the Coast (excluding the slummers) were seafaring men. Sailors of the day had an expression. The world, they said, was divided into three parts: the sea, the ship, and the Barbary Coast. And the Coast catered to their every whim; anything could be bought here for a price, including the establishment's official "virgin."

In more than a few cases the price paid for the fleeting pleasures was life itself. Others, somewhat luckier, lost only their money, health, and a few months' time, as shanghaiing was an accepted custom in these parts.

"The anything but gentle art of crimping seamen was by no means confined to San Francisco," wrote historian Richard Dillon in his book *Embarcadero*, "but during the nineteenth century no port—Valparaiso, New York or Liverpool —bore quite so evil a reputation as it did. The Golden Gate city so far excelled her competitors that a new term for crimping was coined on the Embarcadero, a term which made its way into the English language, including dictionaries, as 'shanghaiing.' . . . Shanghai was less often the destination of a slugged or drugged seaman than was Canton or Mejillones, but a 'shanghai voyage' or a 'shanghai passage' grew to mean a long, roundabout, and usually involuntary deepwater cruise."

The method varied. Miss Piggott, whose establishment was on Davis Street, would simply maneuver an unsuspecting customer over a trap door in the floor of the bar, hit him over the head with a bung starter, and release the trap. Largely because of the madam's brawn many of her victims never survived the voyage to the cellar, much less around the Horn. Her assistant, Nikko, a Laplander, compensated for it; he is credited with introducing the practice of selling corpses to shipmasters instead of live, drugged seamen. Sometimes straw dummies were also sold, with trapped rats inserted in the clothing to give the inert forms the necessary twitches of life.

Usually, however, the "pretty waiter girls," as the

waitress-prostitutes of the saloons and dance halls were called, did it much more simply with doctored drinks. One of the most effective mixtures (seamen never asked for a second) was a potent punch composed of equal parts of brandy, whiskey, and gin, liberally laced with opium. Chloral hydrate, knockout drops, were first used on the Coast. But, as one chronicler of the times said, drugs were not used half as much as some claimed them to be—the liquor was bad enough.

Foremost among the many who doubled as crimps and pimps (many of them boarding the ships and inducing the men ashore as soon as the vessels entered the Golden Gate) were Shanghai Kelly and Calico Jim. Kelly's establishment on Pacific Avenue had three trap doors. It was also conveniently built over the water, so that rowboats below could transport the men directly to the ships. But Kelly's great feat did not occur in his establishment. Once when there was a shortage of seamen in the city and the demand for them was great, Kelly charted the paddle-wheel steamer *Goliath* and invited all his friends from the Coast aboard to help celebrate his birthday. The ship was packed with food, drugged liquor, and free-loading well-wishers. That night when Kelly berthed the empty *Goliath*, three of the worst hell ships of the Pacific sailed out of the Golden Gate fully manned.

Calico Jim's place was down Glen Alley, near Battery Point. The tale is told that when Jim was accused of a murder he had committed six policemen were in turn sent to take him. All six were promptly shanghaied. Some months later, when they made their way back to the city from various points of the globe, Jim fled to South America. The six officers of the law drew lots to see which would have the honor. The chosen tracked Jim to Peru, where, accosting him on the street, he shot him six times.

There were many others—Mother Bronson; Limey Dirk; Jimmy the Pig; Johnny Devine; the Shanghai Chicken, who used his iron-hook hand with deadly precision. It was largely due to their machinations that the Sailor's Union of the Pacific was formed, one of the first steps in bringing order to the waterfront.

Equally well known, in their times, were the various female entertainers who appeared on the boards of the dance halls of the Coast, and whose nicknames describe their talents: the "Waddling Duck," the "Dancing Heifer," the "Little Lost Chicken," the "Galloping Cow" and "Gyp." (Gyp's dance was obscenely lewd, however its effect was tempered by a smile of infantile innocence.) Some sang, some danced, and all earned as much money off stage as on.

In the dance halls on Pacific Avenue (also known as Terrific Street and Battle Acre)—the Thalia, the Midway, Purcells, the Hippodrome, Spider Kelly's, Moulin Rouge, to name only a few—originated, according to Asbury:

"dance steps which practically every dancing young man and woman in America strove to master. For the turkey trot, the bunny hug, the chicken glide, the Texas Tommy, the pony prance, the grizzly bear, and many other varieties of close and semi-acrobatic dancing, which swept the country during the half-dozen years that preceded the World War, despite the scandalized roaring of the nation's pastors, were first performed in the dance halls of the Barbary Coast . . ."

The fire of 1906 almost totally destroyed the Barbary Coast (except, curiously, Ruef's Tower). Though it was the first part of the city to rebuild and open for business, the Coast was now restricted to a relatively small area, this block on Pacific Avenue. The graft prosecutions of 1906, which indicted Ruef, were harbingers of doom for the Coast. The Red Light Abatement Act of 1914, prohibition, and various reform crusades did the rest. In 1921 it briefly but unsuccessfully tried to resurrect itself. As Charles Caldwell Dobie wrote:

"The quarter did what every courtesan does who finds her charms and her following on the wane. It decided to capitalize on its previous reputation, buy a new false front and an extra pot of rouge. The result was a tough quarter maintained largely for the purpose of shocking tourists from the Chautauqua circuit."

By 1935 it was so far gone that one writer called it a "street of dance-halls and imitation vice." Sailors still came here, less by tradition than because of the numerous strip joints. "B girls" had long since replaced the "pretty waiter girls." In the late 1950's, after the street had again been renamed, now as the International Settlement, the last bars closed. Most of them had long since had their liquor licenses revoked and were reduced to selling soft drinks and sweet vermouth at a dollar a glass.

Many of the buildings on both sides of this block of Pacific Avenue date from the post-fire Barbary Coast. Outside 555 Pacific is still another reminder of the quarter's bawdier days and nights: the famed satyr sculptures of Arthur Putnam.

On reaching Montgomery, cross to the other side and walk back to Columbus Avenue.

There are some who view the renovation of this last great center of masculine vice into a street of interior decorator shops (an extension of Jackson Square) as a sad commentary on our times. Most, however, are content to remember but not mourn the passing of the Coast. It was a murderous, vicious, diseased cancer in the body of San Francisco, yet . . .

The *Annals of San Francisco* was published in 1854, a decade before this area became *really* wicked, but Frank Soule's remarks about the sins of San Francisco are perhaps a fitting epitaph for the Coast:

"Though there be much vice in San Francisco, one virtue—though perhaps a negative one, the citizens at least have. They are not hypocrites, who pretend to high qualities which they do not possess. In great cities of the old world, or it may be even in those of the pseudo-righteous New England States, there may be quite as much crime and vice committed as in San Francisco, only the customs of the former places throw a decent shade over the grosser, viler aspects. The criminal, the fool, and the voluptuary are not allowed to boast, directly or indirectly, of their bad, base, or foolish deeds, as is so often done in California."

Walk north on Columbus Avenue to Broadway.

NORTH BEACH.   There is a subtle change as we move from downtown San Francisco into this, one of the city's most colorful neighborhoods, for here the past is a living part of the present. In place of old buildings, sites, and historical markers we have strangely laden shopwindows, foreign tongues, and Old World traditions, mixed, not altogether incongruously, with the past-disclaiming protests of Bohemia. The dozen blocks of Broadway that stretch from the east end of the Broadway tunnel to the bay form the southern boundary of this area.

North Beach, deceptively, isn't a beach at all—although at one time there was one here, a popular pleasure resort of the 1860's and 1870's, before the city began filling in the land along this part of the bay. Rather North Beach is a narrow valley between the slopes of Telegraph and Russian hills, containing most of the Italian, a large part of the Mexican, all of the Basque, and a good measure of the bohemian population of San Francisco, plus a flavoring of peoples from most other parts of the world.

The Italians predominate, eighty thousand strong. The first to arrive and settle were Captain Pietro Bonzi and his son Orazio, who came in 1840. Others followed, and the pattern was almost unvarying. The men came first, worked hard and saved: to bring their families from Italy; to buy their own boats, if they were fishermen, or their own businesses if they were not. (The young unmarried men saved first to return to Italy to pick a wife.) And then, once the family was established, they kept saving, but this time to be able to return to Genova or Milano or Roma to live, although most of them were content with a short visit once they got back. They chose to settle in North Beach because the rents were cheap (from the 1870's until well into the present century a flat could be had for ten to twelve dollars a month, plus a landlord who would do almost anything to keep his tenants); it was close to their work, for most were fishermen; and the bay itself was more than a little reminiscent of the Bay of Naples.

It was not until the latter part of the last century, however, when the Italians began to outnumber the French, Irish, Spanish, Chileans, and Germans—who also chose to settle not far from the point of their debarkation, the long-vanished North Point Docks at the end of Sansome Street—that the area became known as "Little Italy."

The Mexicans, who arrived before the Italians and for many years had the largest foreign colony here, have spread through the Bay Area, leaving only a small settlement of the oldest families in North Beach. Their world is largely centered upon their church, Nuestra Señora de Guadalupe, and a number of shops and restaurants along Broadway.

The Basques have a permanent population of fewer than one hundred; during some seasons, however, especially when the sheepherders come down from the hills of California and adjacent states, more than a thousand congregate around the few Basque hotels, restaurants, and bars still remaining on Broadway.

Outnumbering both the Basques and the Mexicans in the North Beach area are the Chinese, no longer confined by tradition and law to the ten square blocks of Chinatown.

But separating the nationalities in this way gives a partly incorrect impression. For, though their social life is often centered within their own ethnic groups, North Beach itself is a fairly heterogeneous mixture. Any single block in the area is likely to include an Italian or Chinese market (or a combination, such as the Napoli Market, managed by Lloyd Quock), patronized by everyone; apartment houses containing two or three different national groups, and probably owned by a member of an altogether different one; and a laundromat or cleaner's shop under Irish or Jewish management. Even the major Italian celebrations—Columbus Day, celebrated in Washington Square, and the Blessing of the Fishing Fleet, occurring on the first Sunday in October and climaxed by a march from the square to Fisherman's Wharf —are community celebrations. And most of North Beach (most of San Francisco for that matter) heads for Chinatown during Chinese New Year. The relaxed informality of most of North Beach cannot be separated into distinct components. It is a little of each and a little of all, and no other section of the city is quite like it.

This is especially apparent on Broadway, the city's nightclub belt. Here entertainment ranges from Italian opera to jazz to female impersonation to topless. (Since the inception of the latter in 1964, Broadway has been dubbed "Mammary Lane.") Restaurants vary from the most expensive to the cheapest, from prime American beef through a great variety of pizzas to teriyaki. And the bars are as different as the drinks they serve, martinis, camparis, cappuccinos, Irish coffee, and scotch and soda.

Cross Broadway and walk north along Grant Avenue to Union Street.

To many, North Beach is also Bohemia, as it has been since the last quarter of the nineteenth century, during the days

of Joaquin Miller, Jack London, Ina Coolbrith, Rudolf
Friml, Edwin Booth, and George Sterling. In a way the
term is deserved. Over the years the area has attracted a
great number of artists and musicians, entertainers and
writers, though probably no more than could be found in
other parts of the city. But most—contrary to newspaper-
magazine descriptions of the Lost, Silent, and Beat Generations—were individuals independent of literary cults,
groups, or movements; most who actually wrote or painted
or composed or performed, that is. Here, as elsewhere, the
talkers inevitably predominate.

At its best, one suspects, bohemianism is merely a state
of mind, the ability to see things freely and, when necessary,
differently. In the last analysis it is just a label, despite the
fact that some make it a social convention. It fits North
Beach if you don't take it too seriously.

In recent years the informal gathering places of North
Beach's bohemians or *avant-garde* have been the bars and
shops along Grant Avenue, Broadway, and the City Lights
and Discovery bookshops on Columbus Avenue.

Walk west on Union Street to WASHINGTON
SQUARE. *Columbus Avenue, Union, Stockton, and
Filbert streets.*

San Francisco, as has already been noted, is a city of contrasts. Nowhere is this better illustrated than in Washington Square. It is true not only of the people who come here
for the sun—Chinese, Negroes, aged and vested *paesani*,
causeless rebels with or without beards, secretaries, shopkeepers, and children—but also of the square's two statues
and their donors.

The statue of Benjamin Franklin was given to the city
by Dr. Henry D. Cogswell. Dr. Cogswell, a pioneer dentist,

made his fortune shortly after his arrival in the city in 1849 by encouraging a curious form of ostentation. Asbury tells us that many of the miners

"at a loss how else to exhibit their prosperity, employed dentists to put their own gold into their teeth. If they had no teeth that required attention, they had good ones dug out and gold ones substituted. Scores of men had all of their teeth extracted and gold plates installed instead."

Within a few years Dr. Cogswell was twice a millionaire and looking for some good philanthropic cause. Being a teetotaler, he decided to erect a public drinking fountain for every one hundred saloons. Before he quit, he had built several dozen; this is one of the few that still survive, also one of the few on which he erected a statue of someone other than himself.

Contemporaries described Dr. Cogswell as dull and thrifty. Obviously he was also sly—the spigots on the various sides of the fountain labeled "California Seltzer," "Vichy," and "Congress Water" all give forth ordinary drinking water; and more than a little morbid, as attested by the dedication "Presented by H. D. Cogswell to our boys and girls, who will soon take our places and pass on."

It is certain that he had little in common with the donor of the square's other statue.

The Volunteer Firemen's Monument, on the northwest side of the square, a bronze group of three firemen and a rescued damsel, was dedicated to the Volunteer Fire Department of San Francisco, 1849–66, and presented to the city at the bequest of Lillie Hitchcock Coit.

Lillie was the daughter of a prominent surgeon, Charles McPhail Hitchcock, who arrived in San Francisco in 1851. Like Dr. Cogswell in one respect, Lillie had an unusual passion; she liked to chase fire engines, a habit begun as a child and indulged until she was well into her later years. She was especially attracted to Knickerbocker Company No. 5 and while in her teens was formally accepted as mascot of the company. Later, after she married financier B. Howard Coit, she had the numeral 5 embroidered on all of her clothing and always signed her checks, "Lillie Hitchcock Coit 5."

Through all her days she was a nonconformist. While the women of San Francisco affected social pretensions, Lillie smoked, drank, shot pistols, attended cockfights, shaved her head so her colorful wigs would fit better, dressed in men's clothing, and chased fires. When she died in 1924, at eighty-three, she left $50,000 for this monument and $100,000 for the beautification of the city. The latter funds were used for the building of Coit Memorial Tower atop nearby Telegraph Hill.

Neighborhood youths, whether familiar with Lillie's story or not, frequently find the uplifted hand of the fireman too great a temptation. Early-morning passers-by frequently see an empty bottle lifted as if in extolment.

To Telegraph Hill and Coit Tower:

BUS: Catch the No. 39 Coit at the corner of Columbus Avenue and Union Street.

DRIVING: North on Stockton Street two blocks to Lombard Street; east on Lombard to Telegraph Hill Boulevard; follow the same to the summit.

WALKING: As above, except at the end of Lombard Street take the footpath at the base of the hill. (It's uphill all the way, but a fine walk.)

TELEGRAPH HILL. *Loma Alta,* or High Hill, as the Spanish called it before the first Americans came, was a round brown peak, sometimes brightly alive with vegetation —wild blue lupine, yellow mustard, dense chaparral, scrub oak, and the mint yerba buena. Even after the landing of the *Portsmouth* few thought of living here, not on the peak itself. Fort Montgomery was built toward its base, on the eastern side, but was soon abandoned, the cannon and battlements left to rust and time's decay.

In the late 1840's a Scotsman named Joseph MacGregor leased the summit and built a two-story lookout, topped with an observation platform. Through the use of heliograph code he would notify the residents of Yerba Buena of ship arrivals.

The semaphore tower that George Sweeny and Theodore Baugh constructed in 1850 stood atop MacGregor's observation tower. It was an ungainly apparatus, with large black arms, whose signals were known and watched expectantly by most of the children and all of the adults of San Francisco. It was soon connected by telegraph with another tower, built by the same men on Point Lobos, just outside the Gate, often enabling residents to anticipate a ship's arrival by several hours. The signal of two arms outstretched was the most welcome sight, for it meant the arrival of a side-wheel steamer. Schools were dismissed and all business stopped, for these steamers brought the mail.

One night in the 1850's, during a performance of *The Hunchback* at the American Theatre, a performer rushed on stage, threw out both arms, and cried, "What does this mean?" A rogue in the gallery yelled, "Side-wheel steamer!" and brought down the house.

The signals were illustrated on a broadsheet and sold by all the newsboys. Bancroft, in his history, recalls a newly arrived immigrant who

"in applying this chart to the interpretation of signals, mistook a windmill which stood near by for the arms of the telegraph, and counting up the fans concluded that a fleet of clippers was coming in."

The semaphore station was closed down in 1855, and the hill, now named Telegraph, became a popular Sunday picnic spot. Habitations were still few, and confined to the lower portions of the hill. Charles Warren Stoddard, writing of the same year, recalled that

"the hill was not inhabited save by flocks of goats that browsed there all the year round, and the herds of boys that gave them chase, especially of a holiday."

The Irish were the first to populate the hill in large numbers. If the expression "shanty Irish" ever had any real meaning, it was in San Francisco, for their homes were crude wooden shanties, from which came loud happy laughter or the equally loud moanful dirges of the wakes.

A stanza from Wallace Irwin's *Telygraft Hill* perfectly describes the hill during this period:

"For the Irish they live on the top av it,
    And the Dagos they live on the base av it,
    And every tin can in the knowledge of man,
    Is scattered all over the face av it,
    Av Telygraft Hill, Telygraft Hill,
    Nobby owld, slobby owld Telygraft Hill."

The signal tower blew down in 1871. In 1882, a large German castle was built on the top of the hill, baroque, incongruous, more than a little grotesque; however, it had facilities for dining. Nearby was erected a large tower containing a time ball. At exactly noon the ball would fall, enabling the ships in the bay to set their chronometers. The hill knew many strange sights: the wrecks of ships in the bay, riots on Alcatraz, the arrival of great fleets. But perhaps none were quite so strange as the practice of dueling on horseback, the combatants armor-clad and using broadswords, which had a short-lived popularity on the top of the hill during the 1880's, one of the attractions by which the castle owners hoped to make the resort pay. The castle burned in 1903; it had never paid its way.

Gradually the Italians moved up the slopes of the hill. While the fire of 1906 burned most of the surrounding area, the buildings on Telegraph Hill did not burn; residents doused them with buckets of red wine, saving them from destruction.

Bohemia moved onto the hill in the 1890's and stayed through the "lawless decade" of the 1920's. Not until this latter period did the city finally pave a road to the top of the hill. It was perhaps inevitable that in time someone would realize that the magnificent views from the hill were worth money and undertake the building of expensive homes and apartment houses. When they did they faced bitter opposition. The first such building was almost never completed. From the start to the finish of construction, hill residents periodically barraged both the house and the workmen with rocks, tin cans, and dead cats from the slopes above.

Charles Caldwell Dobie wrote despondently of the fate of the hill in 1933:

"The greatest enemy of the Hill as it exists today is not, however, bohemia gone pallid, but wealth seeking new fields to contaminate . . . Telegraph Hill has had a glorious history of picturesque squalor; if it is now in line for something more correct and conventional, it is to be hoped that it will fall into the hands of people who are at least genuine. If they but love the Hill all will be well—if they exploit it or condescend toward it the Hill is doomed."

COIT MEMORIAL TOWER was erected on the summit of Telegraph Hill in 1934. Designed by architect Arthur Brown, Jr., the fluted column at first bothered San Franciscans as much as the invasion of wealth bothered author Dobie, though in the years since it has become an accepted part of the city's skyline. The tower rises 210 feet from its base, the hill is 274 feet above sea level. Vandalism unfortunately has made it necessary to close the lower floor and the stairs to the public, although some of the murals of the Work Projects Administration artists can be seen through the windows on the ground floor. The elevator to the top runs 11–5 weekdays, 10:30–5:30 weekends, at a cost of 25¢.

The view from Pioneer Park, the area at the base of the tower, or from the tower itself is one of the finest in the city on a clear day or night, and one of the most magical when the city is under fog. Along the north, starting at the Golden Gate Bridge, you can see Sausalito and Tiburon on the far shore; Belvedere, which looks like an island but is connected by a sandspit with the mainland; Alcatraz; directly behind it Angel Island; the bay itself; and the piers and ships of the Embarcadero. To the east are Berkeley, the East Bay hills, Oakland; Treasure Island; the San Francisco-Oakland Bay Bridge; and, this side of the bridge, the Ferry Building. To the south are downtown San Francisco and the Mission District, and to the west are Nob Hill and Russian Hill.

MAJOR ISLANDS IN THE BAY

ANGEL ISLAND, the largest island in the bay, one square mile, was the landing place of the first ship to sail through the Golden Gate, the *San Carlos,* which dropped anchor here on August 5, 1775. Its commander, Lieutenant Juan Manuel de Ayala, named the island "Nuestra Señora de los Angeles," six years before a Southern California community was given the same name. It has, over the years, been reputed to be haunted, has served as a dueling ground, a staging area for American soldiers during three wars, a quarantine station from 1892 to 1945, and is now a state park. The island's dense vegetation not only supports considerable wildlife but also sometimes attracts braver animals from the Marin shore. Not too long ago a deer swimming to the island was caught in the swift current and was being pulled out through the Golden Gate when the Coast Guard staged a last-minute rescue.

ALCATRAZ. While exploring the bay Lieutenant de Ayala noticed an island covered with pelicans and named it "Isla de los Alcatraces" (Island of the Pelicans). He had in mind what we now know as Yerba Buena Island, but on a later survey the name was incorrectly given to this island. A lighthouse was built here in 1854 and fortifications were gradually added. During the Civil War it housed its first prisoners, Southern sympathizers who had outfitted a ship and were preparing to sail out the Gate when they were seized. Not long after, state Democratic leaders, who were arrested for criticizing the Republican administration's conduct of the war, were held here for a time. It was not until 1933—after serving as a military disciplinary barracks and a prisoner-of-war camp—that it became the most fearsome of all federal prisons, "The Rock." Among the more noted "incorrigibles" held here were Al Capone and "Machine Gun" Kelley. There were a number of attempted escapes; as far as is known none were successful, though the bodies of several men, *believed* to have drowned, were never recovered. The prison was closed in 1963.

YERBA BUENA ISLAND. The only portion of this island still open to the public is the tunnel through which cars pass between the suspension and cantilever sections of the San Francisco-Oakland Bay Bridge; the balance is occupied by the Navy. Long known as "Goat Island," a host of buried-treasure legends are attached to it.

TREASURE ISLAND is connected to Yerba Buena Island but was not originally a part of it. This large man-made island was created as the site for the 1939–40 Golden Gate International Exposition. After the fair it was to be used as an airport for San Francisco, but with the outbreak of World War II became a naval base instead—"T.I." to millions of swabbies.

From Telegraph Hill to Fisherman's Wharf.

BUS: Return to Washington Square via No. 39 Coit; walk west two blocks to Mason and catch the north-bound cable car; the car stops three blocks from the wharf.

DRIVING: Retrace to Lombard Street; down Lombard to Taylor Street; north on Taylor to the wharf.

WALKING: Same as driving.

FISHERMAN'S WHARF. Foot of Taylor Street. The first Bay Area fishermen were the Costanoans, coast-dwelling Indians, who prior to the advent of the Spanish lived close to the shores of the bay, venturing only a short way for their catch on crude rafts.

During the gold rush, when food was scarce and astronomically priced, a few unsuccessful miners turned fishermen, becoming the first to fish the bay waters for profit. By the mid-1850's fishing was a booming business, the largest catches coming from the Sacramento River, where the salmon ran in great numbers.

The Italians entered the fishing industry early in the 1850's, and, dominating it for over a century, have transformed it into a multimillion-dollar industry.

The Genoese, with their colorful lateen-rigged feluccas, were the first group to move into the business in large numbers. But as the Sicilians began to arrive, the Genoese gradually sold out to them. The Sicilians were born fishermen. Unlike the Northern Italians, most of them were uneducated in any other business or trade. They had one desire, first and foremost: to own their own boats. Since they spoke their own dialect, which the other Italians found hard to understand, they congregated together, holding to their own customs and ways. Today many of the older Sicilians still speak no English.

The Genoese, meantime, went into other occupations, the largest number into the scavenger business. Today they predominate in one of the city's strongest and strangest unions, the Scavengers' Protective Association, which collects a large part of the city's garbage.

While a few of the Northern Italians still fished, most went into other trades, often with conspicuous success. For example, they founded the city's produce markets, developed much of the wine country of Northern California; A. P. Giannini founded the Bank of Italy (now the Bank of America, the world's largest bank); D. Ghirardelli built the chocolate business that bears his name.

About 1865 the square-sailed junks of the Chinese came onto the scene, catching shrimp in large quantities within the bay waters. According to Harold Gilliam in his *San Francisco Bay*, by 1875

"fifteen hundred Chinese were engaged in the shrimp industry around the bay, fishing, shelling, cooking, drying, and selling the little crustaceans. By the end of the century there were twenty six shrimp camps around the bay's shores, each headquarters for a fleet of shrimp boats."

But, as Gilliam goes on to note, strong anti-Chinese sentiment resulted in restrictions on the Chinese fishermen. Today, except for one or two small companies, they play no part in the shrimp industry.

Jack London's short story "A Raid on the Oyster Pirates" has immortalized one phase of the once-important oyster business, which flourished after the transplanting of the Atlantic coast oysters into the bay beds from the 1870's until the 1920's. Then, possibly due to bay pollution, the local oysters began going bad. (Those sold in local markets and restaurants are imported.) Sardines were a major industry from World War I to the end of World War II, when, also for reasons much disputed but still unknown, the sardines disappeared. The huge purse-seiner fleets inhabit the bay no more, though some of the ships are still in use on other parts of the coast.

Since its beginning in the gold rush, almost everything about the fishing industry of the Bay Area has changed—the fish caught, the boats, nets, traps, and gear used, the methods of packaging and distribution. One feature has not changed—the preponderance of Italians in the industry.

But even the fishermen have changed, say the old-timers, as they sit on the wharves, watching sons and grandsons unloading the boats, or as they congregate together, playing cards in the Crab Boat Owners Association. Instinct, sensitivity, and skill aren't so important any more, they complain. Who today can find his traps in a thick fog, without instruments? Before the conversion to gasoline-driven boats, the modern methods of navigation, the radio—back in those days —it was man against the sea. On the other hand, they note, most of the boats that sail out from the wharf today return. In the not-so-distant past this was not always true. Sometimes it was the weather. Sometimes the sea itself. And sometimes, some will admit, it was greed. The Italians are rugged individualists. The Japanese (fierce competitors of the local industry both before and since World War II) have long been inclined to fish as a team, with many small boats unloading their catches into a large boat, then sharing at trip's end. Not so the Italians. Often they would load their boats to capacity, and even a little beyond—why turn fish away when so many days are bad?—a rough sea and the boat would drop out of sight. Sometimes, when they were overloaded and in trouble, they would dump the fish back into the sea rather than transfer them to another boat.

The days of unlimited catches have passed; today the industry is strictly regulated. Shrimp are on quota, only so many can be taken out of an area before the season is declared over. The crab season extends from mid-November to the end of June; salmon from April 15 to the end of September. There is no allowance for bad days.

But the biggest change, the old-timers say, is in the wharf itself.

There were no fish markets on the early wharves. Every Friday a fish peddler would travel through North Beach, pushing his cart, tooting his horn. In those days there was even room to spread out the nets and repair the boats. In time the markets came, with their steaming caldrons for cooking the crabs; this was a valid addition, as were the restaurants. The first, opened in 1916, catered to the fishermen; by 1920 there were several more, and dinner at the wharf became the fine local custom it is today. All this was and is in the wharf's tradition, a part of its meaning.

The chief objection to today's Fisherman's Wharf is that it has lost most of its authenticity. In its place is one of the cheapest, gaudiest, most commercial tourist traps in America. Most visitors to the wharf leave remembering only the junk-laden gift shops, the loudmouthed restaurant barkers, and the crowds. Many never discover why the restaurants are world famous. And a great many leave never having seen a fishing boat.

There is still something of the real Fisherman's Wharf here if you are willing to look for it. Walk on up Jefferson Street, away from Taylor. Find one of the packaging plants; if it is in operation chances are they'll show you through. Explore the narrow side streets. Get out on the wharves, where the crab boats, drag boats, and trawlers are moored. Talk to the fishermen themselves. Each has a thousand stories to tell if he's in the mood. The real wharf may be hidden, but if you're curious you can find it.

HARBOR TOURS. Sightseeing boats run regularly scheduled tours daily from Pier 43½, just east of Taylor Street, starting at 10 A.M. The regular tour is one hour and fifteen minutes and covers a large part of the bay, providing close glimpses of the two bridges and Alcatraz (surprisingly colorful, decked out in seasonal blooms), and remarkable views of the San Francisco skyline (Adults $2, children

75¢). There are also special tours to Angel Island and Tiburon; for information on these call Harbor Tours, 362-5414. Now that the ferryboats are gone, the tours provide, for most residents and visitors, the only opportunity left to get the "feel" of San Francisco Bay.

(The old sailing ship *Balclutha,* maintained by the San Francisco Maritime Museum, is also located in the immediate vicinity. See Chapter Six.)

To Downtown San Francisco:

DRIVING: South on Taylor Street.
CABLE CAR: Catch the Powell Street cable at the turntable three blocks south of the wharf.

For Additional Exploration:

SAN FRANCISCO BAY. By Harold Gilliam. The most comprehensive volume available on the bay, its history and importance.

EMBARCADERO. By Richard Dillon. A lively collection of little-known tales of the San Francisco waterfront.

THE BARBARY COAST. By Herbert Asbury. The sins of San Francisco, from the gold rush to the great fire.

THE MADAMS OF SAN FRANCISCO. By Curt Gentry. A highly irreverent history of the city's parlor house proprietresses, from Belle Cora to Sally Stanford.

CHAPTER THREE:

CHINATOWN

A Walking Tour of a City within the City: including a *joss* house — St. Mary's Square — Grant Avenue — Waverly Place — Old Chinatown Lane — "The Street of the Gamblers" — and the mysterious Chinese Six Companies. With glimpses into the quarter's past: its era of slave girls, tong wars, and opium dens.

In downtown San Francisco the present has been built over the remnants of the past. The village of Yerba Buena is not only hidden, it is mostly forgotten. To many who rush to and from work on Sutter, Montgomery, and Market streets, the past is not only a different time, it is also a different place.

In the Telegraph Hill-North Beach area the past exists almost entirely as a part of the present. Each year a bit of it disappears, with the old-timers go their recollections, but customs, language, and habits survive, and flourish, in "Little Italy," along Columbus Avenue, Stockton, and Filbert streets.

In modern Chinatown the past and the present are in subtle conflict. The quiet clashes between the younger and the older generations, rarely seen by those outside the family groups, are more meaningful and irreparable than the loud alley warfare of rival tongs a half century or so ago. There is an undercurrent of change in today's Chinatown. It is no new thing, it has been going on for more than a century. But each day in a thousand little ways the Old World gives a slight edge to the New.

Many changes are readily apparent. Except on holidays, dress is largely American; there are no more queues, no more lily-bound feet. The closest thing to gunfire you're

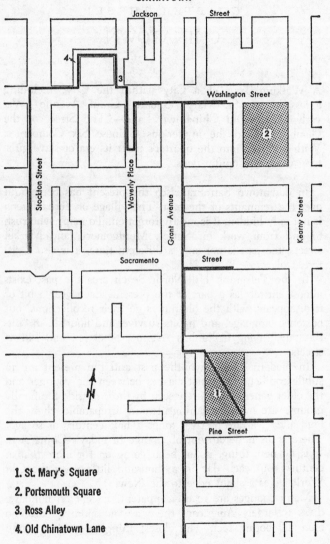

CHINATOWN

Jackson Street

Washington Street

Stockton Street

Waverly Place

Grant Avenue

Kearny Street

Sacramento Street

Pine Street

1. St. Mary's Square
2. Portsmouth Square
3. Ross Alley
4. Old Chinatown Lane

likely to hear are the staccato-bursts of firecrackers. (By a special state law, they are legal during the Chinese holidays). Nor do the Chinese any longer live ghetto fashion, six thousand to a block, limited by law to the confines of a well-delineated quarter. Chinese own property and live in every part of the city, though habit and the nonavailability of Chinese merchandise and foodstuffs elsewhere draw most of them back to Grant Avenue for shopping.

Other changes are subtler. Many parents no longer insist that their children attend both American and Chinese schools. Items once standard no longer appear in the markets. A hundred herb shops have dwindled to half a dozen. Young men no longer limit their futures by the Chinatown boundaries. Assimilation, slow and painful as always, is nevertheless occurring, and often at the expense of tradition.

Many of the changes stem from the break with the Chinese mainland. Since 1948, this has not only suspended goods but also a sense of direct contact with the past. Many of the older Chinese feel cut off; many of the younger ones refuse to take seriously the notion that China is Formosa and Chiang Kai-shek.

Chinatown will always, one is sure, be Chinatown, a place apart. But the world is changing, both along Grant Avenue and far away from it, and modern Chinatown cannot help reflecting these changes.

From downtown walk north along Grant Avenue.

"To the casual tourists, Grant Avenue is Chinatown, just another colorful street in San Francisco; to the overseas Chinese, Grant Avenue is their showcase, their livelihood; to the refugees from the mainland, Grant Avenue is Canton. Although there are no pedicabs, no wooden slippers clip-clapping on the sidewalks, yet the strip of land is to the refugee the closest thing to a home town. The Chinese theatres, the porridge restaurants, the teahouses, the newspapers, the food, the herbs . . . all provide an atmosphere that makes a refugee wonder whether he is really in a foreign land. And yet, in this familiar atmosphere, he struggles and faces many problems that are sometimes totally unfamiliar. . . ."

C. Y. Lee, *The Flower Drum Song*

Walk north on Grant Avenue to Pine Street.

Legend says that individual Chinese were migrating across the Pacific to California before A.D. 500. Hui Shên, a Buddhist priest, is said to have appeared before the Chinese court in A.D. 499, extolling the merits of this quite marvelous new land.

Less romantic chroniclers, not so prone to antecede Columbus, have given honors to a Chinese cabin boy, said to have been on the brig *Bolivar* when it sailed through the Golden Gate in 1838; or to a Cantonese merchant, said to have arrived in 1847; or to two men and a woman arriving on the *Eagle* in 1848.

Whichever is correct, the fact is there were Chinese in San Francisco before the start of the gold rush. And in the months immediately following, many more arrived, driven from China by famine and civil wars in Kwangtung Province, drawn to California by the tales of gold.

In January 1850 there were 789 Chinese men and two Chinese women in San Francisco.

In December of the same year there were 4018 men and seven women.

In December 1851, 12,000 men and the same seven women.

In 1875 there were about 45,000 men and 2000 women, 1900 of whom were prostitutes.

Rather than shock us, these figures should tell something about the Chinese and their attitude toward the new land. The initial absence of women—in a society where the family plays so important a part—indicates that the Chinese did not intend to stay. Like most of the miners, they wanted to make their fortunes and return home. And, also like the others, few were able to do so; most soon had to find other means of support.

In 1863–64 the builders of the Central Pacific Railroad faced a serious labor problem. It was impossible to obtain sufficient workers at the wages they offered. President Lincoln would not supply Confederate prisoners. The idea of using Chinese was said to have been Leland Stanford's. The first crews, solicited in San Francisco's Chinatown, convinced the partners that they had found the perfect solution. Soon every available Chinese in the state was put to work. Though the builders were still far short of the needed number, arrangements were made to import labor crews directly from China, and in 1865 they began arriving in great numbers.

John Steinbeck, who spent a few of his Bohemian years in San Francisco, hauling jute on the docks, living and writing in attics, tells the story of the Chinese and the Central Pacific through the Chinese houseboy Lee, in the novel *East of Eden:*

"I'll have to tell you first that when you built the railroads in the West the terrible job of grading and laying ties and spiking the rails was done by many thousands of Chinese. They were cheap, they worked hard, and if they died no one had to worry. They were recruited largely from Canton, for the Cantonese are short and strong and durable, and also they are not quarrelsome . . ."

Lee goes on to tell how agents for the recruiting companies paid a lump sum of money to each man when he signed his contract. To a man poor or in debt this was a face-saving solution to the problem of supporting his family. It also meant the Chinese worker had to stay in California until his obligation was met.

Lee observed the long-range logic of the railroad barons:

". . . These human cattle were imported for one thing only—to work. When the work was done, those who were not dead were to be shipped back. Only males were brought —no females. The country did not want them breeding. A man and a woman and a baby have a way of digging in, of pulling the earth where they are about them and scratching out a home. And then it takes all hell to root them out. But a crowd of men, nervous, lusting, restless, half sick with loneliness for women—why, they'll go anywhere, and particularly will they go home."

Contrary to expectations, most of the workers neither died nor returned to China. Despite widespread persecution, they decided to stay in California. The most important fact in the statistics of 1875 is not the total of 1900 prostitutes, but those 100 respectable women. For with the establishment of family units was initiated the building of a *permanent* city within the city of San Francisco: Chinatown.

The past of San Francisco's Chinatown has not always been pretty, nor has the past of Caucasian San Francisco during the same period. The slave girls, the opium trade, the tong wars stand out as black spots on Chinatown's past; but they were spots, not the whole fabric, and their eradication reflected, not only a change in the Chinese community, but a related growth toward respectability in the city around it.

Walk one block east on Pine Street to Kong Chow Temple, 520 Pine Street.

KONG CHOW TEMPLE is one of the few surviving joss houses in Chinatown. The long entrance courtyard, the Passageway of Peace, ends in a blank wall, a precaution against evil spirits, who can travel only in a straight line. Around the corner is a stairway. Climbing it to the third floor, you will find one of the oldest Chinese temples in America, established in 1857 by Chinese from the district of Kong Chow and still under the administration of the Kong Chow Benevolent Association, the first Chinese district association in the United States and a member of the Chinese Six Companies. Incidentally, joss houses are always built on top floors, to be nearer to heaven; "joss" is a corruption of *Dios,* the Portuguese word for God, which came to China by way of Portuguese traders to Macao.

The temple, dedicated to Kwan Ti, a military god whose attributes are loyalty and valor, contains many priceless wood carvings and brocades; all the ritual items of worship, including the joss sticks, by which divination is accomplished; and the figure of Kwan Ti, whose rescue in the fire of 1906 (the present building postdates the fire) is accounted one of the temple's many miracles.

Another occurred in 1948 and is still much talked of in Chinatown. During the political campaign that year, President and Mrs. Harry S Truman visited Chinatown. Mrs. Truman, while visiting the temple, was invited to draw one of the joss sticks. Her fortune read: "Don't give up. You are going to gain your goal after all these difficulties. You will reach your destination but you will have an uneasy journey."

Contributions go toward maintenance of the temple.

Retrace on Pine Street to St. Mary's Square. Pine, Anne, and California streets.

ST. MARY'S SQUARE.   Atop one of the city's largest underground garages is one of its most serene squares, presided over by the contemplative twelve-foot statue of Dr. Sun Yat-sen (1866–1925), founder of the Chinese Republic. The statue, of rose-colored granite and stainless steel, is the work of one of America's greatest sculptors, Beniamino Bufano.

The quiet beauty of today's square reveals nothing of its violent past. For many years this block was the location of some of the lowest brothels in San Francisco, set atop a ménage of shooting galleries and saloons. During the 1890's the women of the city, on a crusade to rid Dupont Street (Grant Avenue) of commercial vice, succeeded in having all the Dupont Street establishments moved into this small, already overcrowded area. The result pleased everyone except the Paulist Fathers of Old St. Mary's Church, across California Street. Though the Paulists fought hard for clearing the square, it was not until 1906 that they succeeded, the fire accomplishing it for them. It was then dedicated as a public square.

Nor does the silent strength of Beniamino Bufano's statue give a hint of the sculptor's own hectic past. Born in Italy in 1898, Bufano came to this country in 1901, following his father, a Garibaldian refugee. In the more than half century since then, he has been one of the most disputed figures in the world of sculpture and on the San Francisco scene, a gentle saint with a fiery temper, whose simple Gandhian ideals of peace and world brotherhood provide the major theme for his works, which many believe will in time rank among the major achievements of American art. Bufano lives and works in San Francisco, already as legendary a

SAN FRANCISCO
(*Redwood Empire Association*)

Black Bart

CHARLES E. BOLTON,
ALIAS "BLACK BART"
*(Wells Fargo Bank, History Room,
San Francisco)*

LILLIE HITCHCOCK COIT 5,
society matron and fire buff
*(Wells Fargo Bank, History Room,
San Francisco)*

Emperon Norton

JOSHUA A. NORTON,
Emperor of the United States and Protector of Mexico
(*Wells Fargo Bank, History Room, San Francisco*)

COIT TOWER AND TELEGRAPH HILL,
as seen from Russian Hill
(*Redwood Empire Association*)

FISHERMAN'S WHARF
(*Redwood Empire Association*)

CHINESE NEW YEAR. GRANT AVENUE
(*Redwood Empire Association*)

ST. MARY'S SQUARE,
with Beniamino Bufano's statue of Sun Yat-sen
(*Redwood Empire Association*)

CHINATOWN AT NIGHT
(Redwood Empire Association)

figure as any who have moved through the city's colorful past.

Other Bufano works in the city include his *Peace* statue at San Francisco International Airport; murals at Moar's Cafeteria, 33 Powell Street; seal carvings on the veranda of the Maritime Museum, Aquatic Park, and in Ghirardelli Square; a group of penguins in the fountain of the Stanford Court Apartments at 901 California; and several large animal figures, Valencia Gardens Housing Project, Fifteenth and Valencia streets. His most famous work, his large granite St. Francis statue, for many years a homeless wanderer, was finally given a resting place by Harry Bridges' International Longshoremen's and Warehousemen's Union, at the southeast corner of Taylor and Beach.

OLD ST. MARY'S CHURCH, at California Street and Grant Avenue, was erected in 1854 of granite brought from China and bricks and ironwork brought around the Horn from New England. Despite complaints of parishioners that it was located too far from town, the church soon became the citadel of Catholicism in California. The interior of the church was destroyed by the fire of 1906, but has been similarly reconstructed. Its four-faced clock tower, its booming bells, and the framed motto on the California Street side of the church—"Son Observe the Time and Fly from Evil"—have been familiar to San Franciscans for over a century. It was across from the church, on a foggy night in January 1880, that Joshua Norton, Emperor of the United States and Protector of Mexico, died.

Walk north one block on Grant Avenue to Sacramento Street; walk one-half block east on Sacramento.

NAM KUE SCHOOL, 755 Sacramento Street. Early attempts to educate the Chinese were fought bitterly by those who feared that, once educated, the Orientals would wish to stay in America. Most attempts at education were intended less for instruction in the rudiments of reading, writing, and arithmetic than for conversion of the "heathen Chinee" to Christianity. On August 28, 1850, city officials called a mass meeting in Portsmouth Square, requesting all "China boys" to attend. After several hours of speechmaking the Chinese were presented with tracts written in pidgin English, urging them to forsake their ways and to embrace Christianity. The following day the elders of Chinatown wrote to the city officials, thanking them for their kind attention, in a letter that remains a model of perfect English.

The first mission in Chinatown was established in 1852 and was soon followed by a host of others. At first conversions were few; most were attributed less to the appeal of religion than the desire to learn English. As one Episcopal minister noted at the time: "What the Chinese see of Christianity here, from their viewpoint must impress them unfavorably." Today about one third of the Chinese in the Bay Area are Christians. (According to the 1960 census, there are 36,445 Chinese in San Francisco, 52,984 in the combined San Francisco-Oakland area.)

The Nam Kue School is one of a number of schools in Chinatown that offer children instruction in Chinese language, customs, and culture each day *after* regular public-school classes. Built in 1912, it is also one of the few buildings in Chinatown of pure Chinese design, modeled to the specifications of the Mandarin *yamen*, or courthouse. It is supported by the Nom Hoi Association, another member of the Chinese Six Companies.

Retrace to Sacramento Street and Grant Avenue; walk north on Grant to Washington Street.

In 1835, not long after erecting the first residence in Yerba Buena proper, harbor master William Richardson helped lay out a street to connect the roads leading to the mission and the Presidio. It was named Calle de la Fundación, and a number of early settlers, such as Jacob Leese, built in close proximity to it. With the arrival of Montgomery and American rule in 1846, Spanish street names seemed inappropriate. Calle de la Fundación became Dupont Street.

As already noted, the gold rush and the sudden increase in San Francisco's population did not at first push the city limits westward, but rather to the north and east, onto filled land and wharves extending out over the bay. Early Dupont Street residents moved down to Montgomery and Kearny streets and farther east, to be closer to the commerce of the port. The Chinese moved into the vacated area, gradually filling the ten blocks bounded by Pacific, California, Stockton, and Kearny streets, which were to become the boundaries of old Chinatown.

The succeeding half century brought persecution, prostitution, and tong wars to Chinatown. In the estimation of many white residents the quarter was little better than the Barbary Coast or Morton Street. Just before the turn of the century merchants on the blocks of Dupont nearest Market, in an attempt to disassociate themselves from the street's reputation, changed the name of their portion of the street to Grant Avenue, in honor of Ulysses S. Grant. Following the fire of 1906 (which almost totally destroyed Chinatown) city officials changed the name of the entire street.

Walk east one-half block on Washington.

CHINESE TELEPHONE EXCHANGE, 743 Washington Street. This unusual building has several reasons for historical mention. First, it stands on the site of the office of Samuel Brannan's *California Star*, the first newspaper printed in the city. The *Star's* first number was issued on January 9, 1847; four pages, three columns, 8½ by 12 inches of print; subscription six dollars a year. Just as its fiery owner electrified San Franciscans with his cry of Gold!, so did the *Star* spread the word East. Its April 1, 1848 issue, announcing the discovery, was picked up by the New York *Tribune* in its issue of August 19, and the real rush was on. Like its rival, the *Californian*, the *Star* was forced to suspend publication when all the printers made for the mines.

The triple-tiered, pagoda-style building now houses the Bank of Canton, but was for many years the local office of the Pacific Telephone and Telegraph Company. Prior to 1949, when the dial system went into effect, the office was staffed by twenty young Chinese girls, who handled all of the telephone calls to Chinatown. Phenomenally long memories were required, as many of the older residents refused to use numbers, preferring instead to ask for their parties by name.

BUDDHA'S UNIVERSAL CHURCH is across and down the street, at the corner of Washington and Kearny, on the site of the old Bella Union. The building was constructed entirely by volunteer labor. Each of its members pledged fifty hours of work monthly—businessmen hauled bricks, shopgirls became carpenters, Chinese scholars mixed cement. The finished building, completed in 1961, now contains a large historical library for research into Chinese philosophy and religion, and a growing shoot from what is said to be the Indian boddhi tree under which Gautama Buddha received his illumination.

Retrace on Washington Street to Grant Avenue; cross Grant and walk west one-half block to Waverly Place.

WAVERLY PLACE is a narrow alley that dissects the two blocks between Washington and Sacramento streets. For many years it was inhabited largely by brothels and gambling rooms. "The defenses thrown up to mask these illicit dens," wrote Charles Caldwell Dobie of the gambling rooms:

"strangely anticipated the speakeasy era in these United States. Sometimes entrance was gained through the most innocent of shops. On Commercial street there used to be appropriately a pawn shop that screened a gambling club approach. And one of the notorious gambling clubs was reached through the salesrooms of a most respectable and venerable firm. In other words, even the law-abiding Chinese supported gambling just as the law-abiding white citizens supported bootleggers and blind-pigs during prohibition."

If the gambling clubs, with their deceptive fronts, were the antecedents of the speak-easy, the tong wars were prototypes for the era of gangland warfare. And it was in this alley that Chinatown's first tong war occurred.

TONGS. But first a word of explanation regarding the tongs and other Chinese associations, most of which came into being not in China but in the United States, as a means of solving problems and settling disputes in days when the Chinese were denied protection of the law or access to American courts.

There are in Chinatown today three types of organizations.

First there are the family associations (thirty-three at the present time), created to unite and aid individual family groups in America, open to anyone with the same surname. Most of these associations have their headquarters in San Francisco's Chinatown. Their importance stems from the importance of the family unit in Chinese society.

Second there are the district associations, which represent the people from the various districts of China. Most Chinese-Americans belong to both a family and a district association. Not long after the first large groups of Chinese immigrants came to America, it became necessary to form a final court of arbitration, an organization that would have the last word in any dispute that could not be settled in the family or district associations, or any matter that affected the entire Chinese population. Representatives of each of the district associations then formed the Chinese Six Companies, which we will discuss later in more detail; it was and is still the most important organization in Chinatown. Today there are eleven district associations with headquarters here; seven of them belong to this organization.

Third are the fraternal groups known as tongs. (*Tong,* to add slightly to the confusion, is the Chinese word for "association.") Many of the tongs were (and are) exclusively social; some were organizations of workers in related arts and crafts; a few were revolutionary groups; and some were criminal organizations. Among these last were the Hip Yee tong, formed for the purpose of importing slave girls into the country; the Chee Kung tong, which claimed its origin in the noble Triad Society, an ancient religious-revolutionary organization, but which confined its early activities in this country to blackmail and intimidation; and the Hip Shing tong, which for a time controlled most of the gambling in Chinatown. For each tong that monopolized a certain area of crime there were several others interested in the same territory.

Each of the gangster tongs commanded a force of *boo how doy,* or fighting men, used to extract levies or, when occasion demanded, to battle opposing tongs. Each also employed the services of highbinders or hatchetmen, men who would murder for a fee. The derivation of "hatchetman" is simple: the hatchet was for many years the basic tool of their trade. There have been several explanations for the origin of the term "highbinder." The one most commonly accepted is that it referred to the killer's practice of binding his long queue to the top of his head, under his stiff-brimmed hat, so he couldn't be grabbed by it when fleeing the scene of his crime.

The first of a number of tong wars that took place in the gold fields occurred near Marysville, California, about 1860, between the Hop Sings and the Suey Sings, and, as Herbert Asbury notes:

". . . in common with many of the other conflicts which have since raged in American cities, it started over a woman. The mistress of a Hop Sing man was stolen by a Suey Sing Lothario, and the Hop Sings declared war to wipe out the stain upon their brother's honor. Several men on either side were killed, but the Suey Sings were defeated and compelled to restore the girl to her rightful owner."

A similar occurrence sparked San Francisco's first great tong war, which began in 1875. A member of the Suey Sing tong was murdered for his attentions to a slave girl belonging to a member of the Kwong Dock tong. A *chun hung*, or challenge to battle, was drawn up and posted on the "murderer's bulletin board" at Grant Avenue and Clay Street (so called because the highbinders gathered here to read and consider the fees offered for professional slaughter). Shortly before midnight the following night the fighting members of the two tongs assembled on the two sides of deserted Waverly Place. There were about twenty-five armed and experienced killers on either side. At midnight both began yelling insults and the fight was on. Though police broke it up soon after it started, the final total was four dead and dozens wounded. The Kwong Docks, having lost three of the four, were considered the losers and a peace treaty was signed, with the Suey Sings accepting their apologies and certain indemnities.

This was the first of many battles in San Francisco's Chinatown. Perhaps its most important effect was on a ten-year-old boy who from a third-floor balcony overlooking Waverly Place watched the bloody midnight rites with great fascination. He was Fong Chong, later to be best known by his nickname, "Little Pete."

Years later, when Little Pete was the vice czar of Chinatown, he lived in the same apartment on the third floor above Waverly Place. But this time his room did not look down on the street; with good reason it was windowless. In addition Fong Chong's door was sealed shut at night, a vicious dog chained to either side for extra protection. By day he wore a coat of chain mail and a hat that contained a sheet of steel shaped to fit his head; when he went out he was accompanied by a crew of Chinese and white bodyguards.

It still wasn't enough to save Little Pete.

Today Waverly Place is one of the quieter, more picturesque Chinatown streets, on which are located a number of fine shops and the headquarters of several of the now largely social tongs. If you are still in the mood for joss houses and stair climbing (four flights), the TIN HOW TEMPLE is located at 125 Waverly Place.

Founded in 1875, it is maintained by the Sue Hing Benevolent Association, and dedicated to Tin How, Taoist Queen of the Heavens and Goddess of the Seven Seas. She is said to protect all travelers who call upon her. Early Chinese built the original temple (since destroyed and rebuilt after the 1906 fire) in gratitude for their safe voyages across the Pacific.

It is suggested you send one member of your party up to see if the temple is open. The irregular visiting hours show how little a part joss houses play in today's Chinatown, except during Chinese holidays.

Retrace to Washington Street and cross to Ross Alley.

The ten-year reign of Little Pete was the bloodiest decade in the history of Chinatown.

By his twenty-fifth birthday Little Pete was head of both the powerful Sam Yup tong and the Gi Sin Seer, the latter an organization of paid gunmen as deadly as the minions of Capone. He was active in every form of vice and corruption in the quarter. Needless to say, he made enemies, particularly the members of the See Yup Company, from whom he stole slave girls and gambling locations. The gory battle between the two tongs lasted seven years and took sixty lives. In the midst of it Little Pete attempted to bribe a judge, a jury, and the district attorney. Eighteen months later, when he returned from San Quentin, he resumed command of his two organizations and rekindled the lagging war with the rival tong. Before long he was virtual czar of all crime in Chinatown, controlling the huge slave-girl market, dominating the opium trade, and monopolizing all gambling, from the Chinese lotteries to rigged horse races, all the while working in close alliance with the city's political boss, "Blind Chris" Buckley.

There was another side to Little Pete, that of the musician and playwright, for he not only played the zither, he also wrote comedies, which were performed at the Jackson Street Theatre. (That he owned the theater might have had something to do with it.) He was also very much a dandy, changing his suits and jewelry several times daily, spending two hours each morning brushing and oiling his long queue. The last affectation contributed to his demise.

Late in the afternoon of January 23, 1897, Little Pete, accompanied for a change by only one bodyguard, entered a barbershop on Washington Street. For months there had been a price of two thousand dollars on his head (by now he had alienated thirteen separate tongs), and highbinders watched his every well-protected move. But power sometimes makes a man careless, and Little Pete, anxious to know the latest race results, sent his lone gunman out to buy an evening paper. While Little Pete was leaning forward under a faucet, the barber washing his hair before plaiting it into a queue, two Chinese entered the shop. One remained near the door, the other pushed a revolver under the coat of mail at Little Pete's neck and fired five shots.

The gunmen fled, both eventually escaping to China with their reward. Ironically, they were not highbinders; neither had ever killed a man before. They were miners who heard of the reward, decided to try their luck in another field, and succeeded where the professional killers of Chinatown had failed.

The tong war that Little Pete started did not end with his death. The See Yups attempted to make up for their years of defeat by wiping out the Sam Yups. Only when Kwang Hsu, the Emperor of China, had put all the relatives of the See Yups into prison and threatened their extermination did the two tongs finally sign their treaty of peace.

This was not the last of Chinatown's tong wars, although it was the worst. The last occurred in 1927, although there have been threats of others as late as 1959. On this last occasion it took the mediation of prominent Chinese community leaders from all over North America to avert a reprisal killing when a member of one family group assaulted another.

Walk through the narrow alley next to Tsang's Ricksha Bar, which connects Ross Alley with Old Chinatown Lane.

Will Irwin, in describing Chinatown as it was before the fire, wrote:

". . . Chinatown was the care and vexation of Boards of Health. But always beautiful—falling everywhere into pictures."

In 1895 a young man, arriving in San Francisco for the first time, read in his *Baedeker's Guide:* "It is not adviseable to visit the Chinese quarter unless one is accompanied by a guide." Reacting as one suspects everyone does to guide-book prohibitions, he set out alone to explore Chinatown.

The young man's name was Arnold Genthe, and he was immediately enchanted by the Chinese quarter. When he found there were no photographs or drawings depicting what he had seen, only crudely colored postcards, he tried to sketch the quarter himself, but the people either ducked into doorways or ran.

"Finding it impossible to get pictures in this way, I decided to try to take some photographs. Up to that time I had never used a camera and knew nothing about photography."

Thus began Arnold Genthe's career as a photographer; in his day he was to become one of America's greatest. With a small, cleverly disguised box camera he wandered the streets of Chinatown, catching on film the crowded Street of the Gamblers, the children running single-file holding onto each other's queues, the costumes and celebrations, the high-binders reading the murder offers. It was to be the only pictorial record of old Chinatown; and these were the only Genthe photographs which escaped the fire of 1906. They were later published in a now-out-of-print book called *Pictures of Old Chinatown,* with a text by Will Irwin. More accessible, many of the photographs are on display at the Tao Tao Restaurant, 675 Jackson Street.

For a good half century San Franciscans labored under the misconception that if you changed a street's name you could change its reputation. Dupont Street became Grant

Avenue (it is still *Dupont gai* to older-generation Chinese); the notorious Lozier Street—between Dupont and Kearny, Jackson and Pacific—became the even more notorious Bartlett Alley, and finally Beckett Street, which name it bears today. What we now call Old Chinatown Lane was originally, inappropriately, Church Court, then Cameron Alley (in honor of Donaldina Cameron, friend of slave girls). But to those who came here before the fire its unofficial name was better known and much more fitting—for this was the "Street of the Gamblers."

Today the street is best known for the Chingwah Lee Studio of Orientalia, No. 9 Old Chinatown Lane, open to the public Saturdays, 2–5 P.M.

OPIUM DENS.   No part of old Chinatown was more endowed with myths, misconceptions, and misunderstanding than the hidden, secret Chinatown, the underground labyrinths of the opium dens and the vice trade. Before the turn of the century, writers for periodicals such as the *Police Gazette* successfully gave to this portion of Chinatown the furtive glamour of secret sin.

It was claimed that most of Chinatown was below ground, that there were often seven or eight levels below the street, that catacombs connected all the shops, that monstrous crimes occurred here undetected by the police, who fearfully stayed above ground.

There was more than a little reason for these stories. Packed six thousand to a block in the quarter, the Chinese utilized all available space, including their basements. And there *were* a few underground passages that ran in and out of Chinatown. Both Arnold Genthe and Will Irwin described them from firsthand knowledge. While the fire of 1906 disproved that Chinatown went deeper than the ordinary basement, most of the opium dens were underground. But perhaps the biggest myth of all was that these places were glamorous or decorated in oriental splendor.

Charles Caldwell Dobie wrote:

"There was nothing glamorous about a Chinese opium den either above or below ground. Those underground were reached by narrow passageways lit by flickering gas jets which increased the sense of mystery. Often the den itself did not even boast a feeble gas flame. The light from the opium lamps fed with nut-oil, before each bunk, was sufficient. Someone has spoken of these opium dens of a bygone day as being like 'sepulchers filled with dead.' I can think of no better description."

The stories of heinous crimes committed by the Chinese while under the influence of the poppy seed were mostly fabrications. Dobie makes an important distinction when he says:

"The white man's release was through a positive stimulant—whiskey. The Chinaman's release came through a passive agency—opium. Both of these relaxations were typical of the races indulging in them."

In the years preceding the passage of laws prohibiting the use of the drug, several of the opium dens were kept open solely for the "tourist trade." Genthe tells of one old man he knew whose

"only source of income was the few nickels given him by the guides who brought tourists to his shack to see a smoker in action. His only friend was a cat, who sat on his chest purring contentedly as it inhaled the fumes from his pipe. A woman sightseer reported him to the Society for the Prevention of Cruelty to Animals. The cat was taken to the animals' refuge where, refusing to eat, it almost died of starvation. Another woman who had been in the tourist group, indignant at the attitude of her companion, had followed up the case. When she found out what had happened, she appealed to the higher authorities. The cat was returned to its master where, snoozing peacefully on his chest, it lived happily ever after."

From Old Chinatown Lane walk west on Washington to Stockton Street, cross Stockton and walk south.

THE CHINESE PRESBYTERIAN CHURCH, 925 Stockton Street. Founded in 1853, rebuilt on the same site after the 1906 fire, this was one of the first Protestant churches in Chinatown, active for many years in bettering understanding between the Chinese and American communities.

THE CHINESE PRESBYTERIAN MISSION HOME has had a briefer but far more frenetic history. Established in 1874, in 1895 it came under the direction of Miss Donaldina Cameron, who operated it for forty years. Much of the credit for clearing Chinatown of prostitution belongs to Miss Cameron, or "Lo Mo" (Little Mother), as the Chinese girls called her.

Until Miss Cameron came onto the scene, the lot of the Chinese slave girl was hopeless. Often brought into the country at the age of ten, these girls spoke no English, were never allowed outside their quarters, and had to favor all customers. In order to discourage attempted escapes to the police or the missions, they were told fantastic tales of the white man's torture and barbarity. When a girl did escape, more than likely a prosperous Chinese would appear in court with documents proving she was his legal wife and, once outside police scrutiny, she would be badly beaten, then returned to prostitution. When a girl became seriously ill or incurably diseased she would be locked in an underground room without food and water and removed only after she had died.

Miss Cameron was the slave girls' Carry Nation. During her forty years of militant crusading, she rescued hundreds of girls from the slave dealers of Chinatown. When she heard that a girl wanted to escape a house of prostitution, neither barred doors, armed highbinders, or legal obstacles could keep her from her objective. Her exploits would be unbelievable if recorded in fiction. Genthe described her as a "truly noble and courageous woman . . . not a tight-lipped reformer who wished to make the world over into a monotone. She had respect for the art and literature of China and she saw that the girls she had taken under her wing were educated in its tradition."

Dobie found her "a cultivated woman of gentle voice and even gentler manner, who might be the head of a fashionable girls' school on the Upper East side of New York." He adds, sincerely but erroneously, "One feels sure that she never used any weapon to fight her way out of a tight place more deadly than a silk parasol—or at worst an umbrella."

Largely through her efforts the plight of the Chinese slave girls received world-wide attention, playing no small part in the passage of the Red Light Abatement Act of 1914, which successfully wiped out large-scale prostitution in Chinatown.

Walk south on Stockton Street.

THE CHINESE CONSOLIDATED BENEVOLENT ASSOCIATION, the Chinese Six Companies, is at 843 Stockton Street, and is open to the public, no set hours, although weekday afternoons are generally best.

It is important to remember that this organization was formed to fill a vacuum: during most of the nineteenth century a Chinese was denied access to the American courts, his word could not be accepted as evidence, his rights were limited and rarely upheld, and he was often subject to discriminating legislation. The Chinese Six Companies from its conception therefore had two main functions. The first was to oversee and mediate activities within the Chinese community. The second was to work for the betterment of the lot of the Chinese in America. This included such varied activities as fighting the antiqueue ordinance (a San Francisco law requiring short haircuts, expressly designed to persecute the Chinese); opposing discriminatory provisions of the alien exclusion laws; checking on affairs of immigration, naturalization, and settlement. Often the two objectives were combined, as when the Chinese Six Companies, acting in behalf of the Chinese community, halted the importation of slave girls and worked to eradicate prostitution in Chinatown.

Many of the past activities of this organization are still shrouded in mystery. No impartial history of the Companies has yet been written. Most of the charges brought against it were made in times of anti-Chinese hysteria, when it was believed that Chinese labor would undermine the American economy, times when all things Chinese were anathema. Contrary to one widely accepted legend, the Chinese Six Companies was not responsible for bringing Chinese labor into the country; the trade guilds arranged this. The Chinese Six Companies, however, was frequently called upon to oversee the arrangement, and, supposedly, no Chinese could return to China without first proving that he had met his obligations.

Although the days of its almost unlimited power over the Chinese in the U.S. have passed, this association is still the most important Chinese organization in the nation. Its activities still include mediating disputes within the Chinese communities (those which cannot be settled within the family or district associations); the overseeing of Chinese activities in the United States; and participation in Chinese civic activities.

VICTORY HALL, two doors south of the Chinese Six Companies building, is the community theater of Chinatown. When World War II ended, funds appropriated for

China's war effort were used to build the present structure as a monument to peace. Though various community activities are held here throughout the year, the hall is most crowded during the week of Chinese New Year celebrations, when a troupe of performers from Formosa presents Chinese opera.

The first Chinese opera was performed in San Francisco in 1852; aside from one newspaper, which commented on the "terrible noise, like the wailing of turkey-cocks plus the drum pounding of small boys," white residents ignored this cultural opportunity until the 1890's, when the famed pianist Paderewski attended a performance and declared he had never before heard music so dramatically moving. Performances today, during the holiday seasons, draw audiences as mixed as the population of San Francisco.

CHINESE HOLIDAYS. A number of national celebrations are held in Chinatown during the year. Many are private observances, confined to the family group. These include: the Ming Ching, or Festival of the Tombs, which is similar to Memorial Day and is held in the spring; the Dragon Boat Festival, a summer celebration; and the September Moon Festival. The two largest public celebrations are:

DOUBLE TEN, or Chinese National Day, celebrated on October 10 (tenth day of the tenth month) with dances, fireworks, special events, and climaxed by a dragon parade along Grant Avenue. The famed St. Mary's Drum and Bugle Corps participates, as they do during most public Chinatown demonstrations.

CHINESE NEW YEAR is Chinatown's big week-long celebration, which occurs in late January or early February (it depends on the full moon; call the Chinese Chamber of Commerce for exact dates). In addition to the numerous private observances that precede the New Year—the settling of all outstanding debts, family observances in honor of the ancestors, etc.—public festivities include choosing a "Miss Chinatown U.S.A." from entrants of the American-Chinese communities; dragon and lion dances; and the mammoth several-hour-long Dragon Parade, which draws thousands to Chinatown.

To reach the downtown area, walk south through the Stockton Street Tunnel or catch the No. 30 Stockton Street bus.

For Additional Exploration:

CHINATOWN SAN FRANCISCO. Photographs by Phil Palmer. Text by Jim Walls. A brief but perceptive study of the city's modern Chinese community.

SAN FRANCISCO'S CHINATOWN. By Charles Caldwell Dobie. To date there is no outstanding book on the history of Chinatown, though this comes closest. Out of print but fairly easy to come by in the city's used-book stores.

THE FLOWER DRUM SONG. By C. Y. Lee. A novel dealing with the subtle conflicts within modern Chinatown. The basis for the Broadway musical.

BUFANO. The first of several scheduled volumes on the art of Beniamino Bufano. Printed in Italy but available in local bookstores.

CHAPTER FOUR:

THE HILLS

A Walking or Driving Tour over Two of the City's Many Famed Hills: Nob, the Hill of Palaces — with glimpses into the mansions and pasts of the "Big Four" railroad barons, and the Irish "Silver Kings" of the Comstock Lode — and Russian Hill, Bohemia of the 1890's, possessor of some of the city's most spectacular views — with sidelights on former residents George Sterling, Ina Coolbrith, and Ambrose Bierce.

". . . the next day before the dawn we were lying to upon the Oakland side of San Francisco Bay. The day was breaking as we crossed the ferry; the fog was rising over the citied hills of San Francisco; the bay was perfect—not a ripple, scarce a stain, upon its blue expanse; everything was waiting, breathless, for the sun. A spot of cloudy gold lit first upon the head of Tamalpais, and then widened downward on its shapely shoulder; the air seemed to awaken, and began to sparkle; and suddenly
        'The tall hills Titan discovered,'
and the city of San Francisco, and the bay of gold and corn were lit from end to end with summer daylight."

So wrote Robert Louis Stevenson of his first glimpse of San Francisco's hills in 1879.

Early Chinese, on first catching sight of the city from the crowded boats that brought them from China, christened it *Gum Sahn* or "Golden Hills," a name many of the older Chinese still prefer. One pioneer settler, who preceded even the Chinese, described the chief activity of Yerba Buenans as "getting drunk and falling up and down hills." And of course Rudyard Kipling did not spare the hills his caustic comment. As he walked about the city studying the people,

THE HILLS

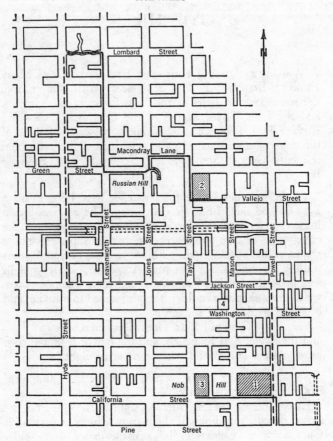

1. Fairmont Hotel   2. Coolbrith Park

3. Huntington Park   4. Cable Car Museum

– – – Northbound Hyde Street Cable Car

endeavoring "to find out in what manner they differ from us, their ancestors," he discovered that

"San Francisco has been pitched down on the sand-bunkers of the Bikaneer desert. About one-fourth of it is ground reclaimed from the sea . . . The remainder is ragged, unthrifty sand-hills pegged down by houses."

The first residents were not too impressed with these tall sand dunes. They preferred to build out into the bay. Early writers lamented that San Francisco had no place to grow, except possibly toward the North Beach region. Build on these hills? Insane.

But up and over they went, pushed by the expanding population, crude shanties that hung precariously to the steep slopes of Telegraph Hill, fine, gaudy mansions set firmly on Rincon Hill or Nob Hill or Pacific Heights, an artists' colony on Russian Hill, a world of quiet statues on Sutro Heights. The move was gradual but constant, until today the "citied hills" with their fantastic views of the city, the bridges, the bay, and ocean are one of the most memorable parts of San Francisco.

For years the legend persisted that San Francisco, like Rome, was built on seven hills: Telegraph, Russian, Nob, Twin Peaks, Mount Davidson, Rincon, and Lone Mountain. But as everyone who lived on any of the other hills knew, it just wasn't so. Not long ago one of the city's newspapers ran a series of articles on the hills and hesitantly listed forty-two. Later published in book form (*Hills of San Francisco*, Chronicle Publishing Company), it listed, in addition to those above mentioned, Alamo Heights, Anza Hill, Bernal Heights, Buena Vista Heights, Candlestick Point, Castro Hill, City College Hill, College Hill, Corona Heights, Dolores Heights, Edgehill Heights, Forest Hill, Gold Mine Hill, Holly Hill, Hunters Point Ridge, Irish Hill, Lafayette Heights, Larsen Park, Laurel Hill, Lincoln Heights, McLaren Ridge, Merced Heights, Mount Olympus, Mount St. Joseph, Mount Sutro, Pacific Heights,

Parnassus Heights, Potrero Hill, Presidio Heights, Red Rock Hill, Strawberry Hill, Sutro Heights, University Mound, and Washington Heights. This did not quite settle it. What of the somewhat smaller hills, such as Tank; how can you label McLaren Ridge one hill when it is really two or three or more? The controversy goes on.

Though disagreeing on their number, San Franciscans take pride in their hills. A package-laden resident will pant up blocks of steep incline every day of the year, and feel adequately compensated, when his visitor, ascending the same route, lags and cries out, "How can you do it?"

The San Franciscan has a penchant the real estate men were strangely late in discovering. He will pay in effort, inconvenience, and money to live with a view. Moreover he will defend his particular choice, honestly believing that his hill offers the best of all possible panoramas.

Each of the city's hills has its history and stories. Each plays its part in that conglomerate entity known as San Francisco. In this chapter we will focus on two hills—Nob and Russian. Telegraph Hill is discussed in Chapter Two; Strawberry Hill appears in Chapter Five; Sutro Heights and Twin Peaks in Chapter Six. All deserve inclusion; George Sterling might have been describing any or all when he wrote:

"At the end of our streets is sunrise;
At the end of our streets are spars;
At the end of our streets is sunset;
At the end of our streets—the stars."

NOB HILL

From downtown San Francisco:

CABLE CARS: Catch either of the northbound cars on
Powell Street; then transfer to the California car at
Powell and California for the one uphill block (west)
to California and Mason Street, or walk it.
DRIVING: Up Powell (steep), or Taylor (steeper), to
California and Mason streets.
WALKING: Same as above.

First solitary builder to erect a home on the crest of this
hill was Dr. Arthur Hayne, who in 1856 cut a path through
the brush to erect a wood and clay house on the present
site of the Fairmont Hotel. Only a few adventurous souls
followed Dr. Hayne's example; most people considered the
hill too steep, too windy, or too far from the business district
for colonization. They built around but not upon it. The
rich for a time preferred Rincon Hill (now partly leveled
and hidden beneath the freeway approach to the San
Francisco-Oakland Bay Bridge), but in the late 1860's there
began a gradual exodus from Rincon to what is now known
as Nob. The name came later, sometime after the 1870's,
when the "Big Four," who built the Central Pacific Railroad, and the "Silver Kings" of the Comstock Lode erected
their palaces. "Nob," most agree, is short for "nabob," a
colloquial term designating any man of great wealth. It fit.
  They were "strong characters," Oscar Lewis wrote of the
Silver Kings, though his description applies equally well to
most of Nob Hill's early residents

"typical of the group that shouldered their way to the top all over America during the final third of the past century. They were men of consuming ambition, resourceful, acquisitive, and uncommonly able, and, like most of their class, relentless in their opposition to whatever stood in the way of their drive toward wealth and power."

Their homes, without exception, were gaudy, garish, and grand; and, as one writer has added, "over-indulgent, as was the age." Architect Willis Polk made still another point:

"They cost a great deal of money, and whatever harsh criticism may fall upon them, they cannot be robbed of that prestige."

Like the Palace Hotel, the mansions were symbols of the city's growth to maturity, culture, and refinement, and for each critic who lambasted them there were a thousand people who rode the new California Street cable past just to stare in wonder and amazement.

Leland Stanford's house, the first of the grand mansions erected by a member of the Big Four, was built in 1875, where the Stanford Court Apartments now stand, on the southwest corner of Powell and California streets.

£eland $tanford (as Ambrose Bierce often designated him) was, in turn, a lawyer, wholesale grocer, railroad baron, governor, senator, and university founder. Though there is still some disagreement as to his importance in the building of the Central Pacific Railroad (Collis P. Huntington once defined his contribution as turning the first shovel of dirt and driving the last spike) there was no mistaking the fact that his Nob Hill mansion was something to behold. Around his two acres Stanford erected a thirty-foot stone wall. The house itself stretched most of the way from California to Pine Street, towered higher than any other home in the city, and was, outside and inside, as Victorian as the age itself, a mammoth creation in which marble and redwood predominated. Moreover it was a pace-setter. Not everyone wanted a house like it, but in the next few years there were many who tried their best to better it.

THE MARK HOPKINS HOTEL, at the southeast corner of California and Mason streets, was built in 1925, upon a site first purchased in 1874 by railroad baron Mark Hopkins for what he envisioned as a "modest" home.

Mark Hopkins was the most conservative, least ostentatious, best-liked member of the generally despised Big Four. He effected the transition from partner in a Sacramento drygoods business (with Collis P. Huntington) to treasurer and business manager of the Central Pacific Railroad and its vast holdings, with almost no increase in his standard of living.

Oscar Lewis in his classic history *The Big Four* remarks:

"That he became possessed of more than twenty millions was 'against his better judgement.' The role of capitalist seemed to make him faintly uncomfortable, and he sometimes acted 'as if he wanted to apologize for his millions.'"

Lewis sagely comments: "The attitude was novel enough to set him apart from other rich men."

"He had defects and eccentricities; he was an unextravagant rich man and therefore a miser. But he was modest and kindly and sometimes quietly humorous, with none of the vanity and little of the ruthlessness of his partners."

For several years he lived in a small thirty-five-dollar-a-month cottage on Leavenworth Street, at the foot of the hill. In 1874, at his wife's instigation, after Stanford's lead, he bought the present site, anticipating building an average-sized home. His wife, Mary, suffering from too many years of his thriftiness, had other ideas. Humoring her, "Uncle Mark" let her go ahead with plans. The result was a many-turreted mansion that resembled a medieval castle and was by far the most ornate and extravagant of the Nob Hill dwellings. Seven architects worked on it at the same time, each with his own concepts of style and design. The kindest thing ever said about the building was that it was "curious."

Mark Hopkins died in 1878, a year before it was completed, and was thereby spared having to live in it. Mary Hopkins herself lived there only a few years before moving East. Later, as the property of the University of California, it housed, ironically, the Mark Hopkins Art Institute (later called the California School of Fine Arts). It was totally destroyed in the fire of 1906, and only with construction of the Mark Hopkins Hotel on this site in 1925 (opening in December 1926) was it discovered that there was a half-million gallon reservoir in the courtyard. Had its existence been known Nob Hill might have been saved from destruction.

"The Top of the Mark," probably the world's most famous bar, located on the nineteenth floor of the hotel, was opened in 1939. To many thousands of servicemen, visitors, and Bay Area residents the bar, with its fifty-mile panoramic view, has become a symbol of San Francisco. It has been closed just twice—on the day President Franklin Delano Roosevelt died, and on V-J Day. It is 537 feet above sea level, 257 feet above ground.

The FAIRMONT HOTEL, *opposite the Mark Hopkins, is at California, Mason, Sacramento, and Powell streets.*

James G. Fair was the most successful of the men who in the 1860's and '70's took close to four hundred million dollars in silver and gold out of Nevada's Comstock Lode. Again our authority is Oscar Lewis, chief chronicler of the city's past, who in his book *Silver Kings* says of Fair:

"Of all the Comstock's conspicuous figures, Fair was easily

the least admired, a fact of which he was aware and which he regarded with complete indifference. The good opinion of his fellows he valued so little that at no stage of his career did he exert himself to deserve it. He aimed rather to please himself, and in that he succeeded even better than most."

Of his partners, the three other Irish Comstock Lords: John W. Mackay was, like Fair, an experienced miner, but, unlike him, modest, sincere, and given to quiet philanthropy; William S. O'Brien and James C. Flood were gold miners turned saloonkeeps turned stockbrokers, getting their start in the market from their ability to discriminate among conversations overheard in their Auction Lunch Saloon. Together the four outwitted some of the shrewdest men in San Francisco when they gained control of the Consolidated Virginia and the California mines and opened the biggest vein of silver in the Comstock Lode.

"Bonanza Jim" Fair subsequently bought himself a seat in the United States Senate, had domestic difficulties that kept him from completing his mansion on Nob Hill, and died in 1894.

Fair's daughter, Tessie, and her husband, Hermann Oelrichs, decided to build a de luxe hotel on the Nob Hill site. Completed except for the installation of windows, the structure burned in the fire of 1906. Only the granite walls were left standing. As an example of the spirit that ran through the city in the months following the disaster, the Fairmont Hotel was rebuilt and opened on April 18, 1907, the first anniversary of the fire.

While few today remember the bonanza king for whom the hotel was named, the Fairmont has established its own reputation as one of the city's luxury hotels. Notable restaurants within the hotel include the Camellia Room, the Tonga Room, the Squire Room, the Venetian Room, Canlis' at the Fairmont, and Blum's; and there are easily a half-dozen noted bars. The twenty-nine-story Fairmont Hotel Tower, completed in 1961 and reached by means of a scenic glass elevator on the outside of the building, stands 544.95 feet above sea level, the tallest hotel in San Francisco and the tallest building on Nob Hill.

Walk west on Mason Street.

THE PACIFIC UNION CLUB, at the northwest corner of California and Mason streets, is said to be the first brownstone west of the Mississippi, and was the residence of silver king James C. Flood. Erected in 1886 at a cost of one and one-half million dollars, it was the only building on Nob Hill to survive the fire of 1906. Today it houses one of the oldest and most exclusive of the city's many private clubs, the Pacific Union Club. This club is the descendant of the first two gentlemen's clubs in San Francisco, the Pacific Club, formed in the 1850's in Steve Whipple's saloon on Commercial Street, and the Union Club, founded in the same decade. Total membership is restricted to 650 residents and 200 non-residents. Called locally, though not altogether sacrilegiously, the P-U, it is known as a stronghold of aged republicanism and as the club that paid for the funeral and burial of Emperor Norton.

Continue west on California Street.

HUNTINGTON PARK, at California, Taylor, and Sacramento streets.

Quiet, peaceful, and dignified, this park is almost totally divorced from its past.

When railroader Charles Crocker began building his several-million-dollar mansion on Nob Hill, in the early 1870's, his closest neighbor, across Taylor Street (on this site), was a redheaded politician named David D. Colton, a former member of the corrupt David Broderick political machine. The two men became close friends, and in 1874, at Crocker's insistence, Colton was taken into partnership with the railroad barons (who then became known as the "Big 4½"). It was a short, not altogether happy association, ending on October 8, 1878, when Colton died mysteriously, either from a fall from a horse, as his family claimed, or by stabbing, as was widely believed.

Hopkins had preceded him in death by a few months. The three remaining members of the original Big Four laid claim to most of Colton's railroad holdings, intimidating his widow with a threat to expose alleged thefts they claimed Colton had committed, if she contested their demand. She at first gave in, but after some hesitation reconsidered and brought suit for four million dollars.

The trial was one of the longest and most sensational in the history of the state. It lasted for eight years, resulting in Colton's vindication, but a denial of the widow's claims. Its most important aspect, for most of the country, was the introduction into evidence of the famous "Colton letters."

The Central Pacific's founders claimed that Colton had never been privy to the real deliberations of the Big Four, that he was in effect a junior executive, and not a partner. The business and personal letters, written to Colton by Collis P. Huntington, proved otherwise. The letters, widely publicized in newspapers across the country, were concerned mainly with railroad politics. They discussed frankly and fully the buying of congressmen and senators, the ways and means by which the railroad manipulated city (San Francisco and Sacramento), state (California and Nevada), and national politics.

Oscar Lewis summarizes their effect:

"Huntington's messages to 'Friend Colton' focused attention on a situation that, even in the free and easy '80s, the general public found hard to accept. The outlines of the

Big Four's political methods had been known long before the letters came to light, but it required their publication to dramatize the situation. It was Huntington's discussion of the cost of votes in the same terms and often in the same letters as the cost of other railroad necessities that first caused thousands to reflect on the possibility that the picturesque captains of industry who were building up the country would bear watching."

The letters and the trial were to cost the railroad monopoly millions in the coming decades, as Washington legislators looked closely at bills involving their interests. Lewis says of its effect on Huntington:

"By the middle '90s he had become a sort of symbol of predatory wealth bent on the corruption of the public servants. It reached a point where Congressmen, fearing the effect on their constituents should they be seen talking to him, were known to dodge down Washington alleys at the old man's approach."

Perhaps it indicates something of Huntington's character that, despite the unpleasant connotations adhering to the Colton name, he purchased from Colton's widow the home of her late husband, and transferred his San Francisco residence here from the Palace Hotel.

Collis P. Huntington died in August 1900. His home burned in the 1906 fire and in 1915 its site was bequeathed to the city by his widow. It was later dedicated as Huntington Park.

Continue west on California Street, cross Taylor Street.

GRACE CATHEDRAL, at California, Taylor, Sacramento, and Jones streets, stands on the sites once occupied by the residences of railroad builder Charles Crocker and a Chinese undertaker named Yung.

Of the Big Four, Charles Crocker was the most active in the actual supervision of the building of the Central Pacific, spending most of his time living in railroad cars on the site of construction. He was a big man, weighing over two hundred fifty pounds, and he carried a corresponding amount of weight in the deliberations and planning of the railroad. Irving Stone, in his remarkable history *Men To Match My Mountains,* places Crocker well:

"Theodore Judah had found the route, engineered the survey, made the detail maps. Collis P. Huntington raised the money, Mark Hopkins kept the books, Leland Stanford wangled the political privileges and licenses. Charlie Crocker actually, physically, corporeally, built the railroad, built it in the face of shattering obstacles, hardships, defeats and delays that stagger the stoutest heart and mind."

In the mid-1870's Crocker bought this site and began construction of a huge baronial redwood mansion. He was able to obtain all of the block except for a twenty-five-foot strip of land on the Sacramento Street side, where stood the residence of a Chinese undertaker named Yung. Crocker tried to buy out Yung; Yung wouldn't sell; Crocker got mad. In a fit of pique he built a fence forty feet high that towered over the Yung domicile on three sides, shutting out nearly all its light. San Franciscans came to watch the construction in great wonder, a few cheering Crocker, most rooting for Yung, all fascinated by "Crocker's Spite Fence." None missed the irony that Crocker, who had bossed thousands of Chinese during the construction of the railroad, was bested by the stubborn, solitary Mr. Yung.

Then Dennis Kearney came onto the scene. Kearney was an explosive Irish labor agitator, a pioneer in the California labor movement. One day he arrived with a crowd numbering into the hundreds, intent upon (1) tearing down the fence, (2) lynching Crocker, and (3) distributing his wealth. Police succeeded in breaking up the mob before any of these things could be accomplished. This situation also had its irony, though it was not humorous and wasn't apparent for some time. Kearney, the champion of under-dog Yung, was soon to become one of the most rabid anti-Chinese spokesmen in the state, responsible for the "sand-lot riots" that resulted in the deaths of a number of San Francisco Chinese and the destruction of numerous homes and businesses.

In time Mr. Yung sold to Mr. Crocker and the fence came down. After Crocker died in 1888, the property was given by his heirs to the Episcopal diocese of California.

Grace Cathedral, one of the city's largest and most beau-tiful churches, has had a long history of its own, going back to the founding of Grace Church in 1850, at California and Stockton streets. Here in 1863 the Right Reverend William Ingraham Kip placed his episcopal chair, estab-lishing the first cathedral seat of the Protestant Episcopal Church in America. The cathedral itself has been under construction since January 27, 1914.

Though all but one of its early mansions burned in 1906, and only a few were rebuilt, Nob Hill retains in its fine hotels, homes, and apartment houses more than a trace of its former opulence. It is still, in both memory and fact, the Hill of Palaces, as Robert Louis Stevenson christened it. The "great net of straight thoroughfares," Stevenson wrote,

"lying at right angles, east and west and north and south over the shoulders of Nob Hill, the hill of palaces, must certainly be counted the best part of San Francisco. It is there that the millionaires who gathered together, vying with each other in display, looked down upon the business wards of the city."

RUSSIAN HILL

From downtown San Francisco:

CABLE CAR: Catch the northbound Hyde Street car
   on Powell Street, debark at Lombard and Hyde streets.
DRIVING: Up Powell to California Street, west on
   California to Hyde Street, north on Hyde to Lombard
   Street.

—or—

From Nob Hill:

CABLE CAR: Catch the northbound Hyde Street car
   at the corner of California and Powell streets. Debark
   as above.
DRIVING: From California Street as above.

Again there are various conjectures as to the name. Some
say it was christened Russian Hill after a colony of Russians
settled on its crest. Others, and this is the most widely held
opinion, believe the name followed the burial of a group of
Russian sailors at the peak of what became Vallejo Street.
But Russian Hill it is, and a different world from Nob. From
the building of its first lone houses in the 1850's through
the Bohemian '90s to the present it has retained a rustic informality. Nob Hill remains austere, pompous, sedate; it
seems to take itself seriously. Russian Hill has equally fine

homes and apartment houses, but likely as not they are neighbored by modest one-story residences with tiny yards or rambling two-story relics of the past, painted in lively contemporary colors. Russian Hill feels relaxed, informal; one suspects its residents have a great deal of fun.

There are few historic sites left on the hill. A tall apartment house now occupies the northeast corner of Chestnut and Hyde streets, where for many years stood the William Penn Humphries house, the first home on the hill, built in 1852 of oak timbers brought around the Horn. Gone too is the haunted house that stood on the northeast corner of Chestnut and Larkin streets, once the residence of John Pool Manrow, chief advocate of the Committee of Vigilance. Some of the city's most respectable citizens ventured here in the 1860's to watch for appearances of the horribly visaged poltergeists who repeatedly attacked the house and grounds. Manrow, in time, came to believe they were victims of vigilante "justice." They were seen, on and off, up to the time the house was destroyed in 1919, long after Manrow had died.

What remains is more than enough: memories, chiefly of the hill's Bohemian days; the conglomerate houses and quaint lanes of one of the most casually beautiful parts of San Francisco; and the spectacular views.

GEORGE STERLING. Before going down the winding Lombard Street hill, you may care to take a short side trip west on Lombard. In the small park is a plaque dedicated to the memory of the poet George Sterling, 1869–1926.

Sterling was but one of the many Bohemians who found congenial and occasionally understanding companionship on Russian Hill during the last quarter of the nineteenth century. It was an informal colony, its members drawn together as much by their differences as their similarities. Among those who lived here, in little houses on the slopes of the hill, were Will and Wallace Irwin, Gelett Burgess, John Dewey, Charles Norris, Charles Caldwell Dobie, Maynard Dixon, Peter B. Kyne. Many more came to visit or to stay for a while. If the group had any center, it was the home of poetess Ina Coolbrith. The unknown and renowned came here, to sit on the floor, drink coffee or wine, and talk. Among the poetess's special friends were Mark Twain, Bret Harte, Charles Warren Stoddard, Joaquin Miller, Ambrose Bierce, Jack London, and George Sterling.

George Sterling was born in Sag Harbor, New York. As a youth, at his father's insistence, he studied for the Catholic priesthood. But unhappy, plagued with a despondent restlessness that he could never overcome, he left the seminary at twenty and came to California, working in Oakland as a real estate salesman.

He also wrote poetry. At twenty-two he was discovered by the fierce Ambrose Bierce, who became his literary mentor. Bierce accepted the Dantesque Sterling not as a friend but as a disciple. He not only guided Sterling's career—his critical praise brought Sterling his first real success—he also wanted to choose the young poet's friends. Especially repugnant to Bierce was Sterling's companion, the young Jack London. Nor did he approve of the new artists' colony at Carmel, where, for six years, Sterling lived with Lincoln Steffens, Charles Rollo Peters, Upton Sinclair, and Mary Austin.

Samuel Dickson, in *Tales of San Francisco*, recalls that Sterling came to him in 1926, when Dickson was editing a children's magazine, with his long narrative poem *The Saga of the Pony Express*. Dickson wouldn't accept it; he couldn't afford to pay for such a major work and refused to publish anything he couldn't pay for. Sterling insisted, wanting the children to read it, finally suggesting that Dickson pay him with a couple bottles of whisky, which he did.

The whisky, Sterling explained, was to help entertain his idol, H. L. Mencken (probably the only man in America whose sardonic wit matched that of Sterling's former mentor, Bierce), en route to San Francisco to visit him.

Mencken was traveling with author Joseph Hergesheimer, who had a weakness for pretty girls and chess. When the pair reached Los Angeles, Hergesheimer met a female chess player who beat him game after game. Mencken kept postponing his arrival; Sterling drank the whisky and a great deal more. By the time Mencken did arrive, several weeks later, Sterling was too sick and despondent to preside at the banquet in Mencken's honor, and another writer, whom Sterling disliked, was elected to take his place. The following morning Mencken went to Sterling's room, to find in addition to many empty whisky bottles a small and empty vial of poison.

Though he was once proclaimed California's greatest poet, Sterling's work is mostly forgotten today. The title of one of his poems, however, will probably survive as long as San Francisco. Sterling called it *The Cool Grey City of Love*.

Walk or drive down Lombard Street to Leavenworth Street.

"THE CROOKEDEST STREET IN THE WORLD," as this section of Lombard is known, is not the city's steepest street. Several others—Filbert, between Hyde and Leavenworth; Union, between Polk and Hyde—better its grade. But with its eight terraced switchbacks and its near-ninety-degree angles, it is one of the city's most picturesque thoroughfares, either close up or viewed from a distance.

THE SAN FRANCISCO ART INSTITUTE, an optional side trip, is north one block on Leavenworth to Chestnut streets, east on Chestnut three quarters of a block. Formerly the California School of Fine Arts, the Institute offers courses in all of the graphic arts. The changing exhibits in the main foyer, the attractive patio with its tiled fountain, and the auditorium with its large Diego Rivera mural are all open to the public.

From Lombard and Leavenworth streets, south four blocks on Leavenworth to Green Street, east on Green Street one-half block.

THE OCTAGONAL HOUSE, at 1067 Green Street, is a well-cared-for reminder of an architectural fad that moved across America in the middle and late 1850's. The chief advantage of the eight-sided structure was that it reputedly caught the greatest possible amount of sunlight. At one time there were eight octagonal houses in San Francisco, four of them on Russian Hill. Today only two remain, this building, which is a private residence, and another, on Gough Street near Union. The latter, sponsored by a historical society, is open to the public.

Walk east approximately one block to the end of Green Street for a scenic view of Telegraph Hill, the San Francisco-Oakland Bay Bridge, Treasure Island, and the East Bay. If driving, park in the vicinity, note location, and walk the remainder of the tour.

AMBROSE BIERCE. Perhaps the strangest and easily the most brilliant man who frequented Russian Hill's bohemia was Ambrose Bierce, America's greatest satirist.

There is much we still don't know about this man. His date of birth like his date of death is unknown; it is thought he was born in 1842 and that he died in 1913, at the age of seventy-one. He arrived in San Francisco in 1866, deeply embittered by the horrors of the Civil War, in which he had served as a Union lieutenant, and began working for various local newspapers—the *Overland Monthly*, the *News-Letter*, the *Wasp*, young Hearst's *Examiner*. He was a cynic, in the very best sense of that word, as well as a lonely, troubled man. Satire was his only sacred cow; with it he attacked everyone and everything:

"It is my intention to purify journalism in this town by instructing such writers as it is worth while to instruct, and assassinating those that it is not."

"A morning paper says three unclaimed gold watches are in the hands of the police, and that it is not definitely known who stole them. It is definitely known who will steal them."

"Stanford and Huntington, so long at outs,
    Kissed and made up. If you have any doubts
    Dismiss them, for I saw them do it, man;
    And then—why, then I clutched my purse and ran!"

He professed to hate women ("Woman: An animal usually living in the vicinity of Man, and having a rudimentary susceptibility to domestication") and loved a larger number of them than most men. He had a clear, sharp, incisive wit ("the salt with which the American humorist spoils his intellectual cookery by leaving it out"), though he often drank from morning through the night—it being said on Montgomery Street that there was not a man in the city who could buy Bierce's last drink. He was an off-and-on-again friend of Ina Coolbrith, Joaquin Miller, George Sterling, Bret Harte (none of whom claimed really to know or understand him), but he could not stand those two great opposites, Oscar Wilde and Jack London.

"Bitter bitter Bierce," they called him. He lived for a time in New York, Washington, London, writing his famous *Prattle* column, which provided the essence for his greatest work, *The Devil's Dictionary*. But mostly he lived in San

Francisco, subjecting every aspect of the city and its inhabitants to his merciless, cutting wit, making innumerable enemies and seeking but never finding a true disciple or friend.

Then in 1913 he disappeared. Later a letter established that he had gone to Mexico "with a pretty definite purpose, which, however, is not at present disclosable." It never became known, for he was never heard from again. And then the legends began. Most agree that he had gone to join Pancho Villa and was later killed by (1) Villa himself, (2) Villa's men, or (3) the opposition. A firing squad figured prominently in most of the tales. His fellow newspapermen, nearly all of whom hated him, were sure that (along with Sterling and probably London) he had committed suicide.

If any ghost now haunts Russian Hill it is likely to be Bierce's. His wit, since then endlessly plagiarized in both style and content, has about it a touch of ghostly laughter. Here are a few samples from the A's in *The Devil's Dictionary*:

Abstainer: A weak person who yields to the temptation of denying himself a pleasure. A total abstainer is one who abstains from everything but abstention, and especially from inactivity in the affairs of others.

Acquaintance: A person whom we know well enough to borrow from, but not well enough to lend to. A degree of friendship called slight when its object is poor or obscure, and intimate when he is rich or famous.

Admiration: Our polite recognition of another's resemblance to ourselves.

Alliance: In international politics, the union of two thieves who have their hands so deeply inserted in each other's pocket that they cannot separately plunder a third.

And perhaps Bierce's best, and, in a way, his saddest:

Alone: In bad company.

Retrace to Jones Street.

Another optional side trip (two blocks south on Jones to Broadway, down Broadway one-quarter block) is the ATKINSON HOUSE, 1032 Broadway, one of the oldest surviving residences in San Francisco. The two-story structure was built in 1853 by contractor Joseph H. Atkinson, who also erected the prison walls at San Quentin. A private residence, it is largely hidden from the street by stone walls. Thanks to a modern coat of plaster, what can be seen looks younger than many of the other buildings on the same street.

From Jones and Green streets north (downhill) one-half block to Macondray Lane. Follow Macondray Lane east to Taylor Street by way of the steps.

There is very little history attached to Macondray Lane, but a great deal of charm. It is included as a sample of the colorful streets and alleys to be found in the Russian Hill and Telegraph Hill areas.

South on Taylor Street one and a half blocks to Vallejo Street. East through Coolbrith Park to Mason Street.

INA DONNA COOLBRITH was an unusual woman. Born in 1842, a niece of the Mormon prophet Joseph Smith, she came to San Francisco in 1862, by way of an unhappy marriage and a short residence in Southern California. Here she wrote poetry, became active in the affairs of the literary

SAN FRANCISCO AND THE EAST BAY,
as seen from Twin Peaks
(*Redwood Empire Association*)

CABLE CAR ASCENDING THE CALIFORNIA STREET HILL
(*Redwood Empire Association*)

JAPANESE TEA GARDEN. GOLDEN GATE PARK
(Redwood Empire Association)

THE GREAT HIGHWAY, OCEAN BEACH, AND THE
PACIFIC OCEAN, as seen from Sutro Heights
(Redwood Empire Association)

CITY HALL, SAN FRANCISCO'S CIVIC CENTER
(Redwood Empire Association)

ONE OF THE LAST GREAT SAILING SHIPS,
THE *BALCLUTHA*, with Alcatraz in the background
(*Redwood Empire Association*)

GIRARDELLI SQUARE
(*Redwood Empire Association*)

GOLDEN GATE BRIDGE IN THE FOG
(*Redwood Empire Association*)

Overland Monthly, was for "thirty-two years a librarian; friend and counselor to three generations of California writers," became the first poet laureate in America in 1919, and died in 1928.

These are all important facts but, like her poetry, mostly long forgotten. Few today remember that she corresponded with some of the leading literary figures of the nineteenth century—Alfred Lord Tennyson, John Whittier, Dante Gabriel Rossetti, George Meredith, Henry Wadsworth Longfellow—and was acclaimed by them; that her salon was the focal point of Russian Hill's Bohemia; that with the aid of her friend Joaquin Miller she fought, unsuccessfully, to have the remains of her favorite poet, Lord Byron, moved from a nondescript grave on a remote island to the stately confines of Westminster Abbey. Even the slight scandals attached to her name are forgotten: that Bret Harte wanted to divorce his wife to marry her; that Charles Warren Stoddard climaxed his marriage proposal to her with a threat of suicide if she refused him.

But her place is assured in California folklore, for during the time she was librarian in the Oakland Public Library, a twelve-year-old youth came in and asked her for something to read. For years she supplied him with books, directed his way through the classics, became his friend and confidante. He was later to write of her, "I loved Ina Coolbrith above all womankind, and what I am and what I have done that is good I owe to her." His name was Jack London.

If driving, retrace to your parking place; if walking, catch the southbound Powell Street cable car on Mason Street to downtown San Francisco.

For Additional Exploration:

THE BIG FOUR. By Oscar Lewis. The story of the builders of the Central Pacific Railroad.

SILVER KINGS. By Oscar Lewis. The story of the men who discovered and developed the Comstock Lode.

THE HILLS OF SAN FRANCISCO. San Francisco *Chronicle*. Brief biographies of San Francisco's "citied hills."

TALES OF SAN FRANCISCO. By Samuel Dickson. The lore of the city by the Golden Gate; three volumes in one.

BUILDINGS OF THE BAY AREA. By John and Sally Woodbridge. A guide to the architecture of the San Francisco Bay region.

CHAPTER FIVE:

GOLDEN GATE PARK

A Driving Tour, including: the Conservatory; M. H. de Young Memorial Museum — the Japanese Tea Garden — the California Academy of Sciences — Steinhart Aquarium — Alexander F. Morrison Planetarium — Simson African Hall — North American Hall — Shakespeare's Garden of Flowers — Strybing Arboretum and Botanical Gardens — Stowe Lake and Strawberry Hill — Portals of the Past — the Buffalo Paddock — and the ship *Gjoa*. With a short history of the park and the men who created it.

From the *Annals of San Francisco*, 1854:

"Over all these square miles of contemplated thoroughfares, there seems no provision made by the projectors for a public park—the true 'lungs' of a large city. The existing plaza, or Portsmouth Square, and other two or three diminutive squares, delineated on the plan, seem the only breathing-holes intended for the future population of hundreds of thousands. This is a strange mistake, and can only be attributed to the jealous avarice of the city projectors in turning every square vara of the site to an available building lot . . . Not only is there no public park or garden, but there is not even a circus, oval, open terrace, broad avenue, or any ornamental line of street or building or verdant space of any kind, other than the three or four small squares alluded to; and which every resident knows are by no means verdant, except in patches where stagnant water collects and ditch weeds grow."

By 1875 the lack that the *Annals* decried had been remedied. In that year Anthony Trollope, writing that "there is almost nothing to see in San Francisco," had to add, with

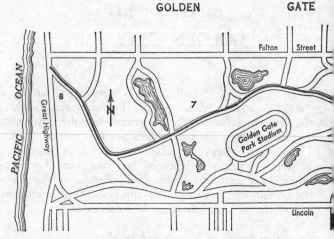

1. Conservatory   3. De Young Museum
2. John McLaren Rhododendron Dell   4. California Academy of Sciences

obvious reluctance, "There *is* a new park, in which you may
drive for six or seven miles on a well made road, and which,
as a park for the use of the city, will, when completed, have
many excellencies."

At that, his admission went a lot further than many residents were willing to go. Just two years earlier, a newspaper
editor, surveying the 1017 acres of sand dunes that com-
prised Golden Gate Park, found it "a dreary waste of shifting sand hills where a blade of grass cannot be raised without four posts to support it and keep it from blowing away."
The loud and highly vocal criticism had begun in 1868,
when the city obtained final rights to the land; it grew more
adamant in 1871, when engineer William Hammond Hall
was appointed first park superintendent and began the job
of transforming the dunes into a green haven that would
surpass New York's 840-acre Central Park in both beauty
and size; and it was to continue well into the present cen-

PARK

5. Strybing Arboretum and Botanical Gardens   **7.** Buffalo Paddock
6. Strawberry Hill   **8.** Amundsen's Ship "Gjoa"

tury, long after Hall had himself fallen martyr to the city's complex politics. (Even today there is periodic talk of uprooting a portion of the park for a freeway.)

Hall's belief that "The value of a park consists of its being a park, and not a catch-all for almost anything which misguided people may wish upon it" was shared by his highly capable successor, Scottish landscape gardener John McLaren, who was appointed in 1887 and thereafter served for fifty-six years as the "presiding genius of Golden Gate Park." It was McLaren who solved the problem of the rolling sand dunes by discovering the varieties of grass and shrubbery that would hold the sand in place; McLaren who drilled the wells that were to make possible the park's lush vegetation; McLaren who mastered the threat of new sand, blown in from the ocean beach, by patiently building a sea wall. It was McLaren also who, stubbornly fighting attempts at political interference—his gardeners and park employees on more than one occasion served as an army to repel invasions of other branches of the city government—succeeded in retaining the area's natural contours, encouraged the planting of more than five thousand varieties of plants, and, fulfilling a lifetime wish, planted over one million trees.

McLaren's separate accomplishments, often effected despite strong opposition, would fill many pages. It is enough to note that there is little in the four-mile-long, one-half-mile-wide park that McLaren himself did not personally supervise or leave room for in his plans.

Two exceptions might be mentioned:

McLaren believed that statues (he called them "stookies") had no place in parks, and for many years he stoutly resisted the erection of each new statue. Eventually realizing that he was fighting an endless battle, he changed his tactics slightly. He quietly assented to the erection of the statues, with all attendant fanfare. Then he effectively barred them from sight by planting shrubbery and trees around them.

The other exception, occurring after his death, was the erection of the park's only "Keep off the Grass" sign. Believing that parks are for people, the dour Scotsman refused to restrict the public from enjoying any part of Golden Gate Park. After "Uncle John" McLaren's death—he died in 1943, at the age of ninety-six, still park superintendent—a statue of him was erected in McLaren Dell. Next to this "stookie" is the park's only prohibitive sign, necessary to protect the rare rhododendrons that surround the statue.

No simple tour can include the whole of Golden Gate Park. To explore it fully takes not one but several leisurely days, for there is much to see in "the world's largest man-made park." This chapter includes a suggested highlight tour, arranged for the visitor or resident with an automobile at his disposal. You may drive it in an hour. However, if you are interested in the various museums and displays, allow yourself the better part of a day.

If your time is limited and you are dependent upon public transportation, catch the No. 5 McAllister Street bus anywhere along Market Street up to McAllister in downtown San Francisco, transfer at Eighth Avenue to the No. 10 Monterey bus, debark in front of the de Young Memorial Museum. A large number of the park's main exhibits are in the immediate vicinity.

Automobile Tour.

Suggested route from downtown San Francisco: From McAllister and Market, drive west on McAllister to Gough Street (two blocks west of Van Ness Avenue); south on Gough one block to Fulton Street; west on Fulton to Baker Street; south on Baker three blocks to Fell Street; west on Fell eight blocks, alongside the park "Panhandle" to Stanyan Street and Fell and the park entrance.

For specialized information on Golden Gate Park—information on the current botanical exhibits, recreational areas, etc.—visit the Park Lodge, near the entrance at Stanyan and Fell streets.

Important: A number of the roads within the park are unnamed. Watch for signs indicating the various buildings and exhibits.

To the north of the Main Drive.

CONSERVATORY (open 8–5 daily). Erected in 1879 (restored after its destruction by fire in 1883), the wood-and-glass structure is modeled after the Royal Conservatories at Kew Gardens, and houses a large and varied collection of tropical plants from all parts of the world. In addition to the permanent collection seasonal blooms are displayed in the exhibition room of the west wing. Special attractions of the garden area in front of the entrance are the floral plaque (an example of the almost forgotten art of carpet bedding) and the floral clock, the latter a gift to San Francisco from the Watchmakers of Switzerland.

To the south, alongside the Main Drive.

JOHN MCLAREN RHODODENDRON DELL.   In addition to the "stookie" of Uncle John, set not on a pedestal but with its feet planted firmly on the ground, are twenty acres of a colorful rhododendron named for him. There are over three hundred other varieties of rhododendrons in the park, the world's largest collection.

Turn left at museum sign. Park in the vicinity of M. H. de Young Memorial Museum.

The buildings grouped around the inclined amphitheater of the Music Concourse form the cultural center of Golden Gate Park. Used first as the site for the California Mid-Winter International Exposition of 1894, the area now contains the West's oldest scientific institution, one of its finest art museums, an aquarium, an African hall, and a planetarium.

THE M. H. DE YOUNG MEMORIAL MUSEUM (open 10–5) was opened March 25, 1895, financed in part by funds from the successful exposition, in which *Chronicle* publisher M. H. de Young played a prominent part. The present building was erected a wing at a time, replacing the original edifice, a heritage of the exposition, the latest addition, completed in 1966, housing the $30,000,000 collection of oriental art presented to the city by Olympic czar and art collector Avery Brundage.

By area population, the de Young is the most popular museum in the world, with 1,500,000 visitors annually. Its galleries and courts house an art collection unrivaled on the West Coast, ranging from acknowledged world masterpieces, such as Rubens' *Tribute Money* and El Greco's *St. John the Baptist,* to a fascinating collection of pioneer Californiana.

Branching out from the sunken Garden Court, the museum is divided into several main sections:

The East Wing is devoted to loan exhibitions from art collections the world over, each generally on exhibit for about a month at a time. The Information Desk will answer queries regarding current or forthcoming exhibitions.

The Central Wing (the galleries grouped around the Great Court) contains a permanent but ever-expanding collection of the arts of Europe and America, with special emphasis given to Egyptian, Greek, and Roman art, and American painting of the nineteenth century.

The West Wing is devoted to Californiana, in particular to the history of San Francisco. On display are a comprehensive costume collection, as worn by Californians from 1760 to the present; four living rooms, as one might have found if visiting the city in 1850, 1865, 1870, and 1885; a collection of ship models, paintings, and navigational gear; as well as other special regional displays. This wing also contains the Armor Room, housing a weapon collection world-wide in scope and stretching in time from the fifteenth century to the present.

The new Brundage collection wing, centered around an interior court with a fountain and looking out over the Japanese Tea Garden, includes ancient Chinese jade, bronzes, ceramics and paintings; Japanese paintings, ceramics and lacquer; Persian pottery and bronzes; and sculpture from China, India, Korea, Japan and Southeast Asia. The collection is believed to be one of the largest of its kind in the world.

Go to the northwest corner of the Music Concourse, a short walk west of the de Young Museum.

JAPANESE TEA GARDEN (open 10–5 daily). The two-storied entrance gate, the winding paths, the tranquil pools, the miniature gardens, the Buddhist and Shinto shrines, the half-moon Wishing Bridge have delighted visitors and residents since the 1894 exhibition. During World War II this five-acre tract was renamed the Oriental Tea Garden and the thatched teahouse was staffed by Chinese maidens, but it has since reverted to its Japanese name and character. A year-round favorite spot for San Franciscans, it draws its largest crowds in the spring when the cherry blossoms are in bloom.

THE MUSIC CONCOURSE, set in a low valley opposite the de Young Museum, also dates from the 1894 exposition. (Old-time residents are unusually exposition-conscious, remembering as best the 1915 Panama-Pacific International Exposition, for which the Marina was created, and the 1939 Golden Gate International Exposition, set on Treasure Island.) On fair-weather Sundays and holidays the Municipal Band gives free concerts here, from 2 to 4:30 P.M. The outdoor auditorium seats twenty thousand.

South of the Music Concourse.

CALIFORNIA ACADEMY OF SCIENCES, the oldest scientific institution on the West Coast. Founded in 1853 in a Montgomery Street office by seven men whose scientific curiosity exceeded their desire for gold, the academy was housed in various buildings downtown until 1906. After the last location, on Market Street, was destroyed in the fire, the city voted funds to set up the academy in its present location. Under its auspices are four major scientific divisions located in the interconnecting buildings: North American Hall, Simson African Hall, Steinhart Aquarium, and the Alexander F. Morrison Planetarium. The academy also sponsors extensive research and exploration in its various fields of inquiry and maintains a large library with research facilities. Entry is through Cowell Hall.

THE STEINHART AQUARIUM (open 10–5 daily), is the most popular of Golden Gate Park's many exhibits, often drawing up to three million visitors a year. Though the aquarium houses over twelve thousand different fresh- and salt-water fish, the largest crowds are invariably seen around the tanks of the dolphins (both fresh- and salt-water varieties); the carnivorous piranha fish; and the noisy talking fish. The alligator swamp in the entrance court also draws a large number of spectators.

THE ALEXANDER F. MORRISON PLANETARIUM is located in the East Wing. A special feature is the planetarium star projector, the first installed in this country. There are regular showings of the heavens daily at 2 P.M.; evening shows, Wed.–Sun. 8:30 P.M.; extra matinees Sat.,

Sun. and holidays 3:30 P.M. Admission is $1 for adults, 50¢ for students, children under 16, and service personnel; there is no charge for the many other exhibits, however.

THE SCIENCE MUSEUM, and SIMSON AFRICAN HALL (open 10–5 daily) are also in this wing. The former includes among its unusual displays a horological collection, showing the evolution of the timepiece; a lamp collection, made up of lamps dating from primitive times to the present; and the Alice Eastwood Botanical Collection. Presented by Leslie Simson, a mining engineer and sportsman, the collection in the African Hall includes animals Simson obtained while hunting in Africa, displayed in realistic simulated habitats.

NORTH AMERICAN HALL, located in the West Wing of the academy buildings (open 10–5 daily), contains the Hall of Mammals, with a large collection of American mammals shown in their natural habitats (this was the first museum to do this), and the Hall of Birds, with an equally impressive collection of birds from this continent. Adjacent is the new Hall of Minerals, devoted to things geological.

At the end of a path to the west of the Academy of Sciences buildings.

SHAKESPEARE'S GARDEN OF FLOWERS. Every tree, shrub, flower and plant here is mentioned in the works of the Immortal Bard.

From the parking area continue driving southwest on South Drive.

STRYBING ARBORETUM AND BOTANICAL GARDENS. Over five thousand varieties of plants—many unique or extremely rare—grow in the open in this forty-acre tract. For the botanically minded this is one of the park's highlights. World-wide in origin, the various species are all plainly classified. Five acres are devoted to more than three hundred species of native California plants. The James Noble Conifer Collection, some three hundred seventy-five species, varieties and cultivars of dwarf and slow-growing conifers, surrounds two lakes connected by a stream; the collection is one of the finest in the western United States. One of the most unusual features is the Garden of Fragrance, where plants which are pleasing to the senses of smell and touch may be enjoyed. Because of their special interest to the blind, identifying labels are printed in Braille.

Turn to the right off South Drive at the sign pointing to Stowe Lake.

STOWE LAKE encircles the base of Strawberry Hill, and is not only the central reservoir for the park's irrigation system, (supplying four million gallons of water daily), but also a favorite spot for weekend boating enthusiasts. Canoes, row boats, and motorboats may be rented here. It is the largest of the park's many artificial lakes, and its islets provide haven for a variety of wild and domestic waterfowl.

STRAWBERRY HILL may be reached by stone bridges set across the narrowest part of the lake. A spiraling path leads up to its 412-foot summit, where there is a panoramic view of much of San Francisco, Ocean Boulevard, the Cliff House, the Pacific Ocean, and Golden Gate Bridge.

North to the Main Drive, then west on this drive past Prayer Book Cross.

PRAYER BOOK CROSS was erected in 1894 by the Northern California Episcopal diocese to commemorate the first use of the Book of Common Prayer on the Pacific Coast by Sir Francis Drake's chaplain, Francis Fletcher, when the *Golden Hinde* landed at Drake's Bay in 1579. It is modeled after an ancient Celtic cross on the island of Iona.

Continue on the Main Drive, crossing Over Drive.

LLOYD LAKE and PORTALS OF THE PAST.   The six marble Ionic columns, reflected in the lake's surface, are a mute reminder of the events of April 1906. This was all that remained of A. N. Towne's mansion on Nob Hill.

Continue on the Main Drive past the baseball diamond (to the left) and Spreckles Lake (to the right).

BUFFALO PADDOCK.   More than a dozen buffalo are in the herd that roams the wooded meadow north of Main Drive. Like the deer and elk, antelope and sheep that also graze in the park, the buffalo were brought here (the original herd in 1890) by man. The large flocks of ducks, geese, and other waterfowl that inhabit the park's lakes flew here. The foxes, raccoons, squirrels, rabbits and skunks are less readily explained. They are not indigenous to dune areas, and no one knows just how they traversed the city unseen, to gather here in large numbers soon after the park was opened. A full-time hunter is employed to keep the more predatory under control.

Continue on the Main Drive to the park's westward limits and the Great Highway.

AMUNDSEN'S SHIP *GJOA*.   This forty-seven-ton sloop was the first ship to sail through the icebound Northwest Passage. Built in 1872 in Norway, she served almost thirty years as a sealer before being purchased by arctic explorer Roald Amundsen, who sailed her to the arctic in 1903 on his famed exploration of the fabled Northwest Passage. Amundsen not only navigated the perilous passage for the first time, he also fixed the location of the North Magnetic Pole. He presented the ship to San Francisco in 1909.

For Additional Exploration:

GOLDEN GATE: THE PARK OF A THOUSAND VISTAS. By Katherine Wilson. The best book available on the history of Golden Gate Park.

CHAPTER SIX

CONTINENT'S END

A Driving Tour. Including the Ferry Building, Embarcadero, Balclutha, Maritime Museum, Palace of Fine Arts, Presidio, Sutro Heights, Cliff House, Fleishhacker Zoo, Twin Peaks, Mission Dolores, and Civic Center.

This chapter, covering a suggested route of approximately thirty miles within the city, is intended as an automobile tour. Information on busses and/or cable cars for reaching the major sites can be obtained by calling Municipal Railway Information, 558-4111.

A major portion of the tour (from Aquatic Park to the Mission Dolores) follows the route of the Downtown Association's 49 Mile Scenic Drive and can be followed easily by watching for the blue-and-white sea-gull signs.

Start at the FERRY BUILDING, *the Embarcadero and Market Street.*

At 5:12 on the morning of April 18, 1906, the large hands on the tower clock of the Ferry Building stopped. Exactly a year later they were set back in motion. For the thousands of commuters who passed through this building daily (fifty million in one busy year), on their way to or from home via the ferryboats, it was more than a mute reminder of the earthquake. It was also something of a sentimental inconvenience, since the commuters and a goodly number of downtown San Franciscans set their timepieces by the Ferry Building clock. For, all geographical considerations aside,

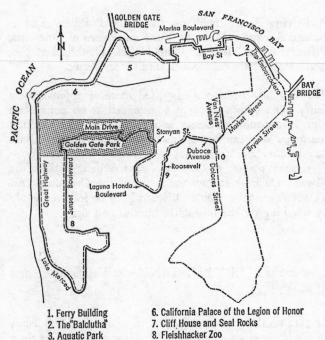

CONTINENT'S END

GOLDEN GATE BRIDGE

SAN FRANCISCO BAY

Marina Boulevard

Bay St

The Embarcadero

BAY BRIDGE

PACIFIC OCEAN

Van Ness Avenue

Market Street

Bryant Street

Main Drive

Golden Gate Park

Stanyan St.

Duboce Avenue

Roosevelt

Dolores Street

Laguna Honda Boulevard

Great Highway

Sunset Boulevard

Lake Merced

1. Ferry Building
2. The "Balclutha"
3. Aquatic Park
4. Palace of Fine Arts
5. Presidio
6. California Palace of the Legion of Honor
7. Cliff House and Seal Rocks
8. Fleishhacker Zoo
9. Twin Peaks
10. Mission Dolores

_ _ _ _ Route of the 49 Mile Scenic Drive

(For the exact route between points 6 and 7 see the text).

the Ferry Building was, and in a sense still is, the sentimental heart of San Francisco.

The ferryboats are gone now, but the building, with its near-empty corridors, remains, and reminds.

The oldest known ancestor of the bay ferryboats was a sloop built in 1826 by a Mr. John Reed, to carry passengers from Yerba Buena to what is now Sausalito. Two schooners joined the list of progenitors in 1835; operated by Captain William Richardson (see Chapter One) they traveled back and forth from Contra Costa (meaning "opposite shore"). The first "regularly scheduled" ferry service is said to have been inaugurated in 1850 by the propeller-driven steamer *Kangaroo*. During the following decades, in addition to the railroad ferries, which, beginning in 1869, conveyed passengers and sometimes entire trains from Oakland to San Francisco, there came a great variety of craft, including stern-wheelers, side-wheelers, oil burners, coal burners, single- and double-enders, with names like *Redwood Empire*, *Yerba Buena*, *Chrysopolis*.

The Central Terminal Building, built in 1877, with only three ferry slips, was soon too small for the traffic. The present Ferry Building was opened in July 1898. Proclaimed "the most solidly constructed edifice in California," it was designed by architect Arthur Page Brown, who modeled its 235-foot tower after the Giralda tower in Seville. Brown died before the building was completed, and his young assistant, Willis Polk ("the man who rebuilt San Francisco"), finished it. It has survived earthquakes, fire, and the millions of rushing commuters for whom it was the gateway to San Francisco.

"The ferryboat was far more than the means of getting to the job," notes Harold Gilliam:

"It was a twice-daily social period, a convivial gathering, a respite in the day's routine only remotely approximated by the modern coffee break or the cocktail hour. In more than a figurative sense the passenger ferries were floating clubhouses. The regular commuters were members of well-defined in-groups with long-established totems, taboos, and folkways."

With the building of the San Francisco-Oakland Bay Bridge and the Golden Gate Bridge in the mid-1930's the ferryboats were doomed. The passage of a state law guaranteed investors in the spans lifelong insurance against competition from water-borne conveyances. The only exceptions were the ferries maintained by the Southern Pacific Railroad, which were allowed to operate for railroad passengers, between Oakland and San Francisco. (Two nearby lines, Richmond-San Rafael and Martinez-Benicia, remained in operation until the late 1950's, until bridges in the vicinity were completed). Considered uneconomical, the last of the Southern Pacific boats, the *San Leandro*, made its final run on the night of July 30, 1958, packed with silent mourners.

Gilliam, in his book *San Francisco Bay*, presents a fine case for the return of the ferryboats, to replace "the high-tension frenzy of rush-hour commutering, the nerve-fraying lane-to-lane infighting among drivers who know each other not as human beings but only by make and model . . .

"To the ferry commuters the bay was more than a fragmentary glimpse of blue water in the distance; it was a direct experience, a working part of their lives. Every morning and every evening they smelled its salt spray from the deck, heard the sound of its waves, breathed its cool winds off the water, sensed its changes as the boat moved in response to the tides and currents.

"The intimate experience of the boat ride, of the bay and its changing beauty created a mood of easygoing friendliness, geniality, and camaraderie which undoubtedly helped mold the character of the community. Quite possibly San Francisco's reputation as a city of serenity and of vision is due in some degree to the effect on three generations of that twice-daily journey across the waters."

From the Ferry Building drive north on the Embar-cadero.

THE EMBARCADERO. San Francisco was and is, first and foremost, a port city, just as Yerba Buena, during its short and sleepy span, was at best a port town.

Without the bay—450 square miles of it, one of the finest natural harbors in the world—there was little more than sand hills, chaparral, fleas, and that sweet-smelling herb *yerba buena.*

The first ships in search of the fabled great bay missed it. The Golden Gate is narrow, at one point less than a mile wide. Fog then, as now, often hid it from view. In 1542 the Portuguese explorer Juan Rodríguez Cabrillo sailed past it, discovering the Farallones, that stretch of lonely islands some thirty miles outside the gate, but missing the bay itself. Sir Francis Drake came next, almost four decades later, in 1579. There is still disagreement as to where he anchored his ship, *The Golden Hinde.* Most historians believe it to have been in a cove now known as Drake's Bay, thirty-odd miles northwest of San Francisco, in present-day Marin County. In 1595 Sebastián Rodríquez Cermeno sailed into a small bay in this vicinity and officially named it La Bahía de San Francisco, in honor of St. Francis of Assisi. But again, evidence indicates that Cermeno merely repeated Drake's mistake.

Seafaring men have never taken too kindly to the next fact, that it was an expedition of landsmen who finally were first to sight the bay, more than one hundred fifty years later.

We can imagine the look of astonishment on the faces of the hunting party led by Spanish Sergeant José Ortega on that first day of November 1769, as, coming from the south, they stood atop a high hill looking down on the immense reaches of San Francisco Bay, realizing that the myths and legends of centuries were now proven true. Ortega's hunting party was part of the larger expedition of Gaspar de Portolá, in search of a site for another of Father Serra's missions, this one to be dedicated to St. Francis. As the priest with Ortega's party put it: "It is a harbor such that not only the navy of our most Catholic Majesty but those of all Europe could take shelter in it."

Then on August 5, 1775, the *San Carlos*, under command of Juan Manuel de Ayala, maneuvered carefully through the narrow gate to become the first ship to enter the bay.

One might suppose that after the initial settlement—the founding of the mission and the Presidio—ships would then come in great numbers. But they didn't, for there was little here to interest them. There were a few Russian ships (despite the bleak barrenness of the place, they had a desertion problem), some British, more Spanish. In 1812 the Russians began a settlement seventy-five miles north of the bay, establishing Fort Ross as a center for their fur trade. By 1841 they had killed off the last of the sea otter and moved on.

Occasionally an American trading ship would call, leaving her goods in exchange for tallow and "California bank notes" (hides). Aboard one of these vessels was a young man named Richard Henry Dana. In *Two Years Before the Mast* (published in 1840) he wrote prophetically:

"If California ever becomes a prosperous country, this bay will be the centre of its prosperity. The abundance of wood and water; the extreme fertility of its shores; the excellence of its climate, which is as near to being perfect as any in the world; and its facilities for navigation, affording the best anchoring-grounds in the whole western coast of America —all fit it for a place of great importance."

Less than a decade later his prediction would suddenly come true.

Continue on the Embarcadero.

THE SAN FRANCISCO BAR PILOTS STATION, an important heritage from the waterfront's past, is located on Pier 7. Since 1850 members of this association have been guiding incoming vessels over the bar outside the Golden Gate and into the bay. Its twenty-five members are all master seamen. Working in alternating shifts, they spend five days at a time aboard the pilot boat, a schooner standing by around the clock—with sails spread to keep an even keel— about ten miles outside the Golden Gate. They are notified by wireless when an incoming ship requires a pilot. One is then ferried to the incoming boat to navigate it over the often treacherous sand bar and through the Gate. Theirs is probably the most exclusive club in the Bay Area; a new pilot is accepted only when death or retirement creates a vacancy.

Continue on the Embarcadero.

In 1848 only fifteen vessels entered the Golden Gate. The following year there were 775 from Eastern ports alone. In less than one year San Francisco was transformed from a sleepy trading post into a world port.

The primary reason, of course, was gold. But the secondary reason, trade, grew in importance. William Martin Camp notes:

"Many a California clipper loaded with San Francisco-bound goods collected freight revenues as high as $125,000 for a single voyage, often more than enough to pay the original cost of the ship."

The ships were of all kinds and from all places. In the first years of the rush, as their crews deserted and headed for the mines, many of them, sturdy vessels, often beautifully built, intended for a long, rich life on the seas, came to stay—to rot, or to be used for building materials or, even worse, as fill, a substitute for land.

Things were never to be the same on the San Francisco waterfront after the gold rush. In the next one hundred years more would happen here than in the last several thousand.

The waterfront itself changed, physically, as the filled-in tidelands pushed the city and the *embarcaderos* (landing places) farther out into the bay. The wharves multiplied, became permanent piers, forty-three in all (those with even numbers are south of the Ferry Building, those with odd numbers to the north). Today the port is a $100,000,000 public utility; it has eighteen miles of ship-berthing space, and 229 acres of wharf area.

The ships changed. Gone are the square-rigged grain ships, the whalers, the great clippers, the purse seiners, and the hundreds of ships—often odd, often beautiful—that plied the river ports, many built in Bay Area shipyards. Gone too are the tough little boats of the oyster pirates, which clashed in the night with their wily counterparts in the fish patrol. They were replaced by heavy dredges and scows for, although the oysters went bad, it was discovered that their shells make excellent cement. Schooners, steamers, fliers, side-wheelers, battleships, cruisers, destroyers, de luxe passenger liners—all have changed as the port and the world itself changed.

Cargoes have changed too. Today the longshoremen who load and unload the boats handle goods from all parts of the world (except Red China). Copra, hides, mail, coffee, cement, borax—name it and with a little exploration you'll probably find it, plus a thousand other items always taken for granted. Stop at one of the piers where a ship is docked and walk through. Economics suddenly comes alive, a subject of vital interest.

It is much more, of course. Upon the cargoes handled here depends the economic stability of the city, the state, and a good part of America. There is no business in San Francisco that is not subject in some way to the tides of the port, that does not feel its fiscal ups and downs. Great fortunes have been made here, by men named Spreckels (sugar), Matson (Matson Lines), Dollar (American President Lines) and by vast, impersonal monopolies such as United Fruit.

Perhaps the men have changed the least—the seamen and longshoremen, who remain tough and independent, seemingly less affected by time than molded by contact with the sea. But working conditions have altered the most, for from the bloody waterfront wars that occurred here—and this port has known the very worst—have come revolutionary changes that have spread through the entire American labor movement. The Embarcadero has its legends too, built around such men as Andrew Furuseth, Harry Lundeberg, and Harry Bridges.

Continue on the Embarcadero to Pier 43.

Berthed alongside Pier 43, just east of Fisherman's Wharf, is the 256-foot-long *Balclutha*, the last full-rigged merchantman that sailed under the American flag, and one of the last remaining square-riggers (open 10–10; adults, 75¢; children 25¢).

Launched in Scotland, the *Balclutha* has had a long and full career. In 1887 she shipped around the Horn to San Francisco on her maiden voyage. She later took part in the California grain trade (for a total of seventeen trips around the Horn), hauled lumber to Australia, served as a salmon-hauling Alaskan Packer, spent twenty unsuccessful years as a showboat, was a movie ship (a historical anachronism in the old *Mutiny on the Bounty* film), then was left as a near-derelict on the flats off Sausalito.

In 1954 San Francisco Maritime Museum Director Karl Kortum conceived the idea of buying and restoring the ship as part of the museum's permanent exhibit. Though the museum itself lacked sufficient funds (an estimated $250,-000 was necessary to restore her), various civic leaders went ahead with the planning. A year later—after more than thirteen thousand hours of skilled labor had been donated by fourteen different unions and over $100,000 in services and supplies made available by a hundred different business firms—the *Balclutha* moved alongside Pier 43, fully and accurately outfitted, one of the major historic attractions of the Bay Area. Photographs, drawings, and descriptive texts arranged in various parts of the ship tell the full story of the *Balclutha* (including her days as the *Star of Alaska* and the *Pacific Queen*) as well as the story of the old salts who sailed her.

A tour of the ship provides many surprises. One is the captain's cabin, decorated not as he probably would have preferred it, but as his wife might have done when the ship was in port to impress the other captains' wives. You can almost see them sitting around, rhapsodizing over the fabrics their husbands brought back from exotic places, or just gossiping.

Drive past Fisherman's Wharf (Chapter Two) on Jefferson Street to Leavenworth. Park in the vicinity and explore the next four attractions on foot. All are within walking distance of Aquatic Park.

THE CANNERY, at Jefferson and Leavenworth, might well have gone the way of numerous other old San Francisco buildings, had it not been for Leonard V. Martin, who saw the brick walls of the pre-earthquake Del Monte Fruit Cannery as a container in which to stir up something extra special. This he accomplished, with the able assistance of architect Joseph Esherick, landscape architect Thomas Church and graphics designer Marget Larsen, in the process contributing significantly to the neo-renaissance of the north waterfront. Even though more than sixty shops are grouped together here, it would anger Martin if you considered the Cannery a shopping complex. To him it is a mood, something to savor and enjoy. Ride the outside elevator; wander the three floors; take in the panoramic views; peek in the stores—one, for example, sells over 200 varieties of cheese; sit in the Cannery concourse and watch the lively passing parade; or listen to Earl "Fatha" Hines, the father of modern jazz piano, whom Martin has signed to a lifetime contract— and chances are you'll agree with his definition. One of the highlights among many is the *Ben Jonson,* a luxurious early seventeenth century English pub, once the Long Gallery of Albyns Hall, designed by Inigo Jones and built by Queen Elizabeth I for her Ambassador to France, Sir Thomas Edmonds, with its impressive Jacobean oaken staircase leading up to two handsome Elizabethan dining rooms. It was among the mammoth art purchases of publisher William Randolph Hearst, who apparently was trying to move Europe bodily to the U.S. Its destination, however, was a warehouse in the Bronx, until rediscovered and purchased by Martin.

THE HYDE STREET PIER is one block west. The idea of restoring this pier as a turn-of-the-century wharf was that of San Francisco Maritime Museum director Karl Kortum. To the California Department of Parks and Recreation goes credit for transforming the idea into reality, and for maintaining it as a state historical monument. Berthed alongside the wharf are the 156-foot three-mast sail schooner *C. A. Thayer;* the 204-foot steam schooner *Wa-*

pama; the 59-foot *Alma,* last of the hay scows; and the *Eureka,* a 300-foot walking beam ferryboat. (Open daily 10–6 winter, spring and fall; 10–midnight summer; adults 50¢; children 25¢.)

Cut across the gaslighted Victorian Plaza—northern terminus for the Hyde Street cable car line—to Beach Street.

THE SAN FRANCISCO MARITIME MUSEUM, Beach at the foot of Polk, established in 1951, today ranks as one of the great maritime museums in the United States, thanks in large part to its remarkable staff and loyal sponsors. Open to the public without charge (daily, 10–5), it is a vast treasure chest of well-displayed nautical lore, ranging from colorful figureheads, anchors, ships' bells, and top-notch ship models to an exceptional photographic history of the San Francisco waterfront. Viewing the latter, the Bay suddenly comes to life as it was in gold-rush days.

If in the mood for a ride, try the double-decked Omnibus, veteran of New York's Fifth Avenue traffic, which tours the whole north waterfront area from the Maritime Museum to the *Balclutha.* (Fare: 25¢.)

GHIRARDELLI SQUARE, across from the Maritime Museum, is an outstanding example of what imaginative planning can do. Once an old chocolate factory, its red brick buildings dating from the late 1850s, it has been transformed, with no loss of original charm, into a gaily off-beat piece of San Francisco—a must for visitors and residents alike. Bounded by Beach, Larkin, North Point and Polk streets, it contains a number of quality restaurants and bars; a variety of shops whose offerings range from straw ponchos to marimekkos to piñatas; the *hungry i* restaurant-nightclub; a little theater; and numerous surprises. Responsible for the tasteful remodeling is the architectural firm of Wurster, Bernardi and Emmons; Lawrence Halprin was the landscape architect; William Roth had the original idea.

Most of the remainder of this tour (from Aquatic Park to the Mission Dolores) follows the route of the 49 Mile Scenic Drive. Laid out by the Downtown Association, this route is clearly marked with large blue-and-white sea-gull signs.

From Aquatic Park drive one block south to Bay Street and follow the signs west on Bay, driving through the residential Marina District, overlooking Yacht Harbor.

THE PALACE OF FINE ARTS, at the foot of Lyon Street, near Marina Boulevard, is the sole surviving edifice of the $50,000,000 Panama-Pacific International Exposition of 1915 and the work of famed architect-designer Bernard Maybeck. Constructed from plaster and lath, it wasn't built to last, but it did, though in crumbling disrepair. Except for maintenance of the lagoon that mirrors the building (and which is home for a variety of wild ducks, geese and swans), little was done in the way of preservation until years of local sentiment to "Save the Palace of Fine Arts" impelled a concerned philanthropist, Walter Johnson, to donate $2,000,000 for this purpose. With another $4,000,000 from the state and a local bond issue, it has been completely restored, and remains one of the most arresting structures in the Bay Area.

A word of warning. The scenery on most of the rest of this route is truly spectacular. Allow yourself enough time to stop and enjoy it periodically.

Follow the 49 Mile Scenic Drive signs.

PRESIDIO. (A detailed map of the Presidio is available without charge at the gatepost entrance at Lombard and Lyon streets. Except for certain clearly marked restricted areas the Presidio is open to the public around the clock.)

This wooded tract, covering 1698 acres in the northwest portion of San Francisco, the present headquarters of the Sixth Army, has had a long and eventful history.

On March 23, 1776, Lieutenant Colonel Juan Bautista de Anza, Lieutenant José Moraga, Friar Pedro Font, and a small party of soldiers left Monterey with instructions to select sites for a mission and a presidio in this area. After some exploration the present Presidio site was chosen on March 28, having all the requirements of a good military fortification: proximity to the bay, timber, fresh-water springs, good pasturage land, and defensibility. On the following day the site for Mission San Francisco de Asís (Mission Dolores) was chosen. Construction of the Presidio buildings and the high surrounding walls commenced on August 18. The ceremonial founding took place September 17, 1776.

From this date until 1820 the Presidio remained under the flag of Spain. But Spain did very little to maintain it, as is evident in the report of Alférez Hermengildo Sal, a storekeeper at the Presidio and later acting commandant, who wrote to his governor in 1792:

"All the structures are roofed with straw and tule, exposed to fire and at the mercy of the winds. All, except the commandant's house and two or three of the soldier's houses . . . are liable to fall at any minute, the church being in a particularly precarious position. None of the structures are those originally built; each year some of them have fallen and have been restored in the same faulty manner with the same perishable materials . . ."

A British officer, seeing it at about the same time, was even more explicit: it looked like a cattle enclosure.

Though Spain occasionally made some effort toward improving the fortifications—in fear of Russian and English expansion—the Presidio itself went from bad to worse. By 1812 storms and earthquakes had all but destroyed it. Nor did it fare better as a Mexican Presidio from 1821 to 1846. Various foreign visitors remarked how easily it could be taken. It was. On the night of July 1, 1846, Captain John C. Frémont, Kit Carson, and fourteen armed men sailed in a borrowed boat from Sausalito, scaled the crumbling walls of the long-abandoned fort (the Castillo de San Joaquín, later the site of Fort Point or Old Fort Scott, now beneath the Golden Gate Bridge approach) and spiked the rusty cannon. They were a bit premature. It was not until a week later that news reached Yerba Buena that American naval forces had occupied Monterey. On July 9, 1846, a few hours after the American flag was raised over Yerba Buena's plaza, a detachment of marines, led by Lieutenant J. S. Misroon, USN, hoisted the colors over both the Presidio and the fort. There was no opposition. They found ten useless cannon at the fort but none at the Presidio.

American occupation of the Presidio has been continuous from that day. But it does not necessarily follow that these were uneventful years.

Perhaps enough has been said of the first troops to occupy the Presidio, Stevenson's First New York Volunteer Regiment, many of whose members gained notoriety as the San Francisco "Hounds" (Chapter One).

Most of the early battles were not against foreign powers, but against local officials. The gold rush had barely ended before the city administration was attempting to take the Presidio out of government hands. This is a recurrent battle, continuing up to the present. Most San Franciscans appear to back continued government ownership, believing that in city hands the beautifully wooded area would be replaced by housing developments, a belief that has more than a little support in past actions.

The gold rush brought its own problems, chiefly desertion, which is not surprising considering that, while prices on everything else skyrocketed, a soldier's pay remained at an uninflationary eight dollars per month.

In July 1848 the Presidio commandant, Colonel Mason, called on the people of California to return deserters. As one writer commented: "He threatened to use the dragoons to enforce their return, an empty threat, since three-fourths of the dragoons had already deserted."

One night the whole Presidio guard, including the corporal in charge, deserted. An officer and escort were sent after them. The escort deserted and the officer returned with only one man, whom he had wounded.

Penalties for desertion grew increasingly severe. In 1857 a private from the 3rd Artillery was sentenced "to forfeit all pay and allowances . . . to be indelibly marked on the left hip with the letter D, one and a half inches long, and ten days thereafter to receive fifty lashes on his bare back well laid on with raw hide, have his head shaved, and drummed out of the service." Fortunately wiser counsel prevailed; a general, reviewing the sentence, remitted both the branding and flogging.

But these are side lights to the Presidio's main function, which, since 1846, has been the defense of the Golden Gate and a large part of the West Coast. The importance of this task was perhaps not fully appreciated by most San Franciscans until December 7, 1941, when the possibility of a Japanese invasion seemed imminent. Troops at the Presidio, however, figured prominently in the Civil War (1861–65), the Spanish-American War (1898), the Philippine Insurrection (1901–03), maintenance of law and order in San Francisco following the earthquake of 1906, the Mexican border troubles (1910–16), World Wars I and II, the Korean War, and the war in Vietnam.

The major historic site within the present Presidio is the Officers' Club, housed in the oldest adobe building in San Francisco, built in 1776, silent witness to Spanish, Mexican, and American rule.

Continue on the 49 Mile Scenic Drive through the residential Sea Cliff area to Lincoln Park (western terminus of the Lincoln Highway).

CALIFORNIA PALACE OF THE LEGION OF HONOR (open 10–5 daily). Presented to the city in 1924 by Mr. and Mrs. Adolph B. Spreckels as a memorial to the dead of World War I, and modeled after the Palais de la Légion d'Honneur in Paris, the building houses one of the major West Coast art museums, and occupies one of the most spectacular scenic locations in the Bay Area. Though other countries are well represented, the highlight of the permanent collections are the French paintings and sculpture. Several of the nineteen galleries are devoted to changing exhibits, with emphasis on contemporary art. Auguste Rodin, a friend of Mrs. Spreckels, is well represented by bronze and marble sculpture that includes the original bronze of *The Burghers of Calais, St. John the Baptist,* and, in the courtyard outside the building, one of the five original bronze casts of *The Thinker.*

*Due to landslides, portions of El Camino del Mar are
closed to traffic. Follow Thirty-fourth to Geary, then
west on Geary, which becomes Point Lobos, to the Cliff
House and Great Highway. Sea-gull signs mark the
route.*

CLIFF HOUSE and SEAL ROCKS. The first Cliff
House got off to a fine start, then had a bit of bad luck.
Erected in 1863, it was for many years a favorite recreation
spot for families, who would spend most of a day traveling
out and back over the dunes to "take the air." But fashions
change and other, more accessible resorts became the rage.
For a time the Cliff House fell into disrepute; its main customers were politicians and their mistresses of the moment.
In 1879, Adolph Sutro bought it, but was unable to reverse
its strange luck. In 1887 the schooner *Parallel* crashed on
the rocks below; its cargo was forty tons of dynamite. The
explosion blew off the north wing and weakened the building's foundations. Then on Christmas Day 1894, in a great,
impressive blaze, it burned to the ground.

The second Cliff House, built by Sutro the following
year, fared a little better, but not much. It attained popular respectability and survived the earthquake of 1906 but
burned to the ground a year later.

The present building was erected soon after the second
burned, and contains the famed Cliff House Restaurant, a
bar, and a large gift shop.

Seal Rocks, lying four hundred feet offshore below the
Cliff House, are the home of a noisy tribe of Steller sea
lions, which, though not seals, belong to the same family
group. Since 1887 they have been legal residents of the city
and can be seen and heard year round, though many leave
during June and the early part of July, when they swim

twenty-five miles south to Año Nuevo Island to breed. Following the earthquake of 1906 they fled to the Farallones, and several years lapsed before they ventured back.

The Costanoan Indians had a legend about them. Once, when their land was threatened with invasion by a hostile tribe, the Spirit of the Land appeared to the twin daughters of the Indian chief, giving them a magic iris. Each of its three petals would make a wish come true. As the enemy Indians sailed toward the gate the sisters tore off the first petal and wished for a dense fog. This accomplished, they wished with the second petal for a great storm, to wreck the boats on the rocks. This too was done, but the warriors swam on. With their third wish the sisters transformed them into animals. You can guess the rest.

SUTRO HEIGHTS, at Point Lobos and Forty-eighth avenues, is at the end of a short uphill walk. Overlooking the Cliff House and a vast expanse of beach and ocean, the Heights was once the home of Adolph Sutro, whose famed five-mile tunnel through the Sierras broke the monopoly of the Silver Kings. His home has been destroyed, but his park remains, its dignified but broken statues remnants of a grand age now passed.

From the Cliff House drive south on Great Highway.

OCEAN BEACH, to the west, is the most popular spot in San Francisco on warm days, though a vicious undertow makes swimming here dangerous. To the east is Playland at the Beach, the city's only Coney Island-type amusement park, offering a host of rides, concessions, and games of skill and chance.

FARALLON ISLANDS. On clear days it is possible to look westward from the Great Highway and see these islands. Even though located thirty-two miles off Point Lobos, since 1872 the Farallones have legally been a part of the City and County of San Francisco. Few of the city's residents have ever visited there, however. The islands are inhabited by millions of birds, hundreds of sea lions, and a lonely Coast Guard station.

Continue on the 49 Mile Scenic Drive past the Lake Merced-San Francisco State College area.

FLEISHHACKER ZOO (San Francisco Zoological Gardens), on Sloat Boulevard at Forty-ninth Avenue (open 10–5, no admission fee).

Begun with a few monkeys and lion cubs in 1929, not a very auspicious year for new beginnings, the zoo has nevertheless managed to expand into one of the finest in the country. Most of the animals, of which there are a great variety, are on display out of doors in realistic-looking natural habitats, with low moats separating them from the public. The zoo covers an area of about seventy acres; to see it all would take a good part of a day, though even a brief visit will prove enjoyable. Most visitors find the Australian koalas especially fascinating. Popular too are the cages at feeding times, which are arranged as follows: lions, tigers, leopards, jaguars and other "cats," 2–3 P.M. daily except Monday; great apes, 1–1:30 P.M. daily; elephants, 4 P.M. daily; seals (sea lions) are fed all day by the public.

Adjacent to the zoo is a large children's playground, with a large assortment of rides and recreational facilities.

FLEISHHACKER POOL is in the vicinity too, the largest outdoor swimming pool in the world: 1000 feet long, 150 feet wide, 3 to 14 feet in depth. It contains 6,500,000 gallons of warmed salt water (open 9–5 April through November 1; adults, 50¢, children 25¢).

*Continue on 49 Mile Scenic Drive through the Sunset resi-
dential district and Golden Gate Park.* (Golden Gate Park is
treated as a separate tour in Chapter 5; though the two approaches differ—this guide east to west, the 49 Mile Scenic
Drive southwest to east—you will have no trouble finding
the major sites if you watch for the park signs.)

*From Golden Gate Park continue on 49 Mile Scenic
Drive to the top of Twin Peaks.*

TWIN PEAKS. Long ago, in the foggy time when legends were born, these two mountains were one as man and
wife, so said the Costanoan Indians. But they quarreled so
loud and long and often that the Great Spirit, unable to
get any rest, created a huge storm and with a bolt of silver
lightning split them in two.

The Spanish, equally romantic and only a bit more realistic, called them Los Pechos de la Choca (The Breasts of
the Indian Maiden), after a tall and very beautiful girl, of
whom N. P. Vallejo, the son of Spanish General Mariano
Vallejo, later said: "Never have I seen a cultured maiden
half so fair as this untaught, uninstructed daughter of the
wilds."

The early settlers were not given to romanticism, and, re-
grettably, it is their name that has stuck: Twin Peaks.

The South Peak is the higher, with an elevation of 910
feet; the elevation of the North Peak is 903; neither is much
short of the elevation of Mount Davidson, which stands to
the south-west and, at 938 feet, is the highest hill in San
Francisco. Its massive cross rises an additional 103 feet.

These peaks were too steep and rocky for early settlers.
Even when Market Street was finally cut through the sand
dunes all the way from the bay to the base of the hills, few
ventured to build very high up on the slopes. There were a

few houses scattered over the hill in 1912, when a park and reservoir were dedicated on the summit (a public ball was held in the reservoir, then, after the last dance, the water was turned in). But it was not until the drilling of the two-and-a-half-mile tunnel under the peaks in 1917 and the subsequent paving of the winding Twin Peaks Boulevard that the hill became the favored residential area it is today.

The best thing about Twin Peaks cannot be described but must be seen: its spectacular view. If you have the time make a special effort to come here both by day and night, and you will know what is meant when it is said there is not one but many San Franciscos.

Continue on the 49 Mile Scenic Drive.

MISSION DOLORES, Sixteenth and Dolores streets (open 10–4 daily).

The Mission San Francisco de Asís, the sixth in the California mission chain of Father Junípero Serra, was established on June 29, 1776, just five days before the Declaration of Independence was adopted. It was formally dedicated on October 3 of the same year and formally opened five days later. During the latter ceremony the noise of the bells, muskets, and cannon so frightened the Indians that they ran away. Later they came back to make one unsuccessful attack on the mission buildings, but were quickly defeated, and their domestication and conversion began. Construction of the present building started in 1782. Under the supervision of the padres the Indians built the four-foot-thick adobe walls, hauled down from the hills the redwood timbers, to be lashed together with rawhide and raised for the ceiling beams, and set the tiles in the roof. The building has been standing ever since, unlike the more modern church next door, surviving the events of 1906 without damage.

The name Mission Dolores, which has replaced the mission's original name, came from a small lake that was once in the vicinity, called by the Spanish Laguna de Nuestra Señora de los Dolores, or Lagoon of Our Lady of Sorrows.

Much of the history of early San Francisco lies at rest in the graveyard adjoining the mission or within the crypts in the mission building. Among those buried here are Captain Louis Antonio Arguello, first governor of Alta California under the Mexican Government; Charles Cora, James P. Casey ("May God Forgive My Persecutors"), and James "Yankee" Sullivan, all victims of vigilante justice; Lieutenant José Joaquín Moraga, who led the small group that chose the sites of the mission and the Presidio; José Noe, last Mexican alcalde of Yerba Buena; William Leidesdorff, pioneer San Franciscan; and, in the unmarked graves, 5515 Indians, many of whom died not long after the founding of the mission, unable to adjust to civilization.

Between the mission and Yerba Buena was the old Mission Road, which Mission Street now follows. "On fine days, especially on Sundays," the *Annals* noted, "the roads to the Mission show a continual succession, passing to and fro, of all manner of equestrians and pedestrians, and elegant open carriages filled with ladies and holiday folk." South of Mission Street is the sprawling Mission District, "South o' the Slot," which one writer has described as "the blood and guts of San Francisco," a largely working-class neighborhood that ranges from the squalor of skid row to some of the oldest and many of the best-kept homes in the city. "The Mission has always been a favorite place of amusement to the citizens of San Francisco," said the *Annals*:

"Here, in the early days of the city, exhibitions of bull and bear fights frequently took place, which attracted great crowds; and here, also, were numerous duels fought, which drew nearly as many idlers to view them. At present there are two race-courses in the neighborhood, and a large number of drinking houses . . ."

Drinking houses of course remain, but most of the rest is gone, along with the restaurant whose sign advertised, "Pistols for two; coffee for one."

From Mission Dolores drive north on Dolores Street to Market Street, east on Market to Van Ness Avenue, north on Van Ness to McAllister Street, east on McAllister to Polk Street, and park.

SAN FRANCISCO CIVIC CENTER. Less than sixty seconds after the first shock of the 1906 earthquake rocked San Francisco, the impressively permanent-looking $7,000,-000 City Hall (located where the main branch of the San Francisco Public Library now stands) crumbled to the ground, with only its bare framework left standing.

This was a visual fact that San Franciscans were to long remember. And, in its own not so small way, the memory was to help change the face, the attitudes, and the government of the city. It was to be recalled during the graft investigations of 1906–07; it was to become a standard platform reminder of every reform candidate during the next decade; and it was this event, not the turn of the century, that came to symbolize the end of the usually indifferently observed government that too often during the nineteenth century pillaged San Francisco. Of course in time it was to be forgotten; not all of the twentieth-century administrations have been noted for their public concern. But for a few years it helped encourage residents to take the elections of their officials a little more seriously. And it was not unremembered when construction of the present Civic Center buildings—all uncommonly solid structures—began in 1913.

CIVIC CENTER PLAZA, Grove, Polk, McAllister, and Larkin streets, its pools, fountains, and cement walks covering a huge underground convention display headquarters, is bordered by four of the major buildings in the Civic Center compound.

THE CITY HALL, Van Ness Avenue, Polk, McAllister, and Grove streets, was completed December 28, 1915. Its gold-embellished dome rises 308 feet above the ground (sixteen feet, two and five-eighths inches above the National Capitol in Washington, D.C., as Mayor "Sunny Jim" Rolph used to boast). The work of Arthur Brown, Jr., and John Bakewell, Jr., it is generally acknowledged to be one of the most impressive and striking examples of classic architecture in America. Architect John Marshall Woodbridge, in his book *Buildings of the Bay Area*, remarks that it "succeeds so far beyond most 20th century efforts at Renaissance grandeur that it invites comparison with its models."

Housed here are the major administrative offices of the city and county of San Francisco.

THE CIVIC AUDITORIUM, on Grove Street between Polk and Larkin streets, was also designed by Arthur Brown, Jr. Seating ten thousand in the auditorium itself, 2400 additional in two adjacent halls, it has been the scene of major dramatic, political, and commercial productions and gatherings since its erection in 1915.

THE STATE BUILDING, at McAllister, Polk, and Larkin streets, built in 1926, houses the local offices of the governor, attorney general, and other divisions of the state government.

THE SAN FRANCISCO PUBLIC LIBRARY'S main branch, located at Larkin, Fulton, McAllister, and Hyde streets (open weekdays 9–9; Saturdays 9–6; closed Sundays) was designed by George W. Kelham, and opened in

1917. The library collection includes over 1,200,000 books and manuscripts. Interesting Californiana and rare books may be found in the Special Collections room on the third floor. Other features include special exhibits, periodic authors' lectures, and an annual book sale of duplicate items, sponsored by the Friends of the Library. There are twenty-seven branches throughout the city.

THE WAR MEMORIAL OPERA HOUSE and VETERANS' AUDITORIUM BUILDING are located across Van Ness Avenue from City Hall, at the corner of Van Ness and Grove, and were erected in 1931–32, Arthur Brown, Jr., architect. The Opera House was the scene of one of the most important occasions of our time, the birth of the United Nations on April 25, 1945.

The only municipally owned opera house in America, it has made San Francisco one of the nation's most opera-conscious cities. The opera season begins, with great flourish, in mid-September and runs for approximately six weeks. The San Francisco Symphony season follows for eighteen weeks, and there is also a summer "pops" series.

THE SAN FRANCISCO MUSEUM OF ART (open Tuesday to Friday 10–10; Saturday 10–5; Sundays and holidays 1–5) is located on the top floor of the Veterans' Auditorium Building (entrance on McAllister Street). Unlike the city's two other major art museums, the de Young and the Legion of Honor, emphasis is on contemporary work—world-wide in scope. The galleries often include in addition to Picasso, Klee, Soulages, and Pollock, a good sampling of work by living artists from the surrounding Bay Area.

For *Additional Exploration:*

SAN FRANCISCO BAY. By John Haskell Kemble. A pictorial
   maritime history.
SAN FRANCISCO: PORT OF GOLD. By William Martin Camp.
   An informal history of the San Francisco waterfront.

EXTRA ADDED ATTRACTIONS

Although San Francisco is a marvelously compact city,
its attractions are so diverse and widespread that many do
not fit into the conventional tour format. Among them, the
following deserve mention:

THE CABLE CAR MUSEUM is located in the car barn
at Washington and Mason streets. If you're curious to know
how this unusual mode of transportation operates, here's
the place to find out. Open 8 A.M.–midnight (no admission).

DRIVING: See the map in Chapter Four.

CABLE CAR: Take either the Powell-Mason or the Powell-
Hyde car. On the northbound route, get off at Jackson and
Mason and walk one block south, or, on the return route
from Fisherman's Wharf, get off at Washington and Mason.

CANDLESTICK PARK.   About the only nice thing that
can be said about Candlestick Park, home of the San Fran-

cisco Giants, is that the stadium is handsomely designed. Otherwise it's windy, there's often a distinct odor from nearby garbage dumps, and it's inconveniently located. The most amazing thing about Candlestick (or "Candlestink," as many local residents call it) is that the city has never conducted an investigation to determine exactly why this location was chosen and who profited by it. It certainly wasn't the baseball fans. But then, when the Giants are winning, which they do on occasion, the fans don't appear to mind.

DRIVING: Bayshore Freeway or Third Street to Paul Avenue.

BUS: Schedules and routes are subject to change. Call Municipal Railway, 558-4111, for information.

HAIGHT-ASHBURY.   San Francisco's North Beach gave birth to the "beats," the Haight-Ashbury to the "hippies." Aside from the psychedelically orientated shops, there is little to see here except the people. But many visitors find them more than sufficient. Most colorful part of the district —i.e., the most densely populated—is Haight Street between Stanyon and Masonic.

DRIVING: From Union Square, Geary to Van Ness to Market to Haight and north on Haight.

BUS: #7 Haight.

JAPANESE CULTURAL AND TRADE CENTER. For the more than 12,000 Japanese-Americans in San Francisco, Nihonmachi or Japantown serves much the same function as does Chinatown for the American Chinese. Focal point of this area is the new Japanese Cultural and Trade Center, three blocks bounded by Post, Geary, Laguna and Fillmore streets, whose attractions include an elegantly landscaped Peace Plaza, a theater-restaurant for Kabuki and other performing arts, a Bridge of Shops over Webster Street, and the luxurious Miyako Hotel. You can find just about any Japanese item you might want, either here or in Nihonmachi, to the north. One store sells only bonzai trees; another, a pet and fish shop, specializes in carp (some priced at $1200 each). In addition, there are a great number of intriguing Japanese restaurants, grocery stores, art, craft and jewelry shops. For information on the dates of traditional celebrations, such as Cherry Blossom Festival, call the San Francisco Convention and Visitors Bureau, 626-5500.

DRIVING: Geary Boulevard to Laguna or Webster.

BUS: #38 Geary to Laguna or Webster.

KEZAR STADIUM. Golden Gate Park. Home of the "49ers," San Francisco's professional football team.

DRIVING: Gough to Fell to Stanyon to Kezar.

BUS: #71 Haight-Noriega or #72 Haight-Sunset.

CURRENT ACTIVITIES. As a helpful service to both tourists and residents, the San Francisco Convention and Visitors Bureau tapes a daily resumé of interesting activities in the city. Call 391-2000 for the recorded message.

PART II

THE BAY AREA—ONE-DAY TOURS

*"To this gate I gave the name of 'Chrysopylae'
or Golden Gate; for the same reason that the
harbor of Byzantium was called 'Chrysoceras', or
Golden Horn."*
JOHN CHARLES FRÉMONT, *Memoirs of My Life*

The following ten tours cover the major points of interest in the San Francisco Bay Area. They are so arranged that each can be taken in a single day, with an extra margin of time thrown in for personal exploration. A number of excellent trips do not fall into the one-day classification; among these would be tours of the Monterey-Carmel-Big Sur-San Simeon area; Yosemite; the gold country of Northern California and Nevada; and the Reno-Lake Tahoe area. If you have additional time these are "musts," but leisurely ones, to be spread over at least two or more days.

For all tours take along a current highway map. Tour directions are explicit; however, new freeway and highway construction may necessitate slight changes in the routes.

1. Bridge Tour, Including Belvedere, Tiburon, and Sausalito.

A circle tour of the three main bridges in the Bay Area: the San Francisco-Oakland Bay Bridge; the Richmond-San Rafael Bridge; and the Golden Gate Bridge.

For a comprehensive and sweeping view of the Bay Area this route is unequaled. Although side trips to nearby points of interest will increase the mileage in varying degrees, the loop covers approximately fifty miles. It is most interesting if covered in leisurely fashion, with a good part of one day given over to it.

From San Francisco, cross the SAN FRANCISCO-OAKLAND BAY BRIDGE (toll 25¢). Opened November 12, 1936, three and a half years after work began, this is the longest bridge in the world, four and one quarter miles long, with four miles of approaches. The towers rise 519 feet above the water; total cost was $77,200,000. It is actually two kinds of bridges in one: the section stretching from San Francisco to Yerba Buena Island is a suspension span; the balance of the bridge, from the island to Oakland, is a cantilever span.

Continue north along the East Bay Freeway (Route 17) to Richmond and cross the RICHMOND-SAN RAFAEL BRIDGE (toll 75¢). This is the world's second-longest over-water bridge, 4.04 miles. Opened in 1956, it connects the Marin and Contra Costa shores, replacing the more picturesque and leisurely ferries.

From the bridge follow Highway 101, passing the entrance to San Quentin State Prison.

For a pleasant break in driving, cut off from the main route and drive or stroll through Tiburon, Belvedere, and Sausalito in turn—lunching, perusing the shops and galleries, watching the small boats in the bay, taking in the varied residential architecture, which, in Sausalito has a Mediterranean aspect, the houses clinging to the sides of the hills beyond the waterfront. All three communities have excellent facilities for dining or early cocktails.

Vista Point, on the northern approach to the Golden Gate Bridge, commands a marvelous view of San Francisco and the bay. You can walk from the spacious parking area onto the bridge itself and have a good eye-level view of the 36½-inch suspension cables. In addition to the spectacular views to the east and south, to the west you can see the Needles, a famous formation of offshore rocks; the Lime Point Lighthouse; Horseshoe Bay and the buildings of Fort Baker.

GOLDEN GATE BRIDGE (toll 25¢). Though most people considered this bridge a technical impossibility, it was opened nevertheless in May 1937, with more than a little of the credit due its engineer, Joseph B. Strauss, who knew it could be done. Until 1964 and the completion of the

Verrazano-Narrows Bridge, it was the longest single-span suspension bridge in the world; it is now second, but only by sixty feet. The towers rise 751 feet above the water; the bridge's total length is 1.7 miles; the cost was $35,000,000. The total of *known* suicides from the bridge is well over 300; probably as many more have jumped undetected.

2. *Muir Woods, Mount Tamalpais, Stinson Beach, Point Reyes.*

After crossing the Golden Gate Bridge follow U.S. 101 to signs indicating cutoff west to State 1. Follow markers to MUIR WOODS NATIONAL MONUMENT (approximately seventeen miles north of San Francisco).

This 485-acre area was donated to the United States by Congressman and Mrs. William Kent in honor of the famous naturalist John Muir. It lies on the south slopes of Mount Tamalpais at an elevation of 2000 feet. It alone of the National Parks preserves a virgin stand of redwoods, including some of the oldest and tallest trees on earth, several 246 feet high, 17 feet in diameter, 2000 years old. The woods are noted for abnormal growths such as burls and natural grafts plus a great variety of ferns. There are numerous shaded trails through the woods and along the banks of Redwood Creek. The Main Nature Trail, three quarters of a mile, can be hiked in twenty minutes; the others, well worth the effort, will require extra time. All the trails have signs identifying the various plants and trees.

Open sunrise to sunset, year round. There are picnic areas and a lunchroom, but no campgrounds. Dogs welcome if on a leash. Guides available.

From here the scenic Panoramic Highway (Route 1) leads to MOUNT TAMALPAIS AND MOUNT TAMALPAIS STATE PARK.

The mountain's two peaks attain heights of 2604 and 2686 feet respectively, and offer marvelous views of the bay, the eastern towns of Marin, the cities of the East Bay, and the city itself.

There are many hiking trails, all plainly marked; most of the mountain area (except where fenced off) is open to the public. There is a restaurant on Ridgecrest Boulevard. And, in addition to picnic areas, there are two campgrounds— Bootjack and Pan Toll—on the western slope. Campers should have night cover, tents or similar, because the fog *drips*.

Panoramic Highway goes on to STINSON BEACH, a favorite swimming and fishing spot.

Farther north, about thirty miles, are DRAKE'S BAY AND BEACH. This is the bay most historians feel Sir Francis Drake discovered when looking for San Francisco Bay. A granite cross is erected behind the beach in his honor. There are wonderful sand dunes here, also a driftwood amphitheater. The rock pools provide interesting studies of marine life.

Yet a little farther is POINT REYES NATIONAL SEASHORE. This is an especially scenic area—with grasslands, steep sea cliffs, abundant wild-flower growth, miles of white beach (unsafe for swimming, however), and lots of driftwood for the gathering. The lighthouse on the tip of the peninsula was built in 1870, and if you're willing to walk down the 400 stone steps—and back up—is open to visitors 2–4 P.M. Saturdays, Sundays, and holidays.

This tour can be ended at any point along the way, depending upon how much time you wish to spend at each place.

3. *Sacramento, Sutter's Fort, State Capitol.*

The most direct route is across the San Francisco-Oakland Bay Bridge and via Interstate 80, approximately eighty-five miles. For a more leisurely drive take State Highway 160 and follow the Sacramento River, crossing the Sacramento-San Joaquin Delta country—rich farmland reclaimed from swamps, interlacing two thousand miles of waterways with a labyrinth of trimly farmed islands. One direction might be followed en route, another returning.

SACRAMENTO (Camellia Capital of the World, and, incidentally, state capital of California) has a population of about 250,000. Major points of interest include:

STATE CAPITOL AND CAPITOL PARK. Capitol Avenue between Ninth and Fifteenth streets. Capitol Park covers forty acres, beautifully landscaped, encircling the Capitol and Annex. The four-story Capitol Building was completed in 1874; the large and lofty dome stretches 237 feet above street level and is topped with a thirty-inch ball plated with gold leaf. Inside the building are the legislative chambers, as well as statuary, murals, and other exhibits. Offices of the governor and the legislators are in the East Wing Annex. The Capitol Building is open to the public daily from 7–9. There are over a thousand varieties of shrubs and trees from all parts of the world on the Capitol grounds, including a collection of trees from Civil War battlegrounds.

SUTTER'S FORT. On L Street between Twenty-seventh and Twenty-eighth streets. This is a careful restoration (accomplished in the early 1900's) of the adobe house built in 1839 by the Swiss immigrant pioneer, John A. Sutter. Operated as a state park and museum, it is open daily, 10–5, without charge. Exhibits include Indian burial mounds, pottery, dugout canoes, spurs of pony-express riders, gold from Sutter's Mill at Coloma, and stagecoaches and prairie schooners that transported the first gold from the Mother Lode.

CROCKER ART GALLERY, at 216 O Street, houses a basic collection of treasures brought from Europe by a prominent lawyer in 1870. The collection is augmented by changing exhibits of sculpture, painting, prints, bronzes, tapestries, and furniture. Open daily except Monday.

GOVERNOR'S MANSION, on the corner of Sixteenth and H streets. No longer used by the state's chief executive, this handsome Victorian structure has been designated an historical landmark. Open to the public 10–5 daily (admission $1).

PONY EXPRESS BUILDING, at Second and J streets. Constructed in 1853 as a post office, this later became a pony-express terminus. The adjacent area, once the Embarcadero, is being restored as OLD SACRAMENTO, and when completed will resemble the city as it was during the years 1849 to 1870.

SOUTHERN PACIFIC STATION AND HUNTINGTON LOCOMOTIVE, at Fifth and I streets. The building contains a series of murals concerning the first transcontinental railroad. The historic Huntington Locomotive, on display in front, dates from 1863. It saw service on the Central Pacific after being shipped via schooner up the Sacramento River.

Interstate 80 (used en route or on return) passes near VALLEJO, onetime state capital (circa 1850), although the original building is no longer standing. Approximately six miles southeast—a departure from the main route—is BENICIA, state capital for one year, 1853–54. The old capitol building still stands and is now the city hall. On display here is a collection of pioneer items—a Wells Fargo safe with a secret keyhole, old lithographs, old music boxes, etc. Also in Benicia, at the lower end of First Street, is a marker indicating the site of Jorgenson's Saloon, a hangout of Jack London during his days as an officer of the fish patrol, 1892–93. London's novel *John Barleycorn* relates to his Benicia period.

4. Mount Diablo, Piedmont.

Start from Oakland; Mount Diablo is thirty-six miles east. Go north on Broadway, which becomes State Route 24, to

Walnut Creek. After that there are good roads, clearly marked, all the way.

This route goes close by the CLAREMONT HOTEL, noted for its beautifully landscaped areas and marvelous view, as well as its dining and cocktail facilities. The route also goes by the PIEDMONT residential area; some might wish to take time to drive through this opulent district.

Mount Diablo is the highest point in the Bay Area, its summit 3849 feet above sea level. On a day free of smog and fog, you can scan eighty thousand square miles—land and sea, including Mount Lassen, Mount Shasta and Yosemite Valley. Since 1851 Mount Diablo has been a geography survey control point for California.

There are many interesting side roads, hiking and riding trails on the mountain, as well as plenty of camping and picnicking sites. There is also a geological museum; the many unusual rock formations in the area are the result of volcanic upthrust. Fossilized shells are easily found.

This tour can be made in less than a full day; however, allow time for winding mountain roads.

5. Berkeley, University of California, Oakland, Jack London Square.

Go over the San Francisco-Oakland Bay Bridge and take the East Shore Freeway to Berkeley's University Avenue; follow the latter to Shattuck Avenue, right on Shattuck to Bancroft Way, left on Bancroft Way to Telegraph Avenue.

SPROUL HALL PLAZA is the most used entrance to the UNIVERSITY OF CALIFORNIA's Berkeley campus. It was here that most of the headline-making activities of the Free Speech Movement took place in 1964–65, and it remains, after many skirmishes, the traditional open discussion area for students.

SATHER GATE once marked the entrance to the university

proper, but now the campus sprawls out over more than nine hundred acres. Maps, prominently displayed, indicate the locations of the major campus landmarks.

CAMPANILE TOWER. The elevator takes you up 307 feet for a spectacular view of the campus, the city across the water, and the whole East Bay area. Open 10–5, Wednesday through Sunday.

GREEK THEATRE. The gift of William Randolph Hearst, this is a large outdoor amphitheater of classic design, with a 133-foot stage and a seating capacity of 6200. Leading artists and actors perform here.

BOTANICAL GARDEN. Above the main stadium is Strawberry Canyon. A thirty-five-acre tract, with unusual plantings, many rare rhododendrons and cacti, among other things. Numerous foot trails and footbridges in the area.

LIBRARY. With more than 2,500,000 volumes, this is the largest library in the West. THE BANCROFT LIBRARY, in the same building, has an unrivaled collection of books and manuscripts relating to Californiana and Western Americana. On display is the brass plate Sir Francis Drake left when he landed in California in 1579.

MUSEUM OF PALEONTOLOGY (Hearst Memorial Building) and GEOLOGY MUSEUM (Bacon Hall). Largest paleontological collection on the Pacific coast. There is a fine display of rocks and minerals, plus diagrams depicting life in the various geological eras.

The entire campus is open to walking and picnicking; the only "Keep off the Grass" signs are on newly seeded areas.

To OAKLAND, follow Telegraph Avenue to Grand Avenue, follow Grand to LAKE MERRITT.

This is the largest natural body of salt water in the world completely contained within one city, 160 acres. More important, it provides excellent facilities for boating (canoeing, regattas, speedboat races), is a national duck refuge (feedings during the afternoon), and is surrounded by beautiful parks and drives.

The Oakland Municipal Center is at the south end. At the north end is a Children's Playground; adults admitted when accompanied by a child. The animated settings of popular nursery rhymes include a fine selection of Mother Goose diversions. Rides include the Oakland Acorn Express, a miniature train that travels over a half-mile route, and *Lil Belle*, a miniature replica of a Mississippi River steamboat, with rotating paddle wheels, old-time whistle, *et al*.

From Lake Merritt, follow Grand Avenue northwest to Broadway, then left, southwest, on Broadway to Oakland Estuary and

JACK LONDON SQUARE. This waterfront and restaurant area has a colorful atmosphere; there is usually an old sailing vessel berthed alongside the dock. There are a number of good eating places, several of them named for London characters or novels. But the chief attraction is the FIRST AND LAST CHANCE SALOON. This dilapidated little saloon, more than seventy years old, was built from the timbers of old whaling vessels, and was originally used as a bunkhouse for oyster-bed workmen. In the 1890's it became a hangout for seafarers. The proprietor, Johnny Heinold, befriended young Jack London. The boy wrote and studied here, and received financial aid from Mr. Heinold. The same bar and furnishings are in use today, including the old gaming table that was London's first desk. Also prominent are a worn old dictionary, also London's first, and various London letters and photographs displayed on the wall. Robert Louis Stevenson, Joaquin Miller, and Rex Beach "watered" here too. The atmosphere is far from historical, however; be prepared for some real surprises.

Time permitting, another "literary" trip is available, JOAQUIN MILLER PARK, 33 Joaquin Miller Road at Mountain Boulevard.

The poet's unusual self-designed retreat, the "Hights," has been preserved by the city as a shrine, in a sixty-seven-acre highland area.

Miller, California's "Poet of the Sierras," lived a colorful, eccentric life, and his estate reflects this.

The area is gorgeously wooded, with more than seventy-five thousand trees—pine and cypress, eucalyptus and acacia—all planted by Miller himself. The Abbey (Miller's home) was built in 1866 and is composed of three one-room structures, each roofed with a shingled peak, interconnected as a single unit.

Outside is the stone funeral pyre where Miller wanted to be cremated. He wasn't. Nearby are monuments he erected out of native rock: "Tower to Browning," "Pyramid to Moses," and "The Frémont Monument." It was from a point in this park that Frémont first saw and named the Golden Gate. In the center of the park there are cypress trees planted in the shape of a cross. There is also a wooded amphitheater where summer civic concerts are given.

6. *Russian River Country, Fort Ross.*

Leave San Francisco over the Golden Gate Bridge and drive north through Marin on U.S. 101 as far as Cotati. From Cotati turn left (west) to Sebastopol and onto State Route 12 which follows the Russian River. The road is good and is tree-lined all the way.

Summer cottages cluster along the riverbank and the highway in great numbers, particularly around the numerous resort areas: Forestville, Rio Nido, Guerneville, Monte Rio, and Jenner. Each of these places affords opportunities for eating, swimming, canoeing, and fishing (smallmouthed bass in summer; steelhead and salmon in winter; striped bass in the sea nearby). For those who have missed other redwood tracts, the Armstrong Redwoods State Park is two miles north of Guerneville and contains four hundred acres of redwoods.

Close by Rio Nido (largely a teen-age resort) is the Korbel Winery, open daily for tour.

Upon reaching Jenner, drive north on State Route 1, 11½ miles to Fort Ross. THE FORT ROSS HISTORICAL MONUMENT (open 9–5 daily) is a restoration of the original buildings of this tiny village, which during the first half of the nineteenth century was an outpost of the Russian Empire. Sutter purchased the fort from the Russians in 1841, after it had served for twenty-nine years as a thriving seal and otter trade center, as well as figuring prominently in international bargaining.

The original fort was destroyed by the 1906 earthquake. The restored buildings cover three acres on both sides of the highway and include: stockade, chapel, blockhouses, and Commander's House, plus a museum. There are still visible traces of the wagon road laid out by the Russians for traffic between Fort Ross and the settlement at Bodega, a few miles down the coast.

BODEGA can be reached by traveling south on the Coastal Highway, State Route 1. It resembles an East Coast farm or fishing resort. The site of the Russian settlement is marked on a hilltop north of the main village by a flagpole designating "Site of Kuskof Settlement." But no buildings remain. Surrounding hills were potato fields then, as now. From Bodega, follow the main road east to Sebastopol and return to San Francisco via 12 and 101. Or, if you have extra time, take the Coastal Highway.

7. *Skyline Drive, Saratoga, Los Gatos, Santa Cruz, and Coast Highway.*

State Highway No. 5, better known as Skyline Boulevard, follows the mountain ridges of the Peninsula (three main ridges: Montara, Cahill, Montebello). It is a route of redwoods and lush greenery, permitting vast views of the ocean on one side and San Francisco Bay on the other, beautiful driving all the way.

This route—south of Hillsborough—passes Crystal Springs Lake, picturesque source of San Francisco's water supply. In this area were some of the vineyards of Colonel Harazthy, the Hungarian nobleman whose wine grapes were growing here by 1852.

The famous WOODSIDE STORE lies on King's Mountain Road, which intersects the boulevard about twenty-five miles south of San Francisco, and can be visited by a five-mile temporary departure from the main route. It dates from 1854 and was a trading center for the sawmills roundabout. Several hundred lumberjacks came here for their mail, liquor, and other necessities. The joists and porch roof posts are hand-hewn. The building is now a museum and displays relics of Peninsula pioneer living.

THE METHUSALEH REDWOOD—a lone giant tree, fifty-five feet in circumference—stands along the main route, near the summit of Sierra Morena, slightly south of Woodside. Its scarred trunk and storm-shattered top bear testimony to the fires and gales that have ravaged this area.

Continue to Saratoga Gap. At this juncture State Route 9 crosses Skyline east and west, and here you may elect two routes to Santa Cruz:

1. The southwest route passes Big Basin Redwoods State Park (great stands of redwoods, picnic sites, *et al*). A little farther along this redwood-bordered route you pass by Brookdale. The inn here, its famed dining room containing a fern-bordered brook and waterfall, is a good place for an atmospheric lunch. Then on to Santa Cruz.

2. The southeast route leads to Saratoga and Los Gatos and the outer fringes of the Santa Clara Valley. This is wine country, and while in these parts you may visit one or all of three wineries that are open to visitors, have noteworthy tasting rooms, and offer their products for sale. They are: Paul Masson, three miles northwest of Saratoga; Al-

madén, and Novitiate, both near Los Gatos and easily reached by well-designated roads. If taking this route, after reaching Los Gatos, go south on Route 17 to Santa Cruz.

SANTA CRUZ is a well-known resort and fishing center. It is also a center for fruit and vegetable processing. There is waterfront fishing off the pier, surfing, swimming, deep-sea fishing in the ocean, and sun-bathing along the wide beach. In addition, there is a casino and playland along the boardwalk.

Municipal Pier extends a half mile into Monterey Bay and permits auto traffic. Along the sides are gift shops, restaurants, and boating concessions.

MISSION SANTA CRUZ is a half-size reproduction of the original. The earlier mission was destroyed by earthquake more than a century ago.

Suggested return: via State Highway No. 1, the Coastal Highway. Be sure to have a full tank of gas and allow plenty of time. The coastal scenery is beautiful and unadulterated —ocean, cliffs and beaches, dunes and bluffs, with, at present, few developed areas. This route goes by Half Moon Bay, an old rum-running port, now the heart of the artichoke country.

8. *Peninsula Tour, Including San Jose, Palo Alto, Stanford University, Santa Clara Mission.*

Drive south via U.S. 101, known as "King's Highway," or El Camino Real (this was the eighteenth-century trail that linked together the California chain of missions and pueblos). It is a lovely meander through the heart of most of the Peninsula towns, a good part of it tree-lined.

The towns follow one another in rapid sequence. Millbrae, Burlingame (Hillsborough to the south and west of Burlingame), San Mateo, Redwood City, Atherton, Menlo Park—there is some industrial activity in nearly all of these communities nowadays, with the move in recent years of plants and firms to suburbia, but they are still primarily residential. A succession of well-kept middle-class homes, stores, and village institutions comprises the view.

Near San Francisquito Creek, the boundary of Menlo Park and Palo Alto (to the west of 101) stands EL PALO ALTO (Tall Tree), a solitary redwood marking the site of the Gaspar de Portolá expedition in 1769, and a landmark for travelers since that day.

PALO ALTO is divided from Stanford University by the highway, but the university is nevertheless the hub of the town's life. The town proper is predominantly Spanish-type architecture, with red tile roofs, airy patios, palm trees, iron grillwork. The Community Center is the same, except on a grand scale, with brick-paved court and tasteful landscaping.

STANFORD UNIVERSITY is on the west side of the highway. Enter via Palm Drive (entrance and main drive)—all buildings mentioned are easily reached by following markers along the way. The grounds as a whole are spacious, well tended, and worthy of over-all scrutiny.

High points:

STANFORD UNIVERSITY MUSEUM (open Mon.–Fri. 10–5; Sat., Sun. 1–5). Egyptian, classical and oriental art; most noted: the Nü-wa-Chai collection of Chinese paintings, the Ikeda collection of Japanese decorative art, the Leventritt collection of Far Eastern and European art; plus contemporary European and American art, prints and drawings.

STANFORD ART GALLERY (open Tues.–Sat. 10–5; Sunday 1–5; closed Monday). Changing exhibitions monthly.

STANFORD MEMORIAL CHURCH. Presented by Mrs. Stanford as a memorial to her husband. Mostly destroyed in the 1906 quake, it was rebuilt without the original central tower. The architecture is Romanesque, and the building is famous for the Italian mosaics inside and on the façade. The Sermon on the Mount is depicted here.

HOOVER LIBRARY AND TOWER. The 280-foot tower, which

gives a fine view of the area, surmounts the library, housing ex-President Herbert Hoover's collection of manuscripts and other printed matter dealing with World War I and the postwar period. The collection has been greatly expanded in recent years.

Leaving Palo Alto, you enter into the Santa Clara Valley, one of the great orchard regions of the world, particularly noted for prunes, pears, apricots, and peaches. This route goes through Mountain View and Sunnyvale, cannery and fruit processing centers. The towns in this area are more industrialized than those farther north.

As you near Santa Clara, you will pass the "Site of the Battle of Santa Clara," better known as "The Battle of the Mustard Stalks." A plaque commemorates the battle fought on a field of mustard stalks in January 1847, between the forces of Francisco Sánchez and a small force of American plunderers.

In the town, the MISSION SANTA CLARA is now the University of Santa Clara chapel. This is the fourth reproduction; prior buildings were destroyed by fire, earthquake, and flood. Some articles from the earlier buildings have been saved and incorporated into the concrete structure. Among them: holy-water fonts, wooden statuary, and reredos over the high altar. King Alfonso XIII, the last Spanish monarch, presented replacements for the three eighteenth-century bells, which were destroyed by fire. The large redwood cross in front of the chapel is the same one erected by Spanish soldiers and Indians in 1777 on the site of the first mission. It has been moved with each change of the mission's location.

Immediately after Santa Clara is SAN JOSE, one of the first cities in the state to be incorporated and also the first state capital (1849–51). Today it is one of the fastest-growing cities in California and an important missile and electronics development area.

Coming in on 101, which becomes Clay Street, then

Grant, turn right on Naglee Avenue, where are located the following:

MUNICIPAL ROSE GARDEN, on Naglee and Dana. Five and a half acres of roses—more than five thousand plants, arranged in a formal garden. Contains every variety known to man, including many seldom seen.

EGYPTIAN TEMPLE AND ORIENTAL MUSEUM OF ROSICRU-CIANS, Naglee between Park and Chapman. Headquarters for the world-wide philosophical brotherhood. The museum has a sizable collection of Egyptian and oriental antiquities, including a complete Egyptian temple, an Assyrian gateway, tapestries, scarabs, mummies, ancient writing tablets and scrolls. Open daily. Free.

From here drive to City Hall Plaza, located in the center of the city, and "Site of the First State Capitol." The present building, three-story red brick with interesting cast-iron work, dates from 1889.

In close proximity, by San Jose State College, is the Edwin Markham Home, 432 S. Eighth Street. An old-fashioned home with clapboard facing, it is preserved in memory of the poet, author of *The Man with the Hoe*. In the 1870's he lived here, and his mother continued to do so long after.

From here go north to Santa Clara Street, turning right (east) and following the street to ALUM ROCK PARK. This municipal park of nearly seven hundred acres is often called "Little Yosemite" because of its many natural formations. It was officially named for the two-hundred-foot cliff—with a surface coating of alum dust—that dominates the lower part of the canyon. Throughout the park, housed in rock grottoes, are twenty-two mineral springs. In pre-Spanish days the Indians used these springs for ritual purposes. Native rock bridges, canyon trails, a deer paddock, and a songbird aviary also enhance the natural beauty of the area.

For people who have started early and made good time, and feel up to seeing more, three interesting side trips are mentioned here:

1. Four miles west of San Jose, on the Los Gatos Highway, is the WINCHESTER MYSTERY HOUSE, 439 Winchester Road (open 9–4 daily; adults $1.50, children 30¢). This fantastic structure covers six acres and contains 160 rooms. It was originally a seventeen-room house, partially constructed when the widow of the millionaire firearms manufacturer purchased it in the 1880's. As it neared completion Mrs. Winchester became obsessed with the belief that, were construction to stop, she would die. And so building went on until her death in 1922, over $5,000,000 later. It is a mystery writer's dream: stairways (usually with thirteen steps) leading to blank walls, blind chimneys, trap doors, secret passageways, rooms within rooms in Chinese-puzzle-box fashion. Mrs. Winchester's private chamber was done entirely in white satin, even the floors.

2. LICK OBSERVATORY, located on the summit of Mount Hamilton (4209 feet). This is twenty miles southeast of San Jose, following the same road that leads to Alum Rock Park, but not taking the park cutoff. The observatory is a property of the University of California, and funds for its construction were bequeathed by James Lick, an erstwhile Pennsylvania piano maker, later a San Francisco real estate giant, who is buried in a crypt under the giant telescope. The observatory has been in operation since 1888. Here many important astronomical discoveries have been made, including more than thirty-three comets, additional satellites of Jupiter, and several hundred nebulae. The initial success in photographing the Milky Way was accomplished here. This observatory has several large telescopes; the largest, a 120-inch reflector, is exceeded in size only by Mount Palomar's 200-inch telescope. Open 1–5 daily, except for national and university holidays. Night visits are permitted on Friday, 7–9, but tickets must be secured in advance by writing to Lick Observatory, Mount Hamilton, California.

3. MISSION SAN JOSÉ DE GUADALUPE, fifteen miles northeast of San Jose on State Route 17. Dating from 1797, this was the fourteenth of California's twenty-one missions. Its

early history was turbulent. The Indians fought when their land was pre-empted and again rebelled under the hard work to which they were assigned. Despite these trials it became one of the leading missions, with one of its prefects, Padre Duran, widely known as a specialist in the making of wines and brandies and in the art of good fellowship. The buildings have gone through the usual ravages of earthquakes and fires; once the building was saved from flames by the use of barrels of wine from the old mission cellar. Today one large common adobe room, with thick, cracked, weather-beaten, cobweb-covered walls, is all that remains of the original extensive group of buildings. It houses a few relics relating to the mission's history—vestments worn by the founders, a baptismal font, and mission bells cast in 1815 and 1826, among other items. Now under custody of the Sisters of St. Dominic, it is open daily 9–5 (Admission 25¢).

Quickest return to San Francisco is via U.S. 101 Alternate or By-Pass, the Bayshore Freeway, offering a good view of the eastern side of the Peninsula.

9. *Santa Rosa, Petaluma, Glen Ellen, Sonoma Mission, Vallejo Home.*

Cross the Golden Gate Bridge and drive north on U.S. 101 approximately twenty miles to Petaluma. The main highway by-passes the town, but the Lakeville Road turnoff (east) just north of Petaluma Creek Bridge (where the sign points to Sonoma and Napa) takes you to the CASA GRANDE OF GENERAL MARIANO VALLEJO. Thought to be the largest Spanish ranch house ever to stand in Northern California, this was the headquarters of Vallejo's 75,000-acre Rancho Petaluma, now designated a state historical monument. Built in 1833–34 by Kanaka workmen imported from Hawaii, the great adobe structure was masterfully conceived to receive the best of sun and shade at the proper times and places. The courtyard is open to morning sun and protected from high winds. Three sides receive inner and outer shade from galleries twelve feet high. The massive walls, although with plaster cracked and crumbling, are the same that Vallejo's workmen erected, with ceilings and balconies supported by the original hand-hewn redwood beams. The workmen, numbering in the thousands, used to gather in the courtyard to hear the general's orders. From the second-story rooms one can look out upon the northern shores of San Francisco Bay—all viewable land was at one time part of General Vallejo's ranch. Open daily 10–5, with rangers for guides.

PETALUMA itself is what its nickname implies, the "World's Egg Basket." It contains probably the only drug-store in the world concerned with chicken medicines alone.

From either Casa Grande or Petaluma proper, 101 is easily regained; follow it north to SANTA ROSA, seat of Sonoma County.

Because of the rich soil and gentle climate the area was selected by Luther Burbank as the site for his experimental farm and served in that capacity for over fifty years, from his arrival here in 1875 until his death in 1926. This one and one-half acre tract is now known as BURBANK MEMORIAL GARDENS, Santa Rosa Avenue and Tupper Street. Maintained by the city, it is open daily, no admission charge. The Burbank home and a wide variety of plants may be seen here, including most of the Burbank discoveries. The grave of the great horticulturist is located in this memorial area, under a massive cedar of Lebanon grown from a seed gift from the Holy Land.

MacDonald Avenue, the city's most elegant residential street, enjoys fame as a much-photographed thoroughfare for movie backgrounds. Wide and tree-lined, it runs through nine blocks of substantial Victorian homes and gardens. In the movies it usually represents a New England location.

Another local point of interest is the First Baptist Church, on B Street between Fifth and Sixth streets in Juilliard Park, built in 1873 from the lumber of a single redwood tree. There was enough wood left over to construct a five-room residence.

Departing Santa Rosa, drive east on State Route 12 until you reach the Glen Ellen cutoff (west). An alternate route is Arnold Drive. Either road is adequate and both give a scenic drive through the "Valley of the Moon" country that London loved.

JACK LONDON STATE PARK is now a forty-acre memorial to London's life in this valley. It is open daily 9–5.

London purchased this land, including the old Kohler and Frohling Winery buildings, which were used for ranch headquarters and temporary living quarters, in the early part of this century. From 1904 until his death in 1916 he spent most of his time here, except for occasional voyages or journeys.

It was his dream to build a virtual castle to match the grandeur of the natural surroundings. This materialized into a three-story structure—WOLF HOUSE—of massive rock quarried in the Sonoma hills and hauled by four-horse teams. London never lived in it, however; it was destroyed by fire of unknown origin on the night of August 22, 1913, just as it was completed and ready for occupancy. The ruins stand among charred redwoods.

One lone boulder stands nearby. This huge chunk of red lava, which was too large for use in the house, three years later became the marker for London's ashes, and remains so today.

The second house—HOUSE OF HAPPY WALLS—was completed by London's widow, Charmian, in 1921. She lived there until her death in 1955. Bearing the same walls of rock as the earlier house and topped with a red tile roof, it is surrounded by the trees London adored—redwoods, manzanita, toyon, madrones, and bay.

Inside the house are tons of London mementos, many from his world travels. These were all presented to the state by London's nephew and are so numerous that it is impossible to display all of them at one time. Consequently, the exhibits are changed frequently, in rotating order. Included in the exhibits are original manuscripts and original drawings and paintings by his illustrators.

A singularly fascinating display item is a chest, the size of a small trunk, full of rejection slips, packed so tightly that they fly out in all directions when the lid is lifted.

Leave Glen Ellen and drive on Route 12—past the mineral hot springs resorts Agua Caliente and Boyes Hot Springs—to SONOMA, one of the most historic spots in California. The streets are painted with golden lines giving clear directions to the historical landmarks in and near the town.

A good starting point is the town plaza. In its northeast corner is the spot where, on June 14, 1846, California was acclaimed a republic and the Bear Flag first raised.

Other landmarks:

MISSION SAN FRANCISCO SOLANO DE SONOMA. The northernmost and last established (July 14, 1823) in the California chain of missions. The present mission building—an adobe, L-shaped, with red tile roof and crude cross—is a restoration. During the nineteenth century the mission buildings and patio endured a series of uses—hay barn, wine cellar, butcher's slaughter yard. At one time a saloon was built against the church's front wall. In 1911 the state undertook the restoration and the mission is now a state historical landmark. The mission museum contains part of the Bear Flag staff, hand-wrought iron hinges from Fort Ross, and various papers and items of interest in California history. Open daily from 10–5.

In the vicinity are a number of buildings which date from the time Mariano Vallejo was commandant general of Northern California, including the barracks of General Vallejo's soldiers, built in 1836; the Blue Wing Tavern, a well-preserved adobe a hundred feet long, with a balcony supported by hand-hewn redwood posts, which dates from 1840; and a Swiss chalet, now a restaurant, which was brought around the Horn in the 1830s. Vallejo, who laid out the town of Sonoma around the plaza and was responsible for its life and rule, continued to be a leading citizen after the declaration of the republic and the attainment of statehood.

LACHRYMA MONTIS, west two blocks to Third Street West, then north, was the General's Sonoma home. The name "Tear of the Mountain" was prompted by the existence of a natural spring nearby. His home, built in 1851, was long the most luxurious in the area, and is now a state historical monument. The timbers and bricks came around the Horn from Europe. The family house looks Victorian, with high-pitched roof, many gables and much gingerbread.

The grave of General Vallejo, who died in 1890, is located in the Sonoma Cemetery and is marked by a black granite monument.

The famous and historical BUENA VISTA vineyards are two and one-half miles east of the plaza. These vineyards date from 1832, when Colonel Agoston Haraszthy, the pioneer wine maker of California, brought scores of grape cuttings from all parts of Europe and set them out in the Sonoma Valley (plus a few on the Peninsula). The original cellars, destroyed by earthquake in 1906, have been restored, with the two stone buildings now designated state historical landmarks. The wine cellars are tunneled into a nearby hill. Open daily 10–5, the winery is still operative and the wine can be sampled.

Leaving Sonoma, go south on 121 and 37 back onto 101 to San Francisco.

10. *The Wine Country, St. Helena, Napa Valley, Petrified Forest, Stevenson Memorial Park.*

Go north over the Golden Gate Bridge, following 101. About eight miles north of San Rafael take State Route 37, then State Routes 121 and 12 to the Trinity Road, slightly north of Glen Ellen. This fourteen-mile stretch crosses the Mayacamas Range to Oakville through beautiful vineyard country. From Oakville, State Route 29, north to Rutherford and St. Helena, passes a number of California's finest wineries, all of which are open for touring, testing, and sale. Most of these wineries number their age upward of half a century, one has reached the century mark. Each has distinguishing characteristics, each noteworthy things to see—old wine presses, old casks, aged bottles, storage tunnels carved deep into hillsides, and the colorful vineyards themselves.

Among the more noted:

In or near Rutherford:

BEAULIEU. Founded in 1900 by Georges de Latour of France, operated continually by the same family. Ivy-covered buildings and gardens.

INGLENOOK. Founded in 1879. Stone buildings, vine-covered, noted for its deep rock cellars and wine antiques.

In or near St. Helena:

LOUIS M. MARTINI. Slightly south of St. Helena, this winery was founded by Louis M. Martini in 1906; his family operates the winery now. Instructive lectures are given concerning the whole wine process.

CHARLES KRUG. A little north of St. Helena, this is the oldest winery in the Napa Valley and a state historical monument. It is now operated by the Mondavi family, but was founded in 1861 by Charles Krug. Winery antiques on exhibit.

BERINGER BROTHERS. North of St. Helena, this winery has been operated by its founding family since 1876. It uses more than a thousand feet of subterranean tunnels for storage and aging.

There are numerous others, and markers will be easily noted.

Four miles north of St. Helena is the OLD BALE MILL.

This is a pioneer gristmill, dating from 1846, restored by the Native Sons of the Golden West.

CALISTOGA is a resort town of the spa variety, patronized for its mineral springs, mud baths, and natural hot-water geysers. Its potentialities were first realized by the Mormon Sam Brannan in 1859. The name is a hybrid of California and Saratoga.

About seven miles north of Calistoga is the ROBERT LOUIS STEVENSON MEMORIAL STATE PARK, located near the summit of the extinct volcano, Mount St. Helena, which rises to a height of 4344 feet. The park commemorates the area where Stevenson spent his honeymoon in 1880 and wrote *The Silverado Squatters*. There is a carved Scottish granite monument depicting the author holding an open book. Open during daylight hours, the park is rather rugged.

Retracking to Calistoga, a turnoff west and five miles of driving will lead to the PETRIFIED FOREST. These trees were unearthed in 1919, and all signs indicate an eruption of Mount St. Helena as the petrifying medium. For example, the trees toppled with the tops pointing *away* from the volcano. The petrified objects show excellent preservation of details. Some trees are as tall as 126 feet. The whole area is one mile long by a quarter mile wide (Admission 70¢).

From here, Routes 101 and 29 lead back to San Francisco.

PART III

SAN FRANCISCO RESTAURANTS, ENTERTAINMENT, SHOPPING, AND TRANSPORTATION GUIDE

"What I like best about San Francisco is San Francisco."

FRANK LLOYD WRIGHT

RESTAURANTS

There are numerous explanations why San Francisco restaurants are world famous. Some credit the cosmopolitan quality of the city (probably a result rather than a cause); others the large and varied foreign groups; still others the fine chefs; and, as good an explanation as any, some believe it is a holdover from gold-rush days, when, wives being somewhat uncommon, everyone got into the habit of eating out. Whatever the reason, San Francisco, rightly, prides itself on the quality of its cuisine.

Dining Information: San Franciscans dress for dinner, not showily but comfortably; for men, coat and tie are expected. Reservations are not always necessary (and not always taken), but it's a good idea to call first, if only to make sure the restaurant is open.

Listed here are a few of the city's many fine restaurants. Don't be afraid to try places not on the list; the odds are in your favor. Each of the major hotels has one or more good restaurants, and for that reason the hotels are not included. Due to occasional price changes and the large selection on most menus the following classifications are approximate at best:

Inexpensive*
Moderate**
Expensive***
Luxury****

American:

BONANZA SIRLOIN PIT, 420 Beach**   On Fisherman's Wharf. Steak dinners char-broiled to order.

BRIGHTON EXPRESS, 580 Pacific*   Satisfying meals at budget prices.

BUENA VISTA CAFE AND BAR, 2765 Hyde**   Local home of Irish Coffee; a favorite lunch and after theater spot.

CARAVAN LODGE, 601 Eddy**   Though little touted, well-prepared meals from a varied menu; close to Opera House and Civic Auditorium.

COOPERAGE, 1980 Union**   Steak and lobster, with quality spirits, in an old San Francisco atmosphere.

GRISON'S CHICKEN HOUSE, 2050 Van Ness**   Along with chicken, prime rib from the cart a specialty; also, lemon chiffon pie.

GRISON'S STEAK HOUSE, Van Ness and Pacific***   Top-grade steaks, succulent Eastern lobster.

HOUSE OF PRIME RIB, 1906 Van Ness**   Enormous prime-rib dinners, with all the trimmings. Extra special salad dressing and sherry pudding.

IRON DUKE, 132 Bush**   Financial district lunch mecca, with the trappings of a Tudor pub.

IRON HORSE, 19 Maiden Lane**   A popular downtown dining place, in the heart of the shopping area.

LEOPARD, 140 Front**   Financial-district steak house in high favor with sports crowd.

LEW LEHR, 3345 Steiner**   Your steak cut to order before your eyes. This Marina spot enjoys city-wide popularity.

Basque:

ELU'S, 781 Broadway** Basque dinners in thoroughly Basque surroundings.

Chinese:

EMPRESS OF CHINA, 838 Grant*** Michelin's rates it first in Chinatown. We don't agree; nevertheless the food is more than good, the surroundings opulent.

FAR EAST CAFE, 631 Grant* Popular among the Chinese for family dining.

GOLDEN PAVILION, Sacramento and Grant** Features a tasty buffet luncheon for the Chinatown traveler.

HANGAH TEA ROOM, 1 Pagoda Place* Light lunches, tea cakes and Deem Sums. *see pg. 93 of yellow Shelton book*

IMPERIAL PALACE, 919 Grant** Art objects from ancient Chinese dynasties surround diners here. Emperor Gourmet dinner a real treat.

KAN'S, 708 Grant*** Pre-eminent. Peking duck (must be ordered ahead) is parchment crisp, and the walnut chicken unsurpassable. Patronized by many Hollywood celebrities.

KUO WAH, 950 Grant** First-rate lobster dishes.

MANDARIN, Ghirardelli Square*** Peking, Shanghai, Szechwan cuisine decorously served.

NAM YUEN, 740 Washington** Another choice spot for family dining.

NORTH CHINA, 531 Jackson* Excellent food at bargain prices.

SAI YON, 641 Jackson* Family style dinners in pleasant atmosphere.

SUN HUNG HUEN, 744 Washington** More of the same.

TAO TAO, 675 Jackson** Arnold Genthe photographs of

No Rice in Tea Rooms

pre-1906 Chinatown enhance the surroundings. Especially good: Chinese chicken salad.

YANK SING, 671 Broadway** Cantonese and Mandarin cuisine, family style or à la carte.

Cosmopolitan—Atmosphere Plus:

ADOLPH'S, 641 Vallejo** French-Italian cuisine, cooked to order, unerringly delicious. Quality service.

ALEXIS, 1001 California**** Menu primarily Near Eastern, but with interesting variations. Luxurious Byzantine setting.

AMELIO'S, 1630 Powell**** Famous for excellent cuisine in cozy surroundings.

BARDELLI'S, 243 O'Farrell** Highly favored by press, theater people, and anyone liking superior food.

BLUE FOX, 659 Merchant*** Dating from speakeasy days, features varied menu and superior wine list.

CAR BARN, 1725 Filbert** Cannelloni par excellence only one specialty among many. Unpretentious, but attractive.

COFFEE CANTATA, 2030 Union** Lunch or dinner served in an art gallery, to the accompaniment of Baroque and classical music.

DOMINO CLUB, 25 Trinity Place*** Run-of-the-mill food overshadowed by collection of nude paintings.

DORO'S, 714 Montgomery*** Continental cuisine in atmosphere of elegance. *Dating Game winners ate here*

ENRICO'S COFFEE HOUSE, 504 Broadway** San Francisco's only sidewalk café. In the heart of North Beach, a delightful headquarters for people watching.

ERNIE'S, 847 Montgomery**** Gourmet dinners served in elegant Victorian surroundings.

HOFFMAN CAFE AND GRILL, 619 Market* An old Market Street standby, resembles a silent movie set.

IRON POT, 639 Montgomery*   Equally popular with Bohemians and millionaires.

JOHN'S GRILL, 63 Ellis**   Another press hangout. "Joe's" (hamburger, eggs and spinach scrambled together) especially tasty here.

KOE'S AUBERGE, 1205 Stockton**   Delicious meals at budget prices, but watch out for scratchy chairs.

LE BOEUF, 545 Washington**   Charcoal broiled steaks in intimate environment.

L'ETOILE, 1075 California****   French gourmet specialties, atop Nob Hill.

OLD SPAGHETTI FACTORY CAFE, 478 Green*   Limited menu, but the food is good. High camp atmosphere.

OWL 'N' TURTLE, 615 Washington**   Fireplace and background music make the well-prepared food taste even better.

PAOLI'S, 347 Montgomery***   One of the most popular financial area restaurants.

ROLF'S SINCE 1960, 757 Beach***   International lunch buffet draws large crowds daily. Marvelous bay view.

Creole:

LAFFITE'S, 2301 Powell**   Setting reminiscent of swashbuckling pirates. Enjoyment of remarkably good food can be hampered by a surly waiter.

LE CREOLE, 1809 Union**   Delicious soups, salads and other Creole dishes.

English:

COACHMAN, 1057 Powell**   Choice steak and kidney pie, mellow sherry.

French:

ALOUETTE, 1121 Polk** A longtime favorite with local French colony.

CHARLES', Montgomery Street**** So exclusive its telephone number is unlisted, there is no sign over its door. Only an "in" person can get you there.

CHEZ MARGUERITE, 2330 Taylor** Every dish cooked to perfection. Cozy.

DES ALPES, 732 Broadway** Daily specials served French family style. A bit noisy, but cheerful.

FLEUR DE LYS, 777 Sutter*** Winner of many awards. A gourmet's delight.

HOTEL DE FRANCE, 780 Broadway** Both family style and à la carte. Very French.

JACK'S, 615 Sacramento*** Among the oldest in the city. Somewhat drab décor cannot dampen one's enthusiasm for the superb cooking.

LA BOURGOGNE, 320 Mason**** Menu is without price listings. Food excellent, but strictly for expense account purses.

LE TRIANON, 242 O'Farrell** Varied French menu, fine service. Wild boar available if you have the time.

LES CREPES, 804 North Point** Traditional and varied crêpe recipes from all over.

MAGIC PAN, 3221 Fillmore and Ghirardelli Square** Crêpes with a wide variety of fillings.

NORMANDIE INTERNATIONAL, 1326 Powell*** Marvelous French cuisine, served with great formality.

L'ORANGERIE, 419 O'Farrell*** In a short period of operation, has already won a *Holiday* magazine award.

PLACE PIGALLE, 3721 Buchanan** Parisian trappings in the Marina.

RITZ OLD POODLE DOG, 65 Post** Dates from 1849. Appeals to all, but old-timers consider it their special property.

Greek:

GREEK TAVERNA, 256 Columbus** Excellent Greek food and wine, flanked by Greek décor, Greek music, Greek dancing. In the heart of North Beach.

L'ODEON, 565 Clay** Greek continental cuisine.

MINERVA CAFE, 136 Eddy** Highly popular with resident Greek-Americans.

Indian:

TAJ OF INDIA, 825 Pacific** Pleasurable chance to sample Indian dishes other than curry.

Indonesian:

BIT OF INDONESIA, 211 Clement*** Classic Indonesian cuisine.

Italian:

FIOR D'ITALIA, 621 Union*** One of the oldest and most popular Italian restaurants in the city.

LA STRADA, 443 Broadway*** Expertly prepared food; lush Mediterranean décor; beautiful harp music.

ORESTE'S, 118 Jones** Highly favored by local politicians,

also by theatergoers. After many years, newly decorated.

JOHN'S, 2060 Chestnut** Neighborhood restaurant worthy of outside attention.

LA PANTERA, 1234 Grant* Italian dinners family style.

LUPO'S, 1042 Kearny** Widely known for fine food and personal service.

O SOLE MIO, 2031 Chestnut* Pizza lovers from all over converge here.

POLO'S, 34 Mason* A good bet for downtown moviegoers. Great minestrone and thick sandwiches.

ROCCA'S, 555 Golden Gate Ave.** Close to Civic Center.

VANESSI'S, 498 Broadway** Best lasagna in the city, but served only on Saturdays. Everything here is among the best.

VENETO, Mason and Bay*** Close by Cost Plus and Fisherman's Wharf. The saltimbocca here known far and wide.

Veal

Japanese:

BUSH GARDEN, 598 Bush** Meals served Japanese style in private rooms. Ever wonder what to do with your feet in a Japanese restaurant? Here they have the perfect solution.

CHO CHO'S, 1020 Kearny** Quiet and comfortable Japanese décor. Widely varied menu. Teriyaki the best anywhere.

EDO, 2268 Chestnut** City-style. Intimate.

HISAGO, 1762 Buchanan* Delicious Japanese bean soup.

MINGEI-YA, 2033 Union** Country style. O-mizu-taki the specialty, but menu is varied. Fine collection of Japanese folk art.

SUEHIRO, 1737 Post*** Japanese steak house. Top grade.

TOKYO SUKIYAKI, 225 Jefferson** Sukiyaki superb, as is all food served here. Tempura bar for snacks. *beef & veg.*

YAMATO SUKIYAKI HOUSE, 717 California*** Most widely known, though not necessarily the best.

Jewish:

DAVID'S DOWNTOWN, 301 Kearny** <u>Automat</u> style for busy office workers.

DAVID'S DELICATESSEN AND RESTAURANT, 480 Geary** Marvelous blintzes, fabulous pastries. Wide variety of Jewish dishes. Across the street from the city's two road show theaters.

LISA'S KOSHER-STYLE RESTAURANT, 149 Taylor** Modern Israeli dining room. Kreplach supreme.

MORI'S KOSHER STYLE, 626 Kearny* Mammoth sandwiches.

Mediterranean:

VASILI'S, 44 Compton Place** A lot of expertly prepared food for a little. Romantic décor. Alley behind Gump's.

Mexican:

EL SOMBRERO, 5800 Geary Boulevard** Top notch Mexican food served with style.

LA PINATA, 1851 Union* Good, solid fare at low cost. Rellenos extra special.

SENOR PICO, Ghirardelli Square** Authentic early California and Mexican cookery. Overlooking the Bay.

SINALOA MEXICAN CANTINA, 1416 Powell*** Mexican dinners to floor show accompaniment.

TIA MARGARITA, 300 19th Avenue** A favorite with aficionados of Mexican cooking.

Middle Eastern:

BALI'S, 615 Sansome***   Armenian cuisine. Luxurious surroundings. Mouth-watering Sedlo (rack of lamb) a specialty.

CAIRO, 77 4th Street**   A bargain for the budget-conscious.

Polynesian:

TIKI BOB'S, 599 Post***   Beachcomber atmosphere. Sumptu-
ous menus.

TRADER VIC'S, 20 Cosmo Place****   World famous.

Russian:

RESTAURANT OPERA, 336 Hayes**   Proximity to Opera
House gives it priority with opera and symphony fans.

RUSSIAN RENAISSANCE, 5241 Geary**   Tasteful surroundings. Interesting Russian menu. String music.

TROIKA, 5145 Geary**   A favorite of the local Russian
colony.

Sea Food:

CASTAGNOLA'S, Jefferson and Jones**   Best on Fisherman's
Wharf. Fine view of fishing fleet.

DORO'S POLK AND SUTTER OYSTER HOUSE, Polk and Sutter**
Serves an excellent oyster loaf.

ERNIE'S NEPTUNE FISH GROTTO, 1816 Irving** Neighborhood restaurant, little ballyhooed, but serving excellently prepared seafood.

TADICH'S COLD DAY RESTAURANT AND GRILL, 240 California** In its second century, though the address has changed. Superb food and service.

Short Orders, Snacks, Sandwiches:

CHAUNCEY MACDUFF'S, 360 Bay* Hamburgers the specialty, with a wide range of side orders.

CLOWN ALLEY, 42 Columbus Avenue and 2499 Lombard* Hamburgers here are as good as you can find anywhere.

HIPPO-HAMBURGERS, 2025 Van Ness Avenue* Hamburgers in many guises (over 50 varieties), with exotic accompaniments.

I-THOU COFFEE HOUSE, 1736 Haight* Refreshments in Hippieland.

MR. CHIPS, 1972 Lombard* English fish 'n' chips, now so popular with Americans, done to perfection here.

MIZ BROWN'S, 2414 Lombard and 1356 Polk* Wide range of short orders, all of them good. Pancakes, waffles, other breakfast items a specialty.

SEARS' FINE FOODS, 439 Powell** Delectable Swedish pancakes make this a favorite breakfast and lunch spot (Daily until 3). Menu covers wide assortment of daytime goodies.

Spanish:

TORTOLA, 1237 Polk** Early California cuisine prepared by an internationally honored chef.

West Indian:

CONNIE'S, 1466 Haight** Coconut bread a specialty, accompanying numerous tasty dishes.

THE TORTUGA, 335 Jones** Caribbean concoctions served beside a waterfall.

NIGHT CLUBS AND BARS

The following is intended as a representative sampling of San Francisco night life, which ranges from cellar bistros serving beer, wine, and fresh new talent to the more formal surroundings for top-name entertainment. Some of the night clubs offer dining and dancing in addition to floor shows. In a few of the bars the only entertainment is the other customers, which is sufficient. For a more complete listing, with information on current attractions, check the Saturday newspapers. Only a few of the more expensive clubs take reservations; however, since not all are open every night, it is a good idea to call and check in advance, unless you happen to be in the neighborhood.

BASIN STREET WEST, 401 Broadway. Music by stellar figures in jazz.

BIMBO'S 365 CLUB, 1025 Columbus. The city's largest night club; extravaganza-type floor shows; the "Girl in the Fishbowl."

BOCCE BALL, 622 Broadway. Operatic entertainment.

BUENA VISTA, 2765 Hyde. Irish Coffee.

BOTH/AND JAZZ CLUB, 350 Divisadero. Featuring new jazz talent.

CLUB EL TENAMPA, 3247 Mission. Thoroughly Mexican.

The excellent mariachi band charges for each number requested.

COFFEE GALLERY, 1353 Grant. Art exhibits, a few ancient Beats.

COMMITTEE REVUE, 622 Broadway. Keenest satirical revue to be found anywhere.

CONDOR, 300 Columbus. Where the San Francisco topless began.

CRYSTAL LIL'S, 674 Broadway. Re-creation of an oldtime parlor house, minus only one important feature.

CURTAIN CALL, 456 Geary. For before- and after-theater drinks.

DRAG ON A GO GO, 49 Wentworth Alley. Chinatown discothèque.

EARTHQUAKE MC GOON'S, 630 Clay. One of the best entertainment buys in the city. Home of Turk Murphy's jazz band.

FILLMORE WEST, Market and Van Ness. Dancing. Psychedelic lighting. Music by leading rock groups. Loud, loud, loud.

FINOCCHIO'S, 506 Broadway. Female impersonators in vaudeville splendor.

FORBIDDEN CITY, 363 Sutter. Chinese show girls.

GOLD STREET, 56 Gold. Leggy waitresses. New Year's Eve every Friday and Saturday night.

GOMAN'S GAY 60's, 345 Broadway. Total topless plus a girl in a cage.

HUNGRY I, Ghirardelli Square. A discovery mecca for the new and off-beat in entertainment.

JAZZ WORKSHOP, 473 Broadway. Another excellent jazz spot.

OFF BROADWAY, 1024 Kearny. Another topless factory.

OLD LIBRARY, 951 Clement. Table-to-table phones simplify introductions.

THE OLD SPAGHETTI FACTORY CAFE AND EXCELSIOR COFFEE HOUSE, 478 Green. Featuring interesting habitués and steam beer, from the world's last surviving steam-beer factory.

PIER 23 CAFE, Embarcadero. Dixieland music. Pianist Burt Bales. Clarinetist Vince Cattolica.

PURPLE ONION, 140 Columbus. A launching pad for bright young talent.

RED GARTER, 670 Broadway. Banjos and booze.

RICKSHA BAR, 37 Ross Alley. A cool, dark hideaway, with exotic waitresses.

TOP OF THE MARK, Hotel Mark Hopkins, Mason and California. A must.

TOSCA, 242 Columbus. Famed for its *cappuccinos,* an after-dinner drink (created in San Francisco and different from Italy's drink of the same name) made with chocolate, brandy and live steam.

VARNI'S ROARING TWENTIES, 807 Montgomery. As explosive as the era it imitates.

VENETIAN ROOM, Fairmont Hotel, Mason and California. San Francisco's Waldorf. High-priced name talent.

VESUVIO'S, 255 Columbus. Bohemian bar specializing in high camp.

THEATERS

Legitimate theaters: Attractions include national companies of Broadway shows, new shows in pre-Broadway runs, Civic Light Opera productions, and the American Conservatory Theatre, repertory.

CURRAN, 445 Geary.

GEARY, 415 Geary.

OPERA HOUSE, Van Ness and Grove.

"Little Theaters": Offering a variety of highly professional theater, usually on weekends. Check a daily newspaper for listings.

COMMITTEE THEATRE, 836 Montgomery.

GHIRARDELLI THEATRE, 900 Northpoint.
INTERPLAYERS, 747 Beach.
LITTLE FOX, 533 Pacific.
PLAYHOUSE REPERTORY, 422 Mason.
Motion-Picture Theaters: San Francisco offers a large number of motion-picture theaters. Most of the first-run theaters are on or near Market Street. The art theaters, concentrating on foreign films, are mostly in the neighborhoods, but only a few minutes by bus or car from downtown. Check a daily newspaper for listings.

SHOPPING GUIDE

Department Stores:

CITY OF PARIS, 199 Geary.
EMPORIUM, 835 Market.
MACY'S, Stockton and O'Farrell.

Women's Apparel:

BARRA OF ITALY, 245 Post.
GUMP'S, 250 Post.
ROBERT KIRK, LTD., 150 Post.
LANZ OF CALIFORNIA, INC., 152 Geary.
H. LIEBES, Grant and Geary.
LIVINGSTON'S, Grant and Geary.
I. MAGNIN, Geary and Stockton.
JOSEPH MAGNIN, O'Farrell and Stockton.
MAISON MENDESSOLLE, St. Francis Hotel.
NELLY GAFFNEY, 272 Post.

PECK AND PECK, Sutter and Grant.
RANSOHOFF'S, 259 Post.
ROOS-ATKINS, Post at Powell and Market at Stockton.
R SAKS FIFTH AVENUE, Grant at Maiden Lane.

Men's Apparel and Furnishings:

JAY BRIGGS, 61 Post.
BROOKS BROTHERS, 201 Post.
BULLOCK AND JONES, 340 Post.
DUNHILL, 290 Post.
HASTINGS, 135 Post and Powell at Geary.
ROBERT KIRK, LTD., 150 Post.
ROOS-ATKINS, Post at Powell and Market at Stockton.
A. SULKA, 278 Post.
TOWN SQUIRE, 1318 Polk.

Gifts, Jewelry, Furnishings, Novelties:

S. CHRISTIAN OF COPENHAGEN, 225 Post.
COST PLUS IMPORTS, 2552 Taylor.
PAUL DE VRIES ET CIE, 300 Post.
S. PAUL GEE, 1546 Grant.
R GUMP'S, 250 Post.
TRO HARPER, 140 Powell.
LAYKIN ET CIE, in I. Magnin.
PETER MACCHIARINI, 1422 Grant.
NANNY'S, 251 Grant.
SHREVE'S, Post and Grant.
TAKAHASHI, Grant at Geary and Ghirardelli Square.

Art Galleries:

ARTISTS COOPERATIVE, 2224 Union.
JOHN BOLLES, 729 Sansome.
DILEXI, 631 Clay.
LUCIAN LABAUDT, 1407 Gough.
MAXWELL, 551 Sutter.
PANTECHNICON, 1849 Union.
PEARSON PRIMITIVE ART, 3499 Sacramento.
SCENE, 1420 Grant.
VORPAL, 1168 Battery.

Bookstores:

ARGONAUT, 336 Kearny.
BONANZA INN, 650 Market.
BOOKS, INC., 156 Geary.
BRENTANO'S, City of Paris.
CHESTNUT BURR, 2164 Chestnut.
CITY LIGHTS, 261 Columbus.
DEPLER'S, 439 O'Farrell.
DISCOVERY, 245 Columbus.
DOUBLEDAY, 190 Post.
PAUL ELDER'S BOOKS, 401 Sutter and 228 Montgomery.
EMPORIUM, 835 Market.
FIELD'S, 1419 Polk.
GHIRARDELLI, 900 North Point.
ALBERT HENRY, 524 Geary.
TRO HARPER, 140 Powell and 974 Market.
JOHN HOWELL, 434 Post.
MCDONALD'S, 48 Turk.
NEWBEGIN'S, 358 Post.

STACEY'S, 581 Market.
TILLMAN PLACE BOOKSHOP, 8 Tillman Place.
UPSTART CROW AND CO., The Cannery.

Sporting Goods:

ABERCROMBIE & FITCH, 220 Post.
LAND BROTHERS, 725 Market.
MARINA SKI, 1909 Union.
ROOS-ATKINS, Post at Powell and Market at Stockton.
VIKING SPORTS, 173 Maiden Lane and 1874 Market.

STREETCARS, CABLE CARS, AND COACH LINES

Routes of Lines

STREETCARS

J—CHURCH. Eastbay Terminal via Fremont, Market, Church
to 30th. Motor Coach Owl service to Ferry.

K—INGLESIDE. Eastbay Terminal via Fremont, Market, Twin
Peaks Tunnel, West Portal Av, Junipero Serra, Ocean to
Phelan (City College Terminal). Owl service Eastbay
Terminal to San Jose & Ocean.

L—TARAVAL. Eastbay Terminal via Fremont, Market, Twin
Peaks Tunnel, Ulloa, 15th Av, Taraval, 46th Av, Vicente,
47th Av, Wawona to 46th Av (S.F. Zoo). Owl service.

M—OCEAN VIEW. Eastbay Terminal via Fremont, Market,
Twin Peaks Tunnel, West Portal Av, 19th Av, Randolph,
Orizaba, Broad to Plymouth. Motor Coach service Eves,
Sun & holidays from west portal of Twin Peaks Tunnel

via West Portal Av, Junipero Serra, Eucalyptus, 19th Av, Randolph, Orizaba, Broad, Capitol, Sadowa, Plymouth to Broad.

N—JUDAH. Eastbay Terminal via Fremont, Market, Duboce, Sunset Tunnel, Carl, Arguello, Irving, 9th Av, Judah to Great Highway. Motor Coach Owl service from Ferry via Market, Haight, Cole, Carl, Arguello, Irving, 9th Av, Judah to Great Highway.

CABLE CARS

59—POWELL-MASON. Powell & Market via Powell, *Jackson, Mason, Columbus, Taylor to Bay (Fisherman's Wharf). *Returns via Washington.

60—POWELL-HYDE. Powell & Market via Powell, *Jackson, Hyde to Beach St (Aquatic Park). *Returns via Washington.

61—CALIFORNIA. California & Market via California to Van Ness.

COACH LINES

1—CALIFORNIA. Sutter & Market via Sutter, Presidio Av, California, 32nd Av, Geary to 33rd Av. Nights & Sun. #1 runs via #3. Owl service from Eastbay Terminal via Fremont, Market, Geary, 2nd Av, California, 32nd Av, Geary, 33rd Av, Balboa, 45th Av, Cabrillo to Great Highway below Cliff House.

2—CLEMENT. Sutter & Market via Sutter, Presidio Av, Euclid, Arguello, Clement, 33rd Av, Geary, *Point Lobos, 48th Av to Terminal. *Return via Geary, 33rd Av. Limited Stops on Sutter, weekdays and Saturday daytime only. Certain trips to (or via) Ft. Miley.

2—CLEMENT EXPRESS. Weekday peak periods only. Express area: Presidio Av to Montgomery, inbound on Bush, A.M. —outbound on Pine, P.M.

3—JACKSON. Sutter & Market via Sutter, Fillmore, Jackson,

Presidio Av to California. Nights & Sun #1 runs via #3.

5—MC ALLISTER. Ferry via Market, *McAllister, Central, Fulton, La Playa to Balboa (Playland-at-the-Beach). *In via McAllister, Hyde, Fulton, Market to Ferry. Eves, Sun & holidays and Owl service from Market & McAllister to Balboa & La Playa. Limited Stop service, weekdays peak periods only.

6—MASONIC. Ferry via Market, Haight, Masonic, Frederick, Clayton, Parnassus, Judah, 9th Av, Ortega, 10th Av, Quintara to 14th Av. (Inbound: Haight, Laguna, Page, Market.)

7—HAIGHT. Ferry via Market, Haight, Stanyan to Waller (Golden Gate Park). Return via Waller, Shrader, Haight, Laguna, Page, Market to Ferry. Weekdays & Sat only. Owl service, see "N" line.

8—MARKET. Ferry via Market, Castro (east portal Twin Peaks Tunnel), 18th, Collingwood, 19th to Castro.

9—RICHLAND. Ferry via Embarcadero, Mission, Richland, Murray, Crescent, Andover to Richland. Eves, Sat, Sun & holidays see #27.

10—MONTEREY. 12th Av & California via 12th Av, Clement, 10th Av, Cabrillo, 8th Av, Golden Gate Park (Main Drive, Academy of Science Drive, South Drive), 9th Av, Lawton, 7th Av, Laguna Honda, (Forest Hill Station), Portola, Miraloma, Yerba Buena, Plymouth, Monterey, Diamond, Chenery, *Whitney, 30th, Mission, Cortland to Bayshore. *Return via Sanchez, Randall. Weekdays, daytime only, extended via Bayshore, Industrial, Barneveld, (Apparel City), Oakdale, Bayshore to Cortland.

11—HOFFMAN. Ferry via Embarcadero, Mission, 22nd, Dolores, 24th, Hoffman, 25th, Fountain, 24th, Hoffman, Grand View, 21st, Douglass to 24th. Eves, Sun & holidays feeder service from 22nd & Mission to 24th & Douglass.

12—MISSION-OCEAN AVE. Ferry via Embarcadero, Mission, Ocean to Phelan (City College Terminal).

14—MISSION. Ferry via Embarcadero, Mission to Daly City. Owl service.

14—MISSION LIMITED. Weekdays off-peak and Sat on above route. Weekdays peak periods, same route, except via Guerrero between 14th & Mission and Randall & Mission.

14—MISSION EXPRESS. Weekdays peak periods via Freeway. Express, 5th & Mission to Trumbull & Mission.

15—3rd-KEARNY. Stockton & North Point via North Point, Powell, Columbus, *Montgomery, *Market, *2nd, *Brannan, 3rd, Bayshore, Visitacion, Hahn, Sunnyvale, Santos, Geneva to Mission. *Return via 3rd, Kearny, Columbus. Express service, weekdays, see #30-Stockton Express. Owl service.

15—NAVY YARD. Broadway & Embarcadero via *Broadway, *Battery, *Pine, *Montgomery, *Market, *2nd, *Brannan, *3rd, Newhall, Palou, Crisp, Spear, Fisher, Van Keuren, Lockwood, to S.F. Naval Shipyard Terminal. *Return via 3rd, Kearny, Bush, Sansome, Broadway, Front, Vallejo, Davis to Broadway. Eves, Sat, Sun & holidays from Montgomery & Sutter to S.F. Naval Shipyard.

16—NORIEGA EXPRESS. Ortega & 48th Av via Ortega, 47th Av, Noriega, 22nd Av, Irving, 19th Av, Golden Gate Park (Cross Over Drive, Park Presidio Drive), *Fulton, *Parker, *Golden Gate Av, Leavenworth, Eddy to Mason. *Return via Mason, Turk, Arguello, Balboa. Express area, 19th Av, & Lincoln Way to Van Ness, peak hours, weekdays only. 48th Av 6 to 9 A.M.; Mason 4 to 6:30 P.M.

17—PARKMERCED. West Portal of Twin Peaks Tunnel via West Portal Av, Junipero Serra, Eucalyptus, 19th Av, Crespi, Gonzalez, Font, Juan Bautista, Font, Tapia, Pinto, Arballo, Garces, Gonzalez, Font, Gonzalez, Crespi, 19th Av, Eucalyptus, Junipero Serra, West Portal to Ulloa.

17—PARKMERCED EXPRESS. Vidal & Arballo via Arballo, Pinto, Tapia, Font, Juan Bautista, Font, Chumasero, Brotherhood, Alemany, Freeway, Bryant, 3rd, Market to 2nd. Return via 2nd, Harrison, Freeway, etc. Express area, Chumasero & Brotherhood to 4th. Weekdays, daytime only.

18—SLOAT. 48th & Pt. Lobos via 48th Av, Geary, 47th Av, Pt. Lobos, Great Highway, Balboa, La Playa, Fulton, Great Highway, Lincoln, *46th Av, *Vicente, *47th Av, Sloat, Junipero Serra, Eucalyptus, 20th Av, Buckingham Way (southerly intersection of 20th Av) to Winston. *Return via 46th Av, Irving, 45th Av, Lincoln. Sun & holidays from 48th & Pt. Lobos to Ocean & Junipero Serra with extension via Ocean Av to City College Terminal, 10 A.M. to 6 P.M.

19—POLK. 2nd & Townsend (S.P. Depot) via Townsend, 4th, Brannan, 9th, Larkin, Post, Polk, Beach, Leavenworth, Jefferson (Fisherman's Wharf), Powell to Beach St. Return via Beach, Polk, Geary, Hyde, 8th, Brannan, 2nd to Townsend. Eves, Sat, Sun & holidays from 9th & Mission to Powell & Beach.

21—HAYES. Ferry via Market, Hayes, Stanyan, Fulton, (Golden Gate Park), 6th Av, California to 8th Av. Return via 8th Av, Clement, 6th Av, Fulton, Stanyan, Hayes, Laguna, Grove, Polk, Market to Ferry. Eves, Sun & holidays from 5th & Market.

22—FILLMORE. Marina via Fillmore, Union, Steiner, Broadway, Fillmore, Hermann, Church, 16th, Kansas, 17th, Connecticut, 18th, 3rd to 20th. Owl service from Broadway & Fillmore to 3rd & 20th.

23—CRESCENT. 26th & Mission via 26th, Folsom, Ripley, Alabama, Bradford, Nevada, Cortland, Folsom, Crescent to Farmers Market. Eves, Sat, Sun & holidays see #27.

24—DIVISADERO. Jackson & Webster via Jackson, Divisadero, Castro, 26th, Noe, Clipper to Castro.

25—BRYANT. 5th & Mission via 5th, Harrison, 11th, Bryant, Precita, Army, Bayshore, Silver, San Bruno, Bayshore, Geneva, Saipan, Iwo Jima, Schwerin, Geneva to Santos. Return via Santos, Velasco, Castillo, Geneva, Schwerin, Iwo Jima, Saipan, Geneva, Bayshore, San Bruno, Alemany Circle, Bayshore, Army, Bryant, 6th, Mission, Mint, Jessie to 5th. Owl service Arleta & Bayshore to Scott & Chestnut via portions of lines #25, #30 and #47.

26—VALENCIA. 5th & Mission via Mission, Otis, McCoppin, Valencia, Mission, 30th, Chenery, Diamond, Monterey, Circular, Baden, San Jose, Alemany, Palmetto, Junipero Serra, 19th Av, to Holloway (S. F. State College). Return via 19th Av, Holloway, Junipero Serra, Brotherhood, Arch, Alemany, San Jose, Baden, Circular, Monterey, Diamond, Chenery, 30th, Mission, Valencia, Market, 10th, Mission, Mint, Jessie to 5th. Express Service, via Guerrero, weekday peak periods only (Express area, San Jose & Cotter to 14th & Mission).

27—NOE. Noe & 29th via 29th, Mission, Army, *Bryant, *4th, Townsend, 2nd, Market, 1st to Minna. *Return via 4th, Brannan, Division, Bryant. Eves, Sat, Sun & holidays from Noe & 29th via 29th, Mission, 26th, Folsom, Ripley, Alabama, Bradford, Nevada, Cortland, Folsom, Crescent, Andover, Richland, Leese, Crescent, Mission to Richland.

28—NINETEENTH AVE. Geneva & Mission via Geneva, Naples, Curtis, Prague, Cordova, Chicago, South Hill, Prague, Geneva, Howth, Mt. Vernon, Grafton, Garfield, Junipero Serra, *Winston, *20th Av, *Eucalyptus, Junipero Serra, Sloat, 19th Av, Golden Gate Park (Cross Over Drive), 25th to California, thence via 25th Av, Seacliff, El Camino del Mar, 25th Av to California and/or 25th Av, El Camino del Mar, Lincoln, Old Lincoln, El Camino del Mar, 25th Av to California. *During business hours in Stonestown.

29—VISITACION. Mansell & Hamilton via Mansell, San Bruno, Wilde, Delta, Tioga, Rutland, *Visitacion, *Bayshore, *Blaken, Candlestick, McKinley and Candlestick to terminal. After 6 P.M. *Arleta, *Blanken.

30—STOCKTON. S.P. Depot via *3rd, *Kearny, *Sutter, Stockton, Union, Columbus, No. Point, Van Ness, Chestnut, Broderick to Beach. *Return via Stockton, 4th, Townsend.

30—STOCKTON. EXPRESS. London & Geneva via Geneva, Santos, Sunnydale, Hahn, Visitacion, Rutland, Arleta, San Bruno, *Bacon, *Bayshore, *Freeway, *Bryant, *3rd,

*Kearny, *Sutter, Stockton, Broadway, Van Ness, Chestnut, Broderick to Beach. *Return via 4th, Freeway, San Bruno. Weekdays daytime only. Express Area, Bayshore & Silliman to 4th and Stockton & Sutter to Chestnut & Van Ness.

31—BALBOA. 33rd & Balboa via Balboa, Arguello, Turk, Divisadero, Eddy, Mason, Market to Ferry. Return via Market, Turk, Leavenworth, Eddy, Divisadero, Turk, Arguello, Balboa, 32nd Av, Anza, 33rd Av to Balboa. Eves, Sat, Sun & holidays and Owl service from 33rd & Balboa to Eddy & Market via Hall of Justice. Limited Stop service, weekday peak periods only.

32—EMBARCADERO. 3rd & King (S.P. Depot) via King, 2nd, Berry, Embarcadero, Jefferson (Fisherman's Wharf), Leavenworth, Beach to Hyde (Aquatic Park). Daily service to 8 P.M. only.

33—ASHBURY. Waller & Stanyan via Stanyan, Haight, Shrader, Waller, Ashbury, Clayton, Market, 18th, So. Van Ness, Howard, 4th to Harrison. Return via Harrison, 14th, Folsom, 18th, Market, Clayton, Ashbury, Waller to Stanyan. Eves, Sat, Sun & holidays, Waller & Stanyan to 16th & So. Van Ness.

34—WOODSIDE. Myra & Dalewood via Myra Way, Reposa, *Teresita, *Portola, Woodside, Laguna Honda Blvd (Forest Hill Station), 7th Av, Warren Drive, Oak Park Drive, Clarendon, Laguna Honda Blvd to Forest Hill Station. *Return via Portola, Fowler, Teresita. Weekdays, daytime only.

35—EUREKA. Castro & Market via Castro, 20th, Eureka, 23rd, Diamond, 28th, Noe, 25th, Church, 24th, Vermont, 23rd, Rhode Island, 26th, Connecticut, Army to Michigan. Return via Army, Connecticut, 26th, Kansas, 23rd, San Bruno, 24th, Church, 25th, Diamond, 23rd, Eureka, Market to Castro.

36—MIRALOMA. Sickles & Huron via Sickles, Plymouth, Ocean, Phelan (City College), Staples, Foerster, Teresita, Portola, Woodside, Laguna Honda (Forest Hill Station), Clarendon, Panorama, Marview, Skyview, Cityview, Panorama, Olympia, Clarendon, Laguna Honda to Forest Hill Station. Return via Laguna Honda Blvd., Woodside, Portola, Fowler, Teresita, Foerster, Staples, Phelan (City College), Ocean, Plymouth, Broad, Capitol, Sagamore, Sickles, Huron, Mission, Sickles to Huron.

37—CORBETT. 17th & Market (designated "Glenview") via Castro, 18th, Eureka, 17th, Corbett, *Portola, *Burnett, *Glenview to terminal at Portola. *Return via Glenview, Portola. 17th & Market (designated "Diamond Heights") via Castro, 18th, Eureka, 17th, Corbett, Portola, Clipper, Diamond Heights, Duncan, Diamond Heights, Addison, loop at Digby, Addison to terminal at Farnum. Weekdays and Saturdays to 10 P.M.—Sundays to 6 P.M.

38—GEARY. Eastbay Terminal via Fremont, Market, Geary, 33rd Av, Balboa, 45th Av, Cabrillo to Great Highway below Cliff House. Limited Stop service, weekdays daytime only. Owl service.

38—GEARY EXPRESS. Weekday peak periods only. Express area: Presidio to Powell. In—Geary, Geary Expressway, Starr King Way, O'Farrell, Market, New Montgomery, Jessie, 2nd to Market. Out—via Post, Peter Yorke Way, Geary Expressway, Geary.

39—COIT. Coit Tower via Telegraph Hill Blvd, Lombard, Stockton, Filbert, Powell, Union to Montgomery. Return via Union, Columbus, Powell, Filbert, Stockton, Lombard, Telegraph Hill Blvd to Coit Tower.

40—COMMUTER. 3rd & Townsend (S.P. Depot) via Townsend, 2nd to Stevenson. Return via Stevenson, New Montgomery, Howard, 4th, Townsend to 3rd. Weekday peak service only.

41—UNION-HOWARD. 26th & Mission via Mission, 25th, So. Van Ness, Howard (Eastbay Terminal), Main, Drumm, Sacramento, Sansome, Washington, Columbus, Stockton, Union, Baker, Greenwich to Lyon. Return via Lyon, Union, Columbus, Montgomery, Clay, Davis, Beale, Howard, So. Van Ness, 26th to Mission. Eves, Sat, Sun &

holidays and Owl service from Greenwich & Lyon to Beale & Howard.

42—EVANS. Sansome & Chestnut via Embarcadero, *Battery, *Pine, *Montgomery, *Market, *2nd, *Brannan, *3rd, Phelps, Fairfax, Mendell, Evans, Jennings, Middlepoint, Innes, Donohue, King, Robinson, Lockwood, Spear to S.F. Naval Shipyard Terminal. *Return via 3rd, Kearny, Bush, Sansome.

43—ROOSEVELT. 14th & Market via Market, 15th, Castro, 14th, Roosevelt, Buena Vista Terr, Buena Vista Av, Upper Terr, Loma Vista Terr, Roosevelt, 17th, Cole, Haight, Masonic, Euclid, Presidio to Sutter. Return via Presidio, Geary, Masonic, Haight, Cole, Carmel, Clayton, 17th, Roosevelt, Park Hill, Buena Vista Av, Buena Vista Terr, Roosevelt, 14th to Market.

45—VAN NESS. Market via Sutter, Van Ness, Union, Steiner, Greenwich, Baker, Lombard (Presidio Gate), Lincoln Blvd to Anza. Downtown Loop 6 A.M. to 6:30 P.M. weekdays only, Sansome, California, Davis, Market to Sutter.

47—POTRERO. Potrero & Army via Army, Hampshire, 24th, Potrero, 16th, Bryant, 11th, Mission, So. Van Ness, Van Ness to No. Point. Owl service by #25 line.

51—SILVER. Silver & Mission via Mission, Maynard, Craut, Silver, Palou, Mendell to Terminal. Return via Mendell, LaSalle, Southridge, Northridge, Harbor, Northridge, Jerrold, Earl, Kirkwood, Kiska, Southridge, Newcomb, Lane, Palou, Silver to Mission.

52—EXCELSIOR. Brazil & Mission via Mission, Excelsior, Naples, Avalon, Moscow, Brazil, Prague, Russia, Moscow, Geneva, Naples, Brazil to Mission.

53—SOUTHERN HEIGHTS. Bryant via 16th, Kansas, Mariposa, Vermont, 20th, Rhode Island, Southern Heights Blvd, 22nd, Wisconsin, 25th, Dakota, 23rd, Arkansas, 20th, Connecticut to 18th. Return via Connecticut, 18th, Missouri, 23rd, Wisconsin, 22nd, So. Heights Blvd, Rhode Island, 20th, Vermont, 17th, Bryant to 16th.

55—SACRAMENTO. Ferry via Sacramento, Arguello, Lake, 6th

Av to Clement. Return via Clement, 7th Av, California, 6th Av, Lake, Arguello, Sacramento, Gough, Clay to Ferry. Limited Stop service, weekday peak periods only.

66—QUINTARA. 31st Av & Vicente via 31st Av, Ulloa, 30th Av, Quintara, 16th Av, Lawton, 9th Av, Judah, Parnassus, Clayton, Frederick, Masonic, Haight, Laguna, Page, Market, 4th, Mission, 5th to Market. Return via Market, Haight, etc., 16th Av, Noriega, 15th Av, Quintara, etc. Line extended via Market to 2nd & Market, weekdays peak periods only. Limited Stop service, weekdays only. Eves, Sat, Sun & holidays feeder service from 31st Av & Vicente to 9th Av & Judah.

71—HAIGHT-NORIEGA. Ortega & 48th Av, via Ortega, 47th Av, Noriega, 22nd Av, Lincoln, Frederick, Stanyan, Haight, Laguna, Page, Market, 4th, Mission, 5th to Market. Return via Market, Haight, etc. Line extended via Market to Ferry, weekdays and Sat peak periods only. Limited Stop service, weekdays and Sat daytime only. Owl service, see "N" line.

72—HAIGHT-SUNSET. Sunset Blvd & Lake Merced Blvd via Sunset, 36th Av, Lincoln, Frederick, Stanyan, Haight, Laguna, Page, Market, 4th, Mission, 5th to Market. Return via Market, Haight, etc. Line extended via Market to Ferry, weekdays peak periods only. Limited Stop service, weekdays and Sat daytime only. Owl service, see "N" line.

80—LEAVENWORTH. Jackson & Fillmore via Jackson, Steiner, Washington, Leavenworth, Bush, Jones, O'Farrell, Mason to Turk. Return via Turk, Leavenworth, Jackson to Fillmore.

81—BACON-FITZGERALD. University & Silver via Silver, Colby Silliman, University, Woolsey, Holyoke, Bacon, San Bruno, Paul to 3rd St. Return via 3rd, Keith, Fitzgerald, Griffith, Gilman, Paul, San Bruno, Bacon, Holyoke, Woolsey, University to Silver.

89—LAGUNA HONDA. Forest Hill Station via Laguna Honda Blvd, Laguna Honda Entrance Road, to Main Entrance

(Laguna Honda Hospital and Rehabilitation Center). Return via Main Office Road, Laguna Honda Blvd, to Forest Hill Station. Daily service 10 A.M. to 3 P.M.

WEEKDAYS, AS USED HEREIN, INDICATES
MONDAY THROUGH FRIDAY, HOLIDAYS EXCEPTED.

SUNDAY HOLIDAY TOUR TICKET

On Sundays and certain holidays a real "transit bargain" is available, a 50¢ Tour Ticket good all day long for an un-limited number of rides. Tickets may be obtained from all cable car conductors and starters at Powell and Market Streets. Immediately prior to the day for which they are issued, tickets may be purchased at all Municipal Railway Divisions and the A/C Transit Ticket Office at the East Bay Terminal. For further information call 558-4111.

TAXICABS

DESOTO SEDAN SERVICE, 673-1414
LUXOR CABS, 673-4040
VETERAN'S CAB CO., 567-1300
YELLOW CABS, 626-2345

INDEX

INDEX

ANCHOR BOOKS

3a

DOLPHIN HOME REFERENCE BOOKS

DOLPHIN RECREATION AND TRAVEL BOOKS

<u>Fish</u>; Tadich Grill

Special French restaurant
   (expensive) → L'Orangerie.

Fisherman's Wharf
         Exposition Grotto

Senor Pico's (Ghirardelli
               Square)

Stores to visit

Gumps
Abercrombie & Fitch
I. Magnins.
Saks 5ᵗʰ Ave.
Maison Mendosohlle (in the
                  St. Francis
                  Hotel)